Down by the River

Down by the River

The Impact of Federal Water Projects and Policies on Biological Diversity

Constance Elizabeth Hunt

with Verne Huser

Foreword by Dr. Jay D. Hair
President, National Wildlife Federation

Published in cooperation with National Wildlife Federation

ISLAND PRESS

Washington, D.C. □ *Covelo, California*

ABOUT ISLAND PRESS

Island Press, a nonprofit organization, publishes, markets, and distributes the most advanced thinking on the conservation of our natural resources — books about soil, land, water, forests, wildlife, and hazardous and toxic wastes. These books are practical tools used by public officials, business and industry leaders, natural resource managers, and concerned citizens working to solve both local and global resource problems.

Founded in 1978, Island Press reorganized in 1984 to meet the increasing demand for substantive books on all resource-related issues. Island Press publishes and distributes under its own imprint and offers these services to other nonprofit organizations.

Funding to support Island Press is provided by The Mary Reynolds Babcock Foundation, The Ford Foundation, The George Gund Foundation, The William and Flora Hewlett Foundation, The Joyce Foundation, The J. M. Kaplan Fund, The John D. and Catherine T. MacArthur Foundation, The Andrew W. Mellon Foundation, Northwest Area Foundation, The Jessie Smith Noyes Foundation, The J. N. Pew, Jr. Charitable Trust, The Rockfeller Brothers Fund, and The Tides Foundation.

For additional information about Island Press publishing services and a catalog of current and forthcoming titles, contact Island Press, P.O. Box 7, Covelo, California 95428.

Drawings by Constance E. Hunt

Library of Congress Cataloging-in-Publication Data

Hunt, Constance Elizabeth.
  Down by the river.

  "Published in cooperation with National Wildlife Federation."
  Bibliography: p. 246
  Includes index.
  1. Water resources development — Environmental aspects — United States. 2. Biological diversity conservation — United States. I. Huser, Verne.
II. Title.
QH545.W33H86   1988   333.91'00973   88-13018
ISBN 0-933280-48-3
ISBN 0-933280-47-5 (pbk.)

To my mother, Constance F.

Contents

Foreword

For a heavily industrialized and urbanized nation grappling with increasing demands for energy and development, the values of a meandering stream or a flowing river are often out of sight and out of mind. The values of riparian habitats—those areas within the 100-year floodplain of a stream—are even further down the list of community priorities. They shouldn't be.

Riparian habitats are among the world's richest ecosystems, as this book so vividly describes. Their distinctive and rapidly disappearing vegetation feeds an equally distinctive array of wildlife, which has an economic and aesthetic value that cannot be outweighed by the construction of another housing project, a new federally financed dam, more unsupervised livestock grazing, or the further channelization of a river. Yet all of these activities have destroyed or harmed riparian habitats, as this book also vividly describes, despite the fact that their values for controlling soil erosion, stream siltation and flooding, and for recreation can be quantified in dollars and cents.

Down by the River is an important book because it defines and describes an ecosystem that is often neglected by citizens and policymakers alike. Most people seldom think of riverbanks as separate, distinctive ecosystems. Even less frequently do people realize that riparian, or riverside, habitats are as vital to the health of our planet as are more exotic ecosystems, such as tropical forests, estuaries, and the Arctic tundra.

Nonetheless, the values of riparian habitats are finally being recognized, although perhaps not soon enough. The United States has approximately 121 million acres of land within the 100-year floodplains of rivers. At one time, most of this acreage contained riparian forests and wetlands. It no longer does.

Today, only about 23 million acres are in their natural or seminatural condition. In some floodplains, only 5 percent of the natural vegetation remains. More than 70 percent of the original floodplain forests have been converted to urban or agricultural use. In some parts of the country, the statistics are even more dramatic.

In California's Sacramento Valley, for example, only 12,000 acres of riparian woodland remain of the 775,000 acres that once existed, a reduction of more than 98 percent. In Arizona's lower Gila Valley, only 5 percent of the natural riparian vegetation remains today.

The areas surrounding some of the nation's mightiest rivers have fared no better. The development and rerouting of the Missouri River, for example, destroyed 309,000 acres of terrestrial wildlife habitat, 100,300 acres of aquatic habitat, and 65,300 acres of islands and sandbars. In 1980, approximately 640 acres of riparian habitat existed for each mile of river. By 1985, the ratio had plummeted to 140 acres per river mile.

Such massive destruction is appalling, yet not really surprising. The great conservationist Aldo Leopold said, "We abuse the land because we regard it as a commodity belonging to us. When we see land as a community to which we belong, then we may begin to use it with love and respect."

The concept of love and respect for land was integral to Native Americans but not to the Europeans, who began to settle this great land two centuries ago. During most of this nation's first two centuries, our forebears spent little time contemplating the frailty of the land. Standing on the shores of a new world, where the territory seemed endless and the resources unlimited, the settlers were more interested in conquering the land than conserving it.

And the New World's settlers did just that, fulfilling their manifest destiny with gusto. In the process, they glorified growth and expansion to the exclusion of conservation and land use planning.

Today, after more than 200 years of growth and construction, we are a land not of wilderness but of subdivisions and shopping centers. More than 75 percent of Americans live in urban settings. Demographers estimate that by the year 2000 the population of the United States will top 300 million; 90 percent of the people will live and work in cities built on land that was once wildlife habitat. We will use nearly 20 million acres of undeveloped land to accommodate our urban sprawl.

In just 200 years, we have transformed a land of wild beauty and untouched natural resources into a world where wildlife and wildlife habitat are becoming ever scarcer. That is especially true of riparian zones.

The results are apparent in our everyday lives. For most Americans, the only contact with wildlife comes from television or at the local zoo. That is a terrible loss because few things give us the pleasure, the sense of well-being, and the respect for life that is imparted when we are surrounded by nature.

In a world where natural resources — such as the serenity of a free-flowing stream — are becoming tragically scarce, the need to protect, properly manage, and restore riparian areas is heightened. We already have enough scientific evidence indicating that degraded riparian ecosystems directly affect the numbers and species diversity of fish and wildlife.

As long ago as 1975, researchers reported that removing 70 percent of the trees in Southwestern riparian areas cut the total number of birds in the vicinity by at least half. Researchers studying grazing practices found that of the 363 terrestrial species known to inhabit the Great Basin of southwestern Oregon, 288, or approximately 80 percent, either are directly dependent on riparian zones or are found nowhere else. Similar statistics can be cited around the country.

But we have an opportunity to save the small amount of riparian habitat still thriving across the United States, and this book is one step in that direction. Unlike its predecessors on the subject, *Down by the River* is the only volume that deals with rivers as whole and complex ecosystems. It helps explain, to scientists and laymen alike, the delicate balance between the health of streamside vegetation and the overall health of a river or stream.

It can well serve as a primer on the subject to all outdoor enthusiasts who find their greatest bounty along the banks of the nation's rivers and streams. At the same time, this book offers fresh insight into the subject for those who have long been concerned and knowledgeable about riparian habitats.

The National Wildlife Federation is among the legions who have long been concerned about dams and other water projects that carry an enormous environmental price tag. In this decade alone, the National Wildlife Federation has adopted numerous resolutions calling for a reasoned approach to water resources development. We have supported cost sharing between the federal and state governments for construction of dams and other projects in the belief that the process would eliminate ill-conceived projects. We have called for an end to overgrazing on federal lands, most of them riparian habitat. We have asked the federal government to appropriate monies to inventory and restore riparian lands, and we have convinced the federal Bureau of Land Management to improve somewhat its management of riparian zones.

Most importantly, we have joined with local citizens to fight such damaging and costly projects as Cliff Dam on Arizona's Verde River and Big A Dam on Maine's West Branch of the Penobscot River. And we have found that educated and concerned citizens are key to saving rivers and their riparian zones.

One segment of a four-part television series aired in 1988 and 1989, titled "Conserving America" and cosponsored by the National Wildlife Federation and WQED/Pittsburgh, looks at how citizens have fought — and won — protection for rivers and streamside habitats. Across the country, small groups of citizens, enchanted by the rivers in their communities, are banding together to fight development and channelization that can spell death to free-flowing rivers and the riparian habitats they create.

Down by the River will help these citizens' groups in their struggle to preserve the history and the natural resources heritage that are a river's gift to humankind. We are proud that Connie Hunt became interested in riparian habitats during her tenure as a research associate in the Water Resources Program of the National Wildlife Federation. Indeed, she wrote the first draft of this book while with the Federation. During her internship, she worked on the issue of endangered species protection and quickly realized that only by protecting habitat can society ensure protection for all species, whether endangered or not. It was only a short intellectual leap to the issue of riparian habitat protection.

Although the National Wildlife Federation is proud to have played a role in the publication of this book, we must note that the opinions expressed here are those of the author and do not necessarily represent the views of the National Wildlife Federation.

Down by the River is an evocative account of the misconceived and misdirected federal programs and policies that have destroyed a valuable part of America's natural resources heritage. It is also a call for a new direction and renewed concern for the protection and restoration of riparian habitats. We can only hope that the call will be heeded.

Dr. Jay D. Hair
President, National Wildlife Federation

Preface

Rivers are marvelous spirits. Perpetually singing and dancing, they amble merrily toward the ocean, where they rejoin their cradle and their grave, lose their identities, and are mystically transported to the tops of the mountains to begin new lives. Throughout their time on earth, they give life to the surrounding landscapes. Groves of trees, beds of ferns, walls of wildflowers, songs of birds, and the laughter of children are thickest and richest beside a free-flowing stream. These strips of gifted landscape are called riparian communities.

Riparian communities are disappearing, victims of the nation's eagerness to harness natural resources. Much of their demise is caused by federal projects and policies that Congress intended to benefit the general public. Such programs include the damming and channelizing of rivers, diversions of flows vital to the maintenance of in-stream and riparian life, and the granting of subsidies that encourage urban, industrial, and agricultural development of flood-prone land. Economically inefficient projects to be funded by the taxpayers are justified with contrived and skewed benefit-cost ratios. The estimated local benefits of many projects are inflated by inclusion of speculative benefits. Such benefits may include increased commerce on underused waterways and increased crop production. These are further inflated through the exclusion of long-term "negative benefits" such as erosion and decreased water quality. The predicted benefits often do not materialize, as illustrated by the lack of anticipated traffic on the Tennessee-Tombigbee Waterway; or they may become social liabilities, such as surplus crops (like soybeans and cotton) that drive down the market prices of farm products and drain the Treasury through deficiency payments and other subsidies. The actual costs excluded from consideration in planning documents are usually greater than anticipated; an example is the elimination of two anadromous fisheries from the Apalachicola-Chattahoochee-Flint waterway in Alabama, Georgia, and Florida as a result of damming and channelizing, or deepening and straightening, the rivers for navigation. Thus, sole reliance on a benefit-cost analysis to determine the public's "best interest" often results in a prodevelopment bias. The natural values of intact ecosystems, as well as the cumulative and indirect environmental effects of their alteration, are simply too difficult to accurately assess. Aldo Leopold once commented that

> a system of conservation based solely on economic interest is hopelessly lopsided. It tends to ignore, and thus eventually to eliminate, many elements in the land community that lack commercial value, but that are (as far as we know) essential to its healthy functioning. It assumes, falsely, I think, that the economic parts of the biotic clock will function without the uneconomic parts.[1]

Because the values of beauty, living species, and intact natural communities evade economic evaluation, these benefits consistently lose out in the benefit-cost evaluation game. The game is fixed.

This book describes the impacts of federal water projects and policies on riparian habitats. Using various river basins as examples of specific types of impacts, I have attempted to illustrate weaknesses in the water resources planning system. This system results in many rivers being controlled as if they were garden hoses. The hands turning the spigot too often make decisions based on impulse and political circumstance rather than on comprehensive planning. Catastrophe results for many living things, including mammals, fish, birds, reptiles, amphibians, and taxpayers.

Riparian ecosystems are one of several valuable biological systems that have suffered as a result of rapid and often reckless development. The following pages describe how some riparian systems have been affected, pinpoint weaknesses in the American political system that allow unnecessary environmental destruction in riparian zones, document what has been lost, and emphasize that there is much worth saving and much that can be restored.

In most of the basins discussed, the rivers have been developed for multiple purposes. In order to more clearly underline the individual project and policy functions, however, one water or related land use is emphasized in each chapter. The Columbia River dams, for example, provide water to croplands and contain navigation locks, but Chapter 3 describes the effects of the huge hydroelectric systems along the

[1] A. Leopold, *A Sand County Almanac* (New York: Sierra Club and Ballantine Books, 1949), 251.

Columbia and Snake rivers. The Colorado River dams are also multi-purpose, but Chapters 4 and 5 dwell on their storage and diversion of water for irrigation. It is important to keep in mind that all of the environmental impacts attributed to hydroelectric facilities on the Columbia, for example, also occur on the Colorado, the Missouri, and other rivers with large dams and hydropower facilities. Similarly, the impacts produced by storage of water for agriculture along the Colorado also occur to some extent on the Columbia and Missouri rivers.

Each chapter contains some description of the natural history of the river basin or basins being discussed. Most chapters also contain some of the human history that has influenced the economic use of the region. Individual rivers, along with their associated riparian habitats, are as different as snowflakes and thumbprints, and each has its own story.

Readers may find this book peppered with biological and water resources jargon. I have tried to keep the technical terms to a minimum and to explain them briefly in the text. A glossary is also included to help clarify some of the terms.

I first became aware of and concerned with riparian ecosystems during my college years. Simply canoeing along a river, admiring cottonwood galleries and noticing an unusual number of raptors and herons gliding near the shores, made me realize that these riverside woodlands were unique and important. As a wildlife biology student in Arizona, I spent many weekends camping along streams, planting and nurturing cottonwood seedlings and willow poles. Natural resource managers in that state seemed to be involved in an all-out battle to save and restore the precious slivers of riparian habitat that had not fallen prey to cattle, all-terrain cycles, and overzealous loggers. This concern spread beyond the desire to snatch a single species of plant or animal from the jaws of extinction. It was rather a concern that entire biological communities were disappearing, unraveling like a loosely knit sweater right before our eyes. Riparian communities are more than groups of plants and animals that just happen to share a distinct habitat type. They are sets of interactions between living things that are, in turn, interacting with other biological communities. These ecosystems are part of one grand puzzle, and each piece is of infinite value.

When I went to work for the National Wildlife Federation in Washington, DC, in 1985, my first assignment was to compile material for use in our testimony on the reauthorization of the Endangered Species Act. As I studied the history of this legislation and the case histories of endangered species that were being managed in accordance with the act, it was clear to me that our approach was completely backward. The law had the Fish and Wildlife Service identifying plant and animal species that were on the brink of extinction, then defining "critical habitats" for these species. Yet most species in modern times become endangered *because of* habitat degradation and elimination; we were treating the symptom rather than the disease. A species in danger of extinction is usually a symptom of a declining habitat type. In habitats where one species becomes extinct, chances are that other species are in danger of extinction and that we need to conserve the habitat.

Riparian zones seem to be ideal areas in which to practice the conservation of an entire ecological community, an approach that may reduce the rate of extinctions worldwide. Riparian zones are essential to wildlife and fish; they are flood prone and therefore are not suitable for most types of development; they are well suited to aesthetic enjoyment and recreation; and they are capable of providing many amenities to human society in the form of flood damage reduction and water quality enhancement. In addition, since these zones are relatively linear, the preservation of small areas of land will go far in terms of habitat protection.

Conversely, since riparian habitats are relatively linear, they have little area and consequently have received scant attention from the conservation community. It is my hope that conservationists who influence public policy, and resource managers who are able to plant trees and plan timber sales, will read this book and realize that riparian habitats exist, that they are important, and that they can be protected. I also hope that biologists will gain insight into the political environment that determines the fates of these ecosystems and realize that some of the customs and institutions involved in the frequently unnecessary destruction of these ecosystems are as fragile as the ecosystems themselves.

Riparian ecosystems are vital biological networks finely tuned to the rhythms of their rivers. They each support a distinctive complement of plants and animals, like so many rich, unique, and endangered ecosystems in the United States and throughout the world. Biological diversity is the key to ecological stability. It is the source of future foods and medicines, the seed of scientific knowledge and aesthetic beauty, and the birthright of our children. Through awareness, knowledge, and action, and through the wholehearted effort and thoughtful coordination of people in communities, government institutions, universities, and corporations, we can ensure the continued existence of riparian and other endangered ecosystems.

Acknowledgments

This book owes its existence to David C. Campbell, the National Wildlife Federation's natural resources economist. David arranged the funding for this project, communicated with the publisher, and spent numerous hours reviewing chapter drafts and providing comments. His friendship and moral support have also been invaluable.

Verne Huser assisted with the editing and pulling together of the manuscript. He directed me to new sources of information and provided helpful comments on the text.

Chris Brown of the American Rivers Conservation Council and Brent Blackwelder of the Environmental Policy Institute allowed me to plunder their libraries. Robert Ohmart and Chuck Hunter, biologists at Arizona State University, provided helpful comments on the Lower Colorado River chapter. Personnel within many state and federal agencies graciously shared their reports, photographs, and insights.

To these professionals engaged in the complicated task of managing our natural resources, and to the many other wildlife biologists, public resource managers, and conservationists who have taught me what I've learned so far, I am extremely grateful.

1

Background:
The Rivers
and Their Management

Riparian ecosystems are those natural associations of soil, flora, and fauna existing within the 100-year floodplain of a stream and dependent for their survival on sufficiently high water tables and/or periodic flooding. This definition encompasses wetlands, such as swamps and marshes, so long as they are dependent on the functions of an adjacent river. The definition, so neat and tidy on paper, tends to fray at the edges when one stands in a streamside forest and watches it grade into upland woods or desert, its overhanging banks providing habitat to aquatic wildlife. Nature rarely draws a straight line. Riparian ecosystems provide habitat for animal species that also use uplands; riparian zones depend on and fortify riverine, or in-stream, environments. Therefore, they are inextricably linked to their neighboring ecosystems, and, because life on earth is one web of energy and matter exchanges, they are linked to all ecosystems.

Rivers are ever-changing entities, and their metamorphoses create unique habitats that cannot exist anywhere but on the floodplain of a river. According to Luna B. Leopold, "the first and most important aspect of the river channel is that it is self-formed and self-maintained. The flowing water carves the groove in which it flows. The water fashions the depth, the cross-section, the areal configuration and the longitudinal profile."[1]

Rivers are much like people. They tend to be narrow, straight-backed, and fastpaced when young, gradually growing broader and slowing their pace as they age. A young river rushes toward the sea in a

1

straight-line dash of mad determination; an older river is more likely to stroll back and forth across its floodplain in broad meanders, as if pausing to enjoy the scenery. The erosive forces of the water, which carved steep canyons in the river's younger days, become directed at the banks, whittling away their outer curves and depositing materials as point bars, where the water on the inside of the curve is forced to slow down and drop its sediment load. These processes of erosion and deposition exaggerate the meanders of older rivers.

Flooding is another characteristic of rivers. Generally, high river flows begin when mountain snow starts to melt in the spring. This frozen water, which was carried to the apex of the landscape by the sun, runs in rivulets to the stream valleys nestled between glistening peaks. Periodic bank overflow is the pulse of the river, as natural and normal as the cycles of the moon.

Flooding serves a purpose, too. Sediments carried by the quickly moving stream drop out of suspension when the water passes over the river's banks and slows its frantic pace. The soils that rivers lay down, known as alluvium, are full of the minerals and nutrients present in the watershed. This soft, fine earth becomes a bank for riparian plant species to colonize. The process of sediment deposition makes it possible for most riparian communities to include a primary succession component. The new soil is colonized by plants such as silver maple, black willow, sandbar willow, salt cedar, and, depending on location, other species that can survive in unstable substrates, stabilizing them for species characteristic of more mature seral, or successional, stages. In reciprocation for the gift of constant renewal from the river, riparian communities donate nutrients to the streams in the form of organic matter.

Riparian communities are among the most valuable and productive ecosystems on earth. The leaves of streamside trees shade the water, maintaining water temperatures suitable for trout and other game fish. With the seasonal shifting of the sun and the thrust of restless winds, the trees shed their verdant plumage, providing organic fodder for the microscopic animals that form the bottom of the aquatic food chain. Compared with dryland ecosystems, riparian communities provide an astounding amount of energy to surrounding ecosystems. This supply of energy and carbon compounds feeds instream fisheries, wetland fish and shellfish nurseries, and estuaries where marine and freshwater organisms pass through various life stages. Riparian vegetation filters runoff from farms and cities that would otherwise cause pollution and eutrophication of freshwater streams and lakes. Anaerobic (oxygen-lacking) soil conditions in riparian communities, present because water fills soil pore spaces that would be filled with air in upland environments, allow vegetation to assimilate nutrients such as nitrogen and phosphorus at rates well in excess of the natural supply. This process prevents the nutrients from being exported in excessive amounts to freshwater ecosystems downstream, where they would cause water quality deterioration. The roots of streamside grasses, forbs, and trees bind the soil of the floodplain and riverbanks, armoring them naturally against erosive forces and reducing the amount of soil that would otherwise pass into the stream.

It is not surprising that evolution has created myriad creatures specifically adapted to the unique ecological conditions of streamside forests and wetlands. Riparian ecosystems in their natural state provide many basic wildlife needs, such as early seral vegetation for foraging, water for drinking, and lush growth for hiding and nesting cover. Amphibians must have a land-water interface to pass from larval to adult form. Aquatic furbearers, such as beavers, river otters, minks, muskrats, and nutria, must have a healthy bank habitat to survive. More specialized ecosystems harbor rare animal species that are highly dependent on one specific type of habitat. Bottomland hardwood forests, for example, provide irreplaceable habitat for alligators, gars, bowfins, and several turtle species that have changed little since prehistoric times. Riparian habitats in the desert Southwest are also highly specialized. Among the few ecosystems with a fairly stable water supply, southwestern riparian communities sport the tallest, most dense, and most complex growth of woody vegetation in very arid climates. In the hottest locations in this region, high-canopied trees such as cottonwoods and willows provide the only available insulation for birds' nests, protecting them from the sweltering summer sun. In areas such as Yuma, Arizona, the eggs of summer tanagers and other birds would literally cook if not for forested riparian communities.

Added to these ecological services are the values of natural riparian communities to people for camping, birdwatching, plant collecting, photography, hiking, hunting, horseback riding, picnicking, ski touring, trapping, gold panning, wading, canoeing, rafting, and kayaking.

By virtue of their biological diversity and density, riparian communities are a priceless national treasure. This treasure has been slipping away from American society virtually unnoticed for two centuries. The time has come for Americans to put the brakes on the destruction of riparian habitat — to stop it cold and, through restoration, to reverse the trend.

Riparian ecosystems have fallen victim to a number of abuses. Overzealous logging practices, such as careless cable logging and buffer strip removal, often alter or destroy riparian forests. Unrestrictive livestock managers allow cattle and sheep to concentrate in riparian communities, where water is available and vegetation is especially succulent. The livestock break down riverbanks, compact the soil, remove the vegetational ground cover, and make hors d'oeuvres of tender saplings, thereby suppressing tree recruitment in the next generation. Cities and farmlands that encroach on floodplain ecosystems often receive their just deserts when the rivers reclaim their turf.

Traditional western water law has also contributed to the decline of riparian habitats in arid lands. Western states developed an appropriative doctrine of water rights—property holders must divert the water from a river and put it to "beneficial use" in order to claim a legal right to the water. Beneficial use has not traditionally included the perpetuation of in-stream flows to sustain fish, wildlife, and streamside ecology, although some western states now recognize in-stream flows as a beneficial use.

Federal alteration and management of waterways in the United States began as a noncontroversial boon to national development. As the number of water projects grows, however, each new project's marginal utility, or increment of benefit accruing to the national economy, decreases. Conversely, the basic economic principle of diminishing marginal utility indicates that each remaining acre of natural stream ecosystem increases in its value to society as more and more of these ecosystems are altered and destroyed. For those water projects that are federally subsidized, the economic benefits they provide to local communities usually exceed the dollar cost to those communities. Thence arises a transfer of wealth from the nation at large to the beneficiary state or congressional district. It is no wonder that senators and congressmen push for water projects and policies that will increase their popularity in their home states and districts.

Congress and Water Development

"Porkbarrel politics" is a term commonly used to refer to the congressional authorization of essentially unneeded public works projects. The term originated in the Deep South, where planters once rolled out barrels of salt pork as a reward for their hardworking, half-starved slaves. The slaves would scramble to carry home as much pork as they could. In a similar manner, legislators have developed a reputation for grabbing at tax dollars and transforming them into concrete party favors, which they proudly cart home to their voters. Congressmen are more cooperative than slaves, however; most vote for their colleagues' pet projects and expect their colleagues to do the same for them.

The "iron triangle" is another bit of political science jargon relevant to the queer business of water projects. The three corners of the triangle are the relevant congressional committees (such as the committees on appropriations, public works, and the interior), the federal agencies responsible for water project construction, and the special-interest groups (project beneficiaries) that stand to gain from the construction of these projects in their neighborhoods. Most water projects are initiated either by the federal agencies, which benefit from expanded budgets and jurisdiction, or by the project beneficiaries, who gain from public subsidy of their private business ventures. The legislators, who benefit from the publicity generated by new public works projects in their districts, and often from the generous financial support of the project beneficiaries, tap the funds that create reality from the dreams of the beneficiaries and the nightmares of environmentalists. The relationship between the three corners of the triangle is "alleged to be impenetrable from the outside and uncontrollable by president, political appointees, or legislators not on the committees in question."[2]

Little Help from the Executive Arm

The executive branch of the U.S. government has made some attempts to overcome water project "back scratching" on Capitol Hill since the Eisenhower administration. These attempts have been insufficient to crack the iron triangle, which swallows presidents much as the Bermuda Triangle swallows ships.

Eisenhower, who referred to the Tennessee Valley Authority as "creeping socialism," promoted a "no new starts" policy for the Bureau of Reclamation. His opposition to federal water projects was pro-private sector, not antidam, however. Ike denied both the Army Corps of Engineers and the Bureau of Reclamation the opportunity to dam Hells Canyon on the Snake River in Idaho, instead granting that honor to the Idaho Power Company. The company's dams, Brownlee, Oxbow, and Hells Canyon, flooded the nation's second deepest canyon and destroyed hundreds of miles of salmon habitat.[3]

Ike finally caved in to congressional proproject pressure and signed the authorization for the massive Central Arizona Project before leaving office.

President Kennedy expressed concern for the environment and encouraged prudent planning, rather than porcine politics, in the use of the nation's water resources. Kennedy was himself seduced by the temptation to use water projects as political wampum, however. He offered his support for the Cross-Florida Barge Canal largely in return for the support of the political machine in Florida.

Lyndon Johnson's support for the Marshall Ford Dam in Texas played a large role in catapulting him from the House of Representatives to the Senate. President Nixon gave his support to the disastrous Teton Dam in Idaho in return for Congress' favorable votes on his foreign policy initiatives. Even river-runner Jimmy Carter, who attempted to smash the iron triangle as soon as he took his seat in the Oval Office, signed the final authorization for Tellico Dam in Tennessee to gain congressional support for the Panama Canal Treaty.[4]

Ronald Reagan made some headway against the triangle in 1985 when he promised to veto the first omnibus water projects bill in a decade if the bill didn't contain rigorous requirements for local interests to share with the Treasury an increased portion of the cost of federal water projects. Congress complied, requesting local sponsors to provide 25 to 100 percent of the funding for construction of newly authorized projects. As a result, many project proposals have been scaled back so that local sponsors can afford to pay their fair share.

The House of Representatives' omnibus water resources bill covering the activities of the Army Corps of Engineers in 1986 was, nevertheless, a heap of favors owed by one colleague to another. The contents of the bill were no real surprise to Americans; the exchange of political favors is an unwritten fraternal rule on the Hill. As Robert A. Roe, chairman of the House Subcommittee on Water Resources, Committee on Public Works and Transportation, stated, "It is all well to go and try to grab something out of the pot, but it is fundamentally wrong if we deny somebody else, and that is the one code this committee has worked on, that is the one code this committee has taken."[5] Economically inefficient and environmentally destructive resource development is the result of water resource management under this code.

Some of the results of the collegial code of water development are irrigation facilities that produce surplus crops and contribute to severe depression of the farm economy; flood control structures that create a false sense of security for real estate developers, who then build on the floodplains; and drastic and expensive alterations of rivers so that they can accommodate the increased commercial traffic that *could* someday travel on the waterways.

Unwise federal water policies and projects drive riverine and riparian species to the brink of extinction, ruin recreational opportunities, annihilate wetland and estuarine seafood "factories," and diminish America's biological diversity.

Federal agencies form the limbs of the executive branch of our government. These agencies are staffed by politically appointed administrators trying to carry out the will of the presidential administration. The chief executives of the last three decades have battled, or at least decried, wasteful government spending on unneeded water development. Yet the agencies take on lives of their own and engage in attempts to expand their budget and authority.

The water project machinery churns out blueprints like the Keebler elves churn out cookies. Yet project planners often overlook or deemphasize the environmental aspects of water development. One factor contributing to the lack of attention paid to the environment in federal water resource planning seems to be the difficulty of estimating values that cannot be marketed. The imprecision of environmental valuation seems to drive economists in the executive branch away from attempts to accurately balance environmental costs and benefits of water development plans. Therefore, benefit/cost analyses become weighted toward readily quantified economic values; environmental values are virtually ignored; the development plans appear profitable; and the proposed projects are constructed, usually with inadequate mitigation for environmental losses.

The American public, once it is informed of resource abuses resulting from federal management, usually rises to the defense of those resources. Such concern over natural resources has triggered the creation of many environmental statutes and programs to protect valuable natural areas.

The same taxpayers who support wild and scenic rivers, wilderness areas, and national parks also pay for a large hunk of the water project development that takes place on our rivers. Federal water projects have provided American society with a wide range of valuable benefits, but as citizens we need to be aware of some of the damages and costs these projects have incurred so that we can participate in wiser use of our dwindling river resources in the future.

The History of Federal Water Development

In historical perspective, the involvement of the federal government in water resource development brings to mind the classic cartoon snowball rolling downhill, gathering bulk, speed, and destructive capacity as it descends. The exploration and development of America's waterways began in pursuit of legitimate national objectives such as geographic expansion and economic development. As waterway development increased, it thrived on its own momentum and was credited with less precise and more localized benefits. By the middle of the twentieth century, water projects were becoming expensive gifts from Congress to influential constituents, but the adverse environmental effects of the projects were growing increasingly apparent. Americans can halt this uncontrolled federal water development snowball if they look up in time to see it ominously bearing down on them.

Many federal agencies are responsible for actions that degrade riparian habitat. Among those agencies not discussed in detail in this chapter are the Tennessee Valley Authority, the Department of Housing and Urban Development, the Bureau of Land Management, and the Forest Service. The following discussion of federal activities and their effects on riparian habitats is not comprehensive, but it should be sufficient to provide a diorama for those who care about natural resources.

The federal government entered the water development picture in 1824, when the General Survey Act authorized the Army Corps of Engineers to maintain navigability on the Mississippi and Ohio rivers by removing obstructive snags (dead trees) and sandbars. The corps, which is America's oldest engineering firm, had already been involved in many aspects of the nation's development. The corps had risen in a moment of glory during the Revolutionary War, rushing to the aid of the new nation. On July 15, 1775, the British warships *Lively* and *Falcon* were firebombing Continental troops at Bunker Hill. On July 16, the army formed the Corps of Engineers, and on July 17, the corps had designed and built an earthen fortification. After the war and until 1824, the major responsibility of the corps was surveying areas for canals, roads, and railroads, but by the late 1800s, it had become primarily a navigation and flood control agency.

Throughout the nineteenth century, federal activities on inland waters reflected the expansion of the United States and focused on navigation as the means to bring settlers into the wild country, furnish them with tools and supplies, and eventually carry to market the fruits of their labor.

The Reclamation Act of 1902 established the Reclamation Service, later renamed the Bureau of Reclamation. The intent of the act was to provide for "the construction and maintenance of irrigation works for the storage, diversion and development of waters for the reclamation of arid and semi-arid lands." The Reclamation Service germinated quickly. By 1903, the agency was building six projects, and by 1907, it was overseeing the construction of twenty-seven projects.

The projects were, at first, intended solely for the storage and diversion of river water to fields in the western United States. These states had long growing seasons and fertile soils; they needed only adequate moisture to be brought into production. This type of federal water development served to help settle the West, but it also triggered an era of multipurpose projects that enhanced national and local economies by providing cheap, government-subsidized commercial transportation, electricity, flood control, and municipal, industrial, and agricultural water.

The Federal Water Power Act of June 10, 1920 created the Federal Power Commission, which was replaced in 1977 by the Federal Energy Regulatory Commission (FERC). The commission was originally charged with regulating the nation's water resources but later assumed responsibility for overseeing the electric power and natural gas industries.

During the 1930s, the United States was trying to yank itself to its feet in the face of a series of problems. The Depression era, the Dust Bowl, and our entry into World War II contributed to immense pressures on the economy. In 1933, the Bureau of Reclamation joined the Public Works Administration in order to carry out federal conservation policies and economic recovery programs. That same year, the bureau began construction on Grand Coulee Dam, which, when completed, generated power primarily for aircraft manufacturing and for the production of aluminum needed for the war effort.

On April 27, 1935, Congress created the Soil Conservation Service (SCS) in the Department of Agriculture. In 1938, the secretary of agriculture assigned to the SCS drainage and irrigation responsibilities and consolidated in the new agency all soil erosion control, flood control, and related activities involving actual physical work on farmlands and on predominantly agricultural watersheds. The SCS was created to alleviate the problems of poor land use that had aggravated the Dust Bowl. Not a water management agency per se, the SCS developed drainage and flood control programs that have greatly influenced land use along waterways.

From the 1930s until the mid-1960s, conventional wisdom viewed water development projects mostly as a means of strengthening the national economy. The benefits credited to these projects expanded from concrete estimates of acres of cropland and miles of navigable waterway to less precise estimates of more job opportunities, increased investments, and greater productivity. The Flood Control Act of 1936 contained the first benefit/cost analysis requirement in the history of federal water development in its statement that "the benefits, to whomsoever they may accrue, [must be] in excess of the estimated costs."[6] This simple phrase was perceived by developers as a constraint on their water-related activities.

Under the benefit/cost analysis requirement of the flood control act, the United States saw some of its first juggling of justifications for expensive water projects. According to William B. Lord, director of the Water Resources Research Center at the University of Arizona,

> the first response to the constraining effect of the benefit-cost rules was to define benefits and costs in such a way as to preserve the appearance of constraint but to eliminate the practical impact. Savings to shippers, secondary benefits, land enhancement benefits, cost of the next best alternative and other concepts were introduced through agency practice, or even through legislative action. They all had the effect of increasing allowable benefits or decreasing costs. They also had the effect of stimulating opposition from the Office of Management and Budget, from water resources development opponents, and from most academic economists.[7]

When the national emphasis was almost solely on economic development, the environment did not receive equal consideration. Although project planners invented indirect water project benefits when jousting for federal funds, the losses to the environment and the demise of natural mechanisms that stabilize banks, control floods, and cleanse water naturally were rarely discussed.

The projects being studied and authorized by Congress were quickly stacking up, and the executive branch was becoming anxious over the huge amounts of Treasury funds that Congress funneled into them. As one means to curb federal spending, President Eisenhower vetoed the omnibus rivers and harbors legislation of 1958 and proposed a "no new starts" policy for the 1959 and 1960 budgets. The House and Senate appropriations committees ignored this policy and approved a huge public works appropriations bill for 1960. Eisenhower vetoed this bill.

Partially in reaction to presidential opposition to new water projects, the Senate established a Select Committee on National Water Resources in April 1959. This committee was to collect information through public hearings, studies, and reports to determine the necessity of further water development. The committee submitted its report to the Senate in January 1961. The report cited anticipated water shortages, decreasing water quality, and flooding among the primary water-related concerns. Among other solutions, the report proposed increased regulation of stream flows by reservoirs, better use of underground water, increased efficiency in water use, and increased water yield through desalinization and weather modification. This report provided the foundation for President Kennedy's future actions regarding water planning.

In July 1961, Kennedy submitted to Congress a draft of a water resources planning act. The draft legislation proposed the creation of a water resources council to be composed of the secretary of agriculture; the secretary of the interior; the secretary of health, education and welfare; and the secretary of the army. Such a council would have the authority to make biennial nationwide water supply-demand studies, which had been recommended by the Select Committee on National Water Resources. The council would also establish uniform standards for the evaluation and formulation of water projects by all federal planners; it would review plans from river basin commissions (these commissions were established to represent all federal agencies, state governments, and interstate or international parties with an interest in each major river basin); and it would study and recommend changes in the entire federal water resources program. After 4 years of congressional debate, the act passed into law with only minor changes.

The mid-1960s triggered a change in water resource planning. Jobs and energy shortages were not a major national issue; society had an increasing awareness of the environment and its own dependence on renewable resources. The relative affluence of the American people, their concentration in urban centers, their increasing supply of leisure time, and their great mobility changed the emphasis of national water development somewhat from economic development of river basins to municipal, industrial, and recreational purposes.

Concerns for environmental quality were manifested in legislation beginning in the 1960s. Among the laws passed were the Wild and Scenic Rivers Act (1968), the National Environmental Protection Act (NEPA)(1969), the Endangered Species Act (1973), and the Clean Water Act (1977). All have significantly influenced federal water resource development.

The Wild and Scenic Rivers Act, which became law in 1968, ensures that qualifying rivers are preserved by prohibiting federal agencies from approving or providing assistance to any water or land resources project that may adversely affect a designated river segment. Individual bills designating wild and scenic reaches establish land corridors subject to use and development restrictions, preventing riparian habitat degradation. Although potentially a powerful means to protect free-flowing rivers and riparian communities, this act has been sluggishly used by Congress in placing rivers into the wild and scenic system. In 1985, only two-tenths of a percent of America's river miles were protected under this act.

President Nixon signed the National Environmental Protection Act into law on January 1, 1970. NEPA declares it a national policy to encourage productive and enjoyable harmony between man and the environment. Section 102(2)(c) of that act requires the preparation of an environmental impact statement for any federal activity that will have a significant impact on the environment. An environmental impact statement must document the perceived need for the proposed plan and its potential damage or benefits to the environment. These documents are reviewed by interested private and public parties.

Section 7 of the Endangered Species Act of 1973 requires federal agencies to consult with the Fish and Wildlife Service before funding, permitting, or constructing any project that may harm an endangered species. If the Fish and Wildlife Service finds, in a "biological opinion," that the proposed action is likely to jeopardize the continued existence of a federally listed endangered species, the project cannot go forward. Jeopardy opinions usually contain "reasonable and prudent alternatives," which are essentially modifications to the plan that would preserve the species while allowing the plan to proceed.

Section 404 of the Clean Water Act of 1977 (formerly the Federal Water Pollution Control Act of 1972) contains provisions that require developers to obtain a federal permit from the Army Corps of Engineers before discharging dredged or fill materials into any waters of the United States. Under regulations promulgated in response to a 1975 lawsuit (NRDC v. Calloway), "waters of the United States" include navigable waters, their tributaries, and their adjacent wetlands. Court decisions resulting from lawsuits in the early 1980s expanded the corps's jurisdiction under this law to include isolated wetlands. In effect, Section 404 is the most important federal program for protecting wetlands. It is jointly administered by the Army Corps of Engineers and the Environmental Protection Agency (EPA). The corps is responsible for issuing or denying permits to fill U.S. waters and for taking enforcement actions when these waters are filled without a permit or in violation of permit conditions. The EPA establishes the environmental standards that projects must meet, decides which waters are within the scope of the program, and has the authority to veto harmful projects permitted by the corps. The Fish and Wildlife Service in the Department of the Interior and the National Marine Fisheries Service in the Department of Commerce also review Section 404 permits, but they have no veto power.

In the early 1970s, water projects were competing for dwindling federal funds. In 1973, the Water Resources Council published its principles and standards for water resources planning and evaluation. These guidelines established environmental quality as a coequal objective with national economic development in water resources planning—a major move forward for environmental protection. The principles and standards were strengthened and published as rules in 1979 and 1980.

During his administration, President Carter closely scrutinized federal water plans on both economic and environmental grounds and proposed that their costs be shared by the local beneficiaries. In 1977, Carter called for the establishment of a national water policy. He ordered a review of federal water plans for which Congress was considering appropriation requests. The review found that many of the proposed projects failed to meet minimum economic, environmental, and safety criteria. As a result of the review, the president opposed any funding for eighteen projects and proposed major design changes in five others. In June 1978, Carter requested Congress to fund twenty-six new water projects. Congress passed a bill that contained funding for nine projects Carter had sliced from the water projects list the year before. Carter vetoed the bill.

When the Reagan administration took office, it influenced water resource development in two major ways. First, it relaxed the tight process for water resource plan evaluation by dismissing the staff of the Water Resources Council and abolishing the nonstatutory regional river basin commissions. The Water Resources Council then repealed its original principles and standards and replaced them with nonbinding principles and guidelines that defined national economic development as the sole objective in water resources planning. The repeal of the council's original principles and standards was a huge setback for the environmental movement.

Second, the Reagan administration continued Carter's tough stance on cost-sharing requirements for water projects, threatening to increase the hurdles for aspiring water developers. Developers would be forced by tougher cost-sharing provisions to find private-sector sponsors who would monetarily back up their claims that their proposed projects were sorely needed by their local communities.

The environmental costs and benefits of federally supported water projects, often eclipsed by the political motives of project pushers, continue to elude objective evaluation of which projects will truly benefit American society. In a report by the Rockefeller Brothers Fund Task Force lies the following summary:

> The whole water supply problem is greatly compounded by the continuing large water-engineering projects of the U.S. Army Corps of Engineers and the Bureau of Reclamation. All too often nowadays, these are "pork-barrel" projects which diminish the overall resource (by enhancing evaporation from impoundments), destroy land, wildlife habitat and recreational opportunities, while providing marginal or negative real net economic benefits. The federal government has for too long subsidized unwise, economically inefficient and environmentally destructive water engineering projects, which in turn have permitted and stimulated unwise settlement and development.[8]

Impacts of Federal Water Projects and Policies on
Riparian Habitat

Two centuries of intensive river development have left their mark on riparian ecosystems. Although the extent of the loss of riparian communities has not been quantified, the Eastern Energy and Land Use Team of the Fish and Wildlife Service issued a report in 1981 that estimated the total losses.[9] According to the service's report, at one time 121 million acres of riparian vegetation may have existed within the 100-year floodplains of rivers of the lower forty-eight states. Currently, only 23 million acres now exist in a natural or seminatural condition.

Seventy percent of the original floodplain forests have been converted to urban or cultivated agriculture uses. In some floodplains, 95 percent of the natural vegetation has been destroyed. The National Park Service, in its nationwide rivers inventory, judged 60 percent of the major stream segments in the contiguous United States to be ineligible for inclusion in the national wild and scenic rivers program.[10] Out of an estimated 6 percent of the land mass in the lower forty-eight states that could support (and in pristine condition, probably did support) riparian vegetation, only 2 percent still does. These communities will continue to diminish if the last drops of western water are used for irrigation, if more intensive navigation improvement programs are implemented, if additional structural flood damage reduction measures are constructed, and if the clearing of floodplains for urban use and agricultural development increases.

In many cases, federal water projects sterilize otherwise productive natural habitats by inundating them, by dredging them out of the floodplain, or by simply starving them of the water and nutrients provided by over-bank flooding. In other cases, these projects simply transform a variety of river and stream ecotypes — their vegetation, their soils, and their wildlife — and leave in their place the ecology of a fluctuating reservoir.

Water resource developers might argue that the impoundment of these rivers increases recreational opportunities and, in some cases, fish and wildlife habitat. Indeed, these reservoirs, with their boat ramps, picnic tables, observation decks, and hatchery-reared bass, do provide recreational opportunities. The price is paid, however, in loss of diversity and in loss of choices of landscape, wildlife, and recreational activities.

All of the large rivers in our country have been severely altered by federal water projects. Some, such as the lower Mississippi and the Apalachicola, have merely been channelized and mechanically stabilized so that over-bank flooding and river meandering no longer occur, a state of affairs that nature could probably correct if left to her own devices for a century or so. Many other rivers, such as the Columbia, the Colorado, the upper Mississippi, and the Missouri, have been transformed into submissive strings of man-made reservoirs. In the wake of the recent boom in small hydroelectric project development, many smaller streams are destined to similar fates.

The end result is that the United States has more and more artificial lakes and fewer and fewer natural streams. The options are decreasing for recreationists; they will have to adjust to the loss of many of their playtime activities. The options for riverine and riparian wildlife are also decreasing, but because living things depend on the generally slow process of evolution to allow them to adapt to changing environmental conditions, and because the pace at which modern society is altering river-dependent ecosystems is much more rapid than the pace of evolution, the wildlife is unable to adjust. Instead, it dies off, species by species, until we are left with a natural heritage that resembles a robbed and vandalized Egyptian tomb.

Riparian zones are ecologically important in their own right, but they also serve as symbols of the interrelatedness of the natural world. Their linear shape reminds us that, like thread, they hold together the many aquatic and upland communities that clothe our planet, providing food, shelter, and buffers from both natural and human-imposed shocks. All ecosystems are dependent on one another, and the economic, as well as mental and spiritual, welfare of human society depends on the availability of fertile land, clean water, open space, and other natural resources. Destruction of natural ecosystems, whether they be isolated wetlands, prairie grasslands, old-growth mixed hardwood forests, or riparian corridors, leads to an unstable, sterile, and downright boring world. It is fortunate that we human beings possess the intelligence to learn from our mistakes and the ingenuity to correct them. Through coordinated protection and restoration efforts, riparian ecosystems can remain an important part of our national heritage.

NOTES

1. L. B. Leopold, "Rivers," *American Scientist* 50 (1962): 511.
2. J. W. Kingdon, *Agendas, Alternatives, and Public Policies* (Boston, MA: Little, Brown and Company, 1984), 36.
3. T. Palmer, *Endangered Rivers and the Conservation Movement* (Berkeley, CA: University of California Press, 1986), 67.
4. M. Reisner, Cadillac Desert: The American West and Its Disappearing Water (New York: Viking Penguin, 1986), 341.

5. C. Peterson, "The Deficit vs. the Pork Barrel: House Considers Giant Water-Projects Bill That Gramm-Rudman-Hollings Could Wipe Out," *The Washington Post*, 13 November 1985.

6. Flood Control Act of 1936 (33 U.S.C.A., sec. 701a).

7. W. B. Lord, "Objectives and Constraints in Federal Water Resources Planning," *Water Resources Bulletin* 17, no. 6 (1981): 1061.

8. L. U. Wilson, *State Water Policy Issues* (Lexington, KY: The Council of State Governments, 1978), 23.

9. M. M. Brinson, et al., *Riparian Ecosystems: Their Ecology and Status*, Fish and Wildlife Service publication OBS-81/17 (Washington, DC: Government Printing Office, 1981), 15.

10. National Park Service, *Nationwide Rivers Inventory* (Washington, DC: Government Printing Office, 1982).

Common Impacts
of River Development

L et's start with the basics: a dam, for example. A modern dam is a monolithic monument, gracefully arched yet with as stark and imposing a face as a towering cliff, and strong enough to turn a powerful, churning, bedrock-devouring river into a meek and obedient reservoir. Dams have transformed life-styles and landscapes throughout the United States; they have also transformed tens of thousands of ecosystems.

Effects of Dam Construction

In order to construct a dam, engineers first drive a diversion tunnel through the wall of the river canyon from a point upstream of the dam site to a point downstream. They then line the tunnel with concrete and build inlet and outlet sections to minimize flow turbulence. Cofferdams (watertight structures that allow exposure of the riverbed) are placed across the river above and below the dam site to divert the water into the tunnel and prevent it from backing up into the dam site. Construction of the cofferdams requires excavation of the river bottom to a level bed and construction of cutoff trenches in each canyon wall for stream flow diversion.

These activities completely alter streamside communities. The river can no longer supply water to flora and fauna along the natural stream course, and organisms that move with the stream flow have no natural bank habitat to supply them with nutrition and cover.

After they divert the stream, work crews clear the vegetation from the dam construction and reservoir areas. Thus, riparian habitat is directly destroyed. Masonry dam construction requires excavation of foundation and abutment areas of the dam. First, workers dredge the area and remove all earth, sand, gravel, and loose rock. This directly destroys some riparian vegetation; more is lost under disposed spoils from the excavation. Digging of the stream bottom may lower the water table and make water inaccessible to established vegetative root systems. Additional rock must be drilled, blasted, excavated, loaded, and removed so that the dam may be constructed on solid bedrock.

Impacts of the excavation phase on riparian ecosystems include loss of vegetation; disturbance of wildlife populations, which leads to animal stress and area abandonment; and loss of topsoil, which prevents immediate vegetative regeneration.

The project crew must have facilities such as roads, buildings, minor utility pipelines, surfaced areas for parking, and storage areas available to them during the construction period. Construction and maintenance of these facilities disrupts and destroys additional natural communities.

Dams designed to produce hydroelectric power entail further disruption in the construction of appurtenances such as powerhouses and turbines. Dams used for navigation require locks, the passages through which boats may pass. In order for a dam to supply water for agricultural, municipal, and/or industrial uses, diversion structures must be built. Overflow spillways, dam gates, large conduit pipes (penstocks), and pumphouses are other common features of large dams.[1]

Dam Operation and the Destruction of Riparian Vegetation

Filling of the reservoir and operation of the dam severely interfere with vegetation, both in the project area and downstream. When the reservoir fills, riparian habitat becomes inundated, directly destroying the submerged vegetation. Many of the plant species that are not submerged in the initial filling are unable to tolerate the subsequent water level fluctuations typical in reservoirs and die off, reducing habitat for wildlife. Terrestrial habitat shrinks in acreage as a direct result of inundation. The land-water interface in the project area increases, resulting in shifts in flora and fauna as the ecology changes from that of a river to that of a lakelike impoundment.[2]

Soil moisture may accumulate in the drawdown zone of the reservoir (that area periodically but not permanently inundated by the reservoir) to the extent that marshes and swamps form.[3] Vegetation in this zone then shifts from riparian species intolerant of prolonged flooding, such as cottonwood and willow, to flood-tolerant emergents, such as cattail and bulrush.

Evaporation from reservoirs decreases stream flows below the dam and concentrates salts in the remaining water. Fluctuation of reservoir water levels, particularly when a dam is used for production of hydropower, leaves barren mud flats on previously vegetated banks. The shorelines of these reservoirs change constantly; water levels can drop 10 to 20 feet in 8 to 12 hours. In the upper end of a reservoir, where the water is shallow, such a drop will in some instances leave a mud flat several hundred acres in size. These muddy areas may last for weeks or months, depending on the seasonal rainfall and recharge capacity of the river.

Riparian habitat in the reservoir area may further be reduced by erosive water forces cutting away banks and submerged hills. Waves created by winds and by barge or boat traffic aggravate the erosion caused by water level fluctuation. In general, erosion increases as water level fluctuation increases. Grand Coulee Reservoir illustrates this trend; 74 landslides were recorded at the reservoir in 1967 and 135 were recorded in 1974. The water level fluctuations in the reservoir were gradually increasing within that time span. Entire islands have been leveled or significantly reduced in size by erosion in John Day, McNary, and Ice Harbor reservoirs in the Columbia River basin.[4]

Sediments swept from the land by runoff are carried to rivers. These particles drop out of suspension as a river enters a reservoir and its flow velocity decreases. Sediment deposition may build up the streambed, elevating both the stream bottom and the level of the water table. This increase in water table elevation may cause changes in riparian vegetation and drainage requirements. Most irrigation, hydropower, and flood control reservoirs are large enough to trap almost 100 percent of the sediments carried into them by a stream.[5] In fact, sediments may fill up a reservoir so quickly that they drastically decrease the life expectancy of the dam. For example, Lake Wasco on the Brazos River in Texas suffered a loss of over half of its water-retention capacity, from 39,378 acre-feet to 15,427 acre-feet, in just 34 years. (An acre-foot is the volume of water necessary to cover 1 acre to a depth of 1 foot.) Ocoee Dam No. 3, on the Ocoee River in North Carolina, decreased in capacity from 14,304 acre-feet in 1942 to 3,879 acre-feet in 1972. Black Butte Reservoir on Stony Creek in California decreased from its 1963 capacity of 160,009 acre-feet to a 1973 capacity of 147,754 acre-feet.[6]

Because sediment is entrapped in the reservoir upstream, the downstream system receives essentially clear, "sediment-hungry" water. The clear water derives its equilibrium load by entraining bed sediments and eroding riverbanks.[7] These actions decrease the flood-plain width and therefore decrease the area available for establishment of riparian habitat. The degradation of the main stream channel also increases the gradient of local tributary streams. When the tributary gradients increase, they too are subject to bank erosion. Channel stabilization, the lining of bed and banks with rock or concrete, may be required in the main channel and tributaries to protect riparian land and adjacent developments. Degradation of the channel network reduces the water table level in the floodplain and causes shifts in vegetative composition.[8]

If the normal pattern of seasonal flooding is altered as a result of dam operation, long-established patterns of soil fertility relationships will change as well.[9] For example, riparian vegetation that depends on spring deposition of silt for seedling establishment, such as cotton-woods and sandbar willow, will not regenerate. Floodplain lakes, marshes, swamps, and ponds may not receive annual or seasonal replenishment of water and nutrients. Use of a dam for hydroelectric generation can produce fluctuations downstream that shift conditions from those of a large stream to those of a small headwater in a short period of time.[10]

The House of Cards

Soils and vegetation are the foundations for all forms of animal life. As ecologists and other prophets have long acknowledged, all life is inextricably woven together. Energy and nutrients change form and place, passing from river to forest and back again, within the complex structure devised by nature over the vast span of geologic time. Man cannot simply yank the carpet out from under this magnificent house of cards without inflicting negative consequences on plants, animals, and grandchildren.

Effects of Dams on Aquatic Life

Streamside vegetation is essential in maintaining the aquatic ecosystems that support fisheries. Roots of riparian plants stabilize banks, prevent erosion, and occasionally create overhanging banks that serve as cover for fish.[11] Streamside trees and herbs decrease the amount of sediment passing into the water and keep water temperatures cool enough to support cold-water fisheries. Sedimentation blocks fish gill filaments and results in fish death by anoxemia and carbon dioxide retention. Sedimentation also decreases the oxygen supply to fish eggs, resulting in their death, and alters the habitat of the aquatic invertebrates that form the prey base for many fish. F. H. Everest estimated that destruction of all riparian vegetation along the 5.3-mile Waters Creek in Oregon would result in an 80 percent loss of the stream's fishery because of thermal pollution and increased sedimentation.[12]

Riparian vegetation serves as a source of large organic debris, which distributes sediments in a stream and creates pool and riffle habitat for aquatic organisms. Organic debris is an important source of nutrition for aquatic ecosystems as well.

Stream organisms may feed on herbaceous debris as soon as it enters the water, since it is low in fiber but high in nutrients. Coniferous leaves may require between 180 and 200 days of "processing" by the stream before aquatic organisms can consume them.[13] Thus, a stream passing through an older, stratified forest contains rich and diverse populations of aquatic insects that are keyed to the timing and varied quality of the detrital food base. In short, riparian vegetation regulates the energy base of the stream.

Effect of Dams on Terrestrial Life

Streamside woodlands provide irreplaceable habitat for species within every class of animal life. Many larger animals use this habitat seasonally, such as during the harsh winter months, when uplands are incapable of providing food and thermal shelter. Strips of dense vegetation along rivers are particularly important to large animals during the winter as a barrier against merciless winds and blizzards and as a source of food. Elk give birth in riparian zones, where dense vegetation creates camouflage and streams provide drinking water.

Some smaller animals are inextricably bound to healthy floodplain ecosystems throughout the year. Destruction of these habitats results directly in the decline of these animals. Examples include voles, minks, muskrats, beavers, river otters, and nutria, as well as mice, rabbits, and other common upland species that winter near streams.

Many birds use the shores and banks of streams and rivers for nesting. Although reservoirs can increase the area of land suitable for nests, dam operation often causes unexpected fluctuations in water levels that wash away eggs or inundate nest sites.

Other birds use riparian trees for nesting, roosting, and hunting. Reservoirs often make open-water habitat out of streamside forests, killing the trees. The effect is beneficial for snag-loving birds, so long as the dead trees are left standing, but detrimental for birds that use living trees during their various life stages.

Reptiles and amphibians commonly lay their eggs on stream banks or in river shallows. Reservoir fluctuations prematurely end their development as the eggs are either inundated or dessicated beyond their tolerance.

The wildlife native to any ecosystem reflects the health of that ecosystem. Declines in wildlife populations signal a diseased ecosystem, which is as detrimental to the welfare of human beings as it is to that of other living creatures.

Using the Dam

Hydroelectricity

The natural force of river water as it moves downstream toward the ocean is a form of kinetic energy. To harness this energy, dam planners place turbines in the path of the flowing water. The water turns blades in the turbines, creating mechanical energy. The turbines then turn generator rotors, which produce electricity.

The steeper the gradient down which the water moves, the greater the force it generates and the more power it can produce. The height from which the water flows into the turbines is called the "head." The height of the dam often determines the head of a hydropower generating facility.

Currently, several different methods exist for producing hydroelectricity. One of these is the "run-of-the-river" method, in which the amount of water passing through the turbines is always approximately equal to the amount entering the reservoir behind the dam. These projects use "low-head" dams, typically less than 65 feet in height, and generally are less environmentally destructive than other generation methods because their reservoirs are small and the dams do not alter the natural rhythm of the river.

Pumped storage, a second method for hydropower generation, is becoming increasingly common. Water downstream of the dam is pumped up into the reservoir in the middle of the night, when customer demand for electricity is low. When demand for power increases, the water is allowed to flow back down through the turbines. Pumped storage reservoirs are relatively small, but the complete manipulation of river flows to maximize the economic efficiency of power generation can have severe effects on river and riparian ecology.

The third method of hydroelectric generation is "store and release." With this method, huge dams impound lake-sized reservoirs and release water as demand dictates. This type of dam and reservoir system totally transforms riverine ecology. Store-and-release dams are quite common because the large quantities of water they impound can be used for other purposes, such as irrigation and navigation. They are also popular because the money generated by sales of power from the dams can be used to finance the other, less lucrative uses of the dam.

Navigation

From a barge's perspective, dams are built to regulate river flows in order to maintain a navigable waterway for as much of the year as possible. The timing of releases from a dam used primarily for navigation generally involves annual cycles rather than the daily release cycles more appropriate to the generation of hydroelectricity. Much of a river's winter runoff is stored by navigation dams so that the river may run deep enough to support traffic in the drier summer months.

Additionally, navigation and power production often are at odds because river flows are lost through lockages, when the gates on the dam are held open to allow barge passage. Lockages can result in costly losses of hydroelectric power.

The environmental impacts of river navigation in general are many and extensive. Rivers are often dredged and channelized to increase their depths, decrease their lengths, and remove in-stream debris such as large rocks and tree limbs that could damage a barge. These alterations decrease the natural features on which fish depend, such as pools for cover and riffles for water re-aeration. Such alterations disrupt the bottom rung of the aquatic food chain by decreasing the substrates on which aquatic invertebrates, the fishes' filet mignon, cling to avoid being swept to their deaths by the current.

Once people remove sediment and debris from a river, they must deposit it elsewhere. This "elsewhere" frequently consists of riparian woodlands and wetlands. Dredged spoils, when piled up in sufficient quantities, are lethal to vegetation and destroy wildlife habitat.

Other impacts result from the movement of barges through the channel. The currents created by the barges cause bank and bottom erosion. The use of a river for navigation creates public pressure for the establishment of ports on the river, which in turn demand workers, which in turn demand housing, stores, restaurants, roads, laundromats, and other facilities. The presence of a navigable river has the potential to spur the development of communities and entire towns on its banks, yet history reminds us repeatedly that such floodplain development is neither safe nor wise.

Flood Control

As river floodplains become inhabited, public pressure grows for federal agencies to use dams and other facilities to prevent flood damage. The major environmental impact associated with the use of dams, levees, and other structural measures to reduce flood damage is inducement of further human habitation. As structures intended to make the floodplain a safer place to live become more numerous, more people develop homes and businesses on it. The development of floodplains displaces wildlife populations.

From a human perspective, a more severe effect of floodplain development results from the paving of generally porous floodplain soils. Floodplain land, originally capable of absorbing large quantities of sheet flow as if it were made of sponge, becomes coated with impervious substances such as asphalt and concrete. Instead of soaking up runoff from storms and releasing water gradually after the storms have passed, paved floodplains transmit nearly 100 percent of the water that rolls over them directly to the nearest drainage. Pavement therefore temporally shortens and intensifies flood peaks. Stream channelization often compounds this effect. Governments frequently channelize rivers in order to eliminate the friction created by meanders, rough bottoms, and vegetation. The peak flush of water during a storm may then pass more quickly downstream, creating a larger volume of water and thus inundating more of the floodplain more quickly than would occur if the stream were in a natural condition.

Nonstructural measures for reducing flood damage, such as keeping development off the floodplain, often make more economic, environmental, and safety sense than do most structural measures. Nonstructural flood damage reduction measures are beginning to attract the attention of responsible government agencies throughout the United States, but they are often met with resistance by those who believe that restrictions on floodplain development violate the right of a property owner to "reasonable" use of his or her land.

The use of a dam for flood control purposes conflicts with both hydroelectric and navigation uses. The purpose of a flood control dam is to capture high flows before they become damaging floods; for this purpose, the reservoir behind the dam must be kept as empty as possible. Hydroelectric and navigation dams are most useful if they can store copious amounts of water, which can be released as the demand arises.

Irrigation

Both large storage dams and smaller diversion dams often exist primarily to provide farmers with irrigation water. Environmental impacts associated with irrigation frequently include dewatering of streams and rivers, increased salinization of soil and stream flow, and displacement of wildlife habitat in favor of an agricultural monoculture. Stream dewatering occurs as water is diverted from the stream and applied to crops. The cumulative effect of many such diversions may make a waterway uninhabitable by game fish species and cause the dessication and destruction of riparian areas. Increased salinity occurs as water leaves the stream through an upstream diversion, spreads across croplands, percolates through agricultural soils, and eventually returns to the river, to be diverted again at a lower point. Each time the water passes through the soil, it picks up dissolved minerals, such as salt, and carries them back to the stream. When the stream flow comes to a temporary halt behind a dam, fresh water evaporates and the salts become concentrated. The same phenomenon occurs with heavy metals such as selenium and with agricultural pesticides and fertilizers. Farm soils ultimately suffer from the imposition of this toxic brine. If a farm field contains an impervious layer of clay below its topsoil, the poisoned water may sit and soak into the roots of the crops, stunting their growth and eventually killing them.

The use of dams and reservoirs for irrigation may compete with hydropower production and with navigation, since irrigation farming requires large diversions of water from the stream and releases at times that may not coincide with hydropower demand or navigational needs. Irrigation use may also conflict with flood control uses of dams, since most farmers would like to see the dams that supply them kept full of water, in case of a dry spell.

Most federal dams are built with several or all of these purposes in mind. Each dam now standing had a constituency crying for its construction, and the benefits of the dams have been reaped by regions, states, municipalities, and private landowners. The construction of these dams has not benefited everyone who depends on the rivers, however. Many people have been relocated as their homes and villages were inundated. Others have lost their livelihoods as fishermen, and many have lost sources of recreational pleasure. But the effects are most devastating for the river customers who cannot speak our language, such as trees, frogs, hawks, and bears.

NOTES

1. R. M. Darnell, *Impacts of Construction Activities in Wetlands of the United States* (Corvallis, OR: Environmental Protection Agency, Office of Research and Development, Corvallis Environmental Research Lab, 1976)
2. K. F. Lagler, "Ecological Effects of Hydroelectric Dams," in *Power Generation and Environmental Change*, ed. D. A. Berkowitz and A. M. Squires (Cambridge, MA: The MIT Press, 1969).
3. Ibid.
4. J. L. McKern, *Inventory of Riparian Habitats and Associated Wildlife along the Columbia and Snake Rivers* (Walla Walla, WA: Army Corps of Engineers, North Pacific Division, 1976).
5. D. B. Simons, "Effects of Stream Regulation on Channel Morphology," in *Ecology of Streams*, ed. J. V. Ward and J. A. Standord (New York: Plenum Press, 1978).
6. M. Reisner, *Cadillac Desert: The American West and Its Disappearing Water* (New York: Viking Penguin, 1986), 491.
7. Simons, "Effects of Stream Regulation."
8. Ibid.
9. Lagler, "Ecological Effects of Hydroelectric Dams."
10. Darnell, "Construction Activities in Wetlands."
11. W. R. Meehan, F. J. Swanson, and J. R. Sedell, "Influences of Riparian Vegetation on Aquatic Ecosystems with Particular Reference to Salmonid Fishes and Their Food Supply," in *Importance, Preservation and Management of Riparian Habitat* (Fort Collins, CO: Forest Service, Rocky Mountain Forest and Range Experiment Station, 1977).
12. F. H. Everest, *A Method of Estimating the Value of Streamside Reserve Trees* (Siskiyou National Forest, OR: Forest Service 1975).
13. Ibid.

3

The Columbia— A Piqued River

The development of a thriving power system on the Columbia River and its tributaries brought many backwoods communities into the twentieth century and helped the United States to win World War II by powering aluminum production. The construction and operation of major dams inflict serious damage on natural ecosystems, however. Stress caused by human intrusion and noise during construction of these projects is often enough to drive animals from the river valley or lower their reproductive rates. Changes in the characteristics of stream flow quantity, quality, and timing caused by dam construction and operation disrupt finely tuned associations of plants and animals both upstream and downstream of the project site. Reservoirs inundate riparian habitat and the streamside nest and den sites that are essential to many types of wildlife.

Hydropower reservoirs have inundated half a million acres of floodplain and river valley land in the state of Washington alone. Jack Howerton, a biologist with the Washington Department of Game, estimates that hydroelectric projects have submerged more than 268,000 acres of prime wildlife habitat along the Columbia River and its tributaries, excluding the Snake.[1] Many wildlife populations have declined as a result of the gradual destruction of riparian zones, but the losses remain largely undocumented and unmitigated.

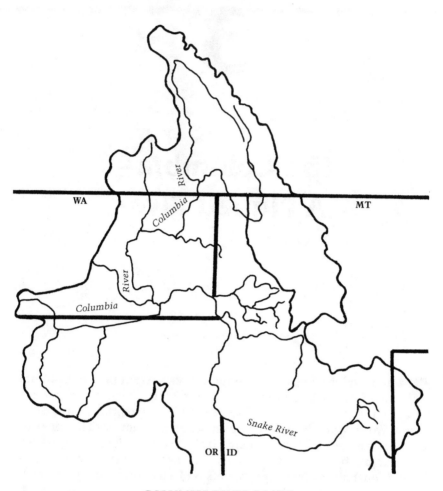

COLUMBIA RIVER BASIN

The Columbia River's Natural History

The Columbia River rises from Columbia Lake in Canada and flows north until it reaches Mica, Canada. From Mica, the river flows south for 680 miles to the mouth of the Snake River, its largest tributary, at Pasco, Washington. The two rivers merge and head west to Bonneville Dam, then onward to the sea.

The 1,210-mile-long Columbia River drains approximately 259,000 square miles of the North American continent. Canada contains 39,000 of these square miles; the rest are in the states of Washington, Oregon, Montana, Idaho, and Wyoming. The Columbia discharges about 187 million acre-feet of water annually into the Pacific Ocean. Most of this water is snowmelt from the Rocky Mountains in British Columbia, western Montana, northern Idaho, northwestern Wyoming, and the Cascade Range. Peak flows on the Columbia are reached in June or July; high flows occur throughout the summer and fall, and the lowest flows occur during the winter months.

The Columbia first passes through the Columbia River plains, or the Columbia Plateau, which comprises about 100,000 square miles in central Oregon, central and eastern Washington, and British Columbia. The plateau's elevation ranges from 4,000 to 7,000 feet, its height contributing to the aridity of its climate. This land is built of layered lava flows, largely basalt. The major vegetation types in this region are sagebrush and rabbitbrush; very little timber grows on the plateau.

The Columbia River gorge cuts through the Cascades and Coast Range downstream of the confluence of the Columbia and Snake rivers. The gorge is characterized by towering walls and powerful waterfalls until it reaches Bonneville Dam at the head of tidewater, about 42 miles east of Portland, Oregon. The shores of the gorge are adorned with thin strips of coastal conifer woodlands. Stands of Douglas-fir, the dominant tree species, ares underlaid with a lush growth of vines and berries. The first floodplain habitat on the Oregon side of the river occurs in the lower end of the gorge at the confluence of the Columbia and Big Sandy rivers. Here, the 1,000-acre floodplain, dissected by old oxbow lagoons from the Sandy River, supports cottonwoods, willow brush, berries, vines, and reed canary grass. Below Bonneville, the basalt cliffs that form the gorge give way to broad lowlands and terraces. The river passes through the Coast Range below Longview, Washington, in another gorge. Beyond the Coast Range gorge, the river widens into a tidal estuary 5 to 7 miles wide and glides into the Pacific Ocean between a sandy peninsula on the Oregon side and a low, rocky headland on the Washington side.

History of Hydropower Development on the Columbia

Although development of hydropower facilities in the Columbia River basin allowed for the creation of an empire of energy-intensive industries, it transformed a powerful, free-flowing river into a string of reservoirs, with significant impacts on the ecology of the region.

The momentum for water project construction began to build during a time in America's history when environmental consciousness was low, ecology was just beginning to emerge as a science, and the economy was the public's number one priority. Very little data had been gathered on the wildlife populations and vegetative composition of the Columbia River before construction began on the early hydropower dams. Therefore, the losses of natural communities were not documented.

The voluminous flows and steep topography of the Columbia and her tributaries provide great hydropower potential for a power-hungry American society. Hydropower was providing 40 percent of U.S. electricity in the 1930s when the federal government began to develop the Columbia Basin Project.[2] The project began in 1933 when the National Industrial Recovery Act authorized funds for the multipurpose Grand Coulee Dam. The Rivers and Harbors Act of 1935 specifically authorized construction of the project, which was reauthorized in 1943 by the Columbia Basin Project Act and brought under the scope of the Reclamation Project Act of 1939.

Grand Coulee Dam, completed in 1942 on a portion of the Columbia where the river forms the southern border of the Colville Indian Reservation, backed up the Columbia 151 miles. The dam's reservoir inundated 68,000 acres of land adjacent to the original riverbed and 20 to 30 miles of free-flowing creeks. Almost 5,000 miles of associated canals, laterals, drains, and dumping ditches drastically altered the desert biota of this area and devastated the habitats of minks, weasels, and many other wildlife species.[3] The Columbia Basin Project was off with a bang.

In 1937, Congress authorized the then-temporary Bonneville Power Administration (BPA) to construct transmission lines and sell power from the Bonneville and Grand Coulee dams. The Army Corps of Engineers completed Bonneville Lock and Dam on the lower end of the Columbia in 1938. The BPA, spurred on by a strong economy and growing public demand for power, increased sales and expanded its system on the Columbia River.[4] From 1940 until 1973, the wholesale rate for the BPA's public utility customers dropped from $.017 to $.005 per kilowatt-hour (adjusted for inflation). Commenting on the history of rapidly expanding power facilities, the Northwest Power Planning Council, an entity formed in 1981 to encourage conservation and development of renewable resources in the Northwest, stated that

> power planning in the 1950's and 1960's involved minimal risk of being wrong. If the supply of electricity exceeded demand, demand was certain to catch up soon. The far greater risk, so it was perceived, was to underbuild; to have demand for electricity exceed the supply.[5]

On the lower Columbia River, the corps constructed four multi-purpose dams. Congress authorized the BPA to market the hydro-power generated by these dams. The first, Bonneville Dam, is the farthest downstream. McNary, the second dam constructed, was operational by 1957. The Dalles Dam, at river mile 192.5 (192.5 miles upstream from the Columbia's mouth), was completed in 1960. The last lower Columbia dam constructed was John Day, at river mile 216; it was operational by 1968. In addition, Congress ratified the Columbia River Treaty in 1964, which obligated Canada to build three dams (Mica, Keenleyside, and Duncan) for power production and flood storage. A fourth dam required by the treaty, Libby Dam on the Kootenai River in Montana, was constructed by the corps. By 1975, the federal Columbia River power system was complete. Twenty-eight dams on the Columbia and its tributaries used over 20 million acre-feet of water to provide the Columbia River basin with 13,000 megawatts of hydropower.

Profiles of Some Columbia River Residents

Beavers The cosmopolitan beaver, distributed over most of the United States and Canada, is certainly not restricted to the Columbia River basin. In fact, much of the original human exploration and settlement of the Pacific Northwest may be attributed to human covetousness of the beavers' thick, brown fur.

The beaver's major claim to fame, however, is not its coat but its engineering ability. Beaver lodges have walls built of excavated dirt and vaulted roofs constructed of branches and sticks and cemented with dirt, mud, moss, and/or grass. Beavers build their lodges above water level but include at least one underwater emergency exit as a standard feature. Many beavers are bank dwellers, digging out spacious, round dens, usually in the root wad of a streamside tree. Beavers may burrow underground tunnels several yards long in riverbanks to serve as entrance and exit halls.

Beavers build dikes and dams to divert and store stream flows. These structures, made of trimmed logs and branches cemented with mud and reinforced with rocks, may be as much as 325 feet long and 10 feet high.

Unlike some man-built structures, beaver dams and dikes often benefit the biological community. The dams, usually built on small headwater streams, can increase the surface water area, forcing water into riparian aquifers, where it moistens the soil and increases the width of the riparian zone. Water stored in these aquifers provides source of recharge for the streams during dry summer months, adding stability to flows that would otherwise fluctuate or disappear. Because the dams themselves also provide some storage capacity, the activities of beavers may decrease runoff during storms and lessen the effects of floods downstream. The storage capacity becomes significant when a watershed contains many beaver dams.

Harlequin Ducks   If streams are graced by the industrious beaver, they are amused by the harlequin duck. This duck borrowed its name from the buffoon in comedy and pantomime with a shaved head, masked face, and parti-colored tights. The male harlequin nearly matches this description. He is a small, bluish-black duck with reddish sides and clownlike white stripes and spots on his head, neck, and shoulders.

The harlequin duck ranges along the West Coast from Alaska south to northern California. Harlequins are completely dependent on cold, rushing, turbulent streams for their survival in summer, and they prefer to occupy streams with heavily forested banks. Harlequins nest in dense brush or in rocky crevices in banks or on islands, always using dense vegetation to conceal their nests from predators. These ducks are skillful divers and swim under mighty currents in search of tasty invertebrates.

Northern Flying Squirrels   These mammalian marvels do not actually fly; they glide through the air buoyed by flaps of skin stretched between their forelegs and hind legs. The northern and southern flying squirrels are the only known nocturnal squirrels. At dusk, the squirrels leave the safety of their treetop homes in abandoned woodpecker holes or nests built of leaves, twigs, and bark to forage for seeds, nuts, insects, and bird eggs. Northern flying squirrels range from Canada south to California in the West and as far south as North Carolina in the East.

Northern flying squirrels live in conifer and mixed forests. They are not completely dependent on riparian forests for their survival but exhibit a strong preference for riparian zones.

Northern flying squirrels are not unique among small northwestern mammals in this preference. In the Pacific Northwest, riparian zones are richer in small mammals in general than is any other habitat type. One biologist reported that on his study sites in southwestern Oregon and on the western flank of the Cascades, all the small mammal species found in either upland or transitional habitats were also found in riparian zones. However, many species found in riparian zones were absent from either upland zones, transition zones, or both. Species such as Siskiyou chipmunks, voles, and marsh shrews are riparian dependent.[6]

Hydroelectric Dams and Transformation of the Columbia River

Hydroelectric dams in the Columbia River basin have had a number of impacts on resident wildlife. Dams and reservoirs cause a direct loss of critical wintering and fawning or calving areas for big game. Full reservoirs inundate crucial island "nurseries"; low water levels create land bridges that provide access to the islands, permitting predators to cross over and feast on fawns and calves. Especially in arid regions where upland vegetation is sparse, as it is in much of the Columbia River basin, riverside vegetation provides thermal and hiding cover not available elsewhere. For example, the Columbian white-tailed deer, federally listed as an endangered species, once existed at a stable population level along the lower Columbia. These deer depend on floodplain forests and meadows, especially pastures that are highly interspersed with cover.[7] Their habitat is dwindling as a result of human encroachment; at present their range is virtually limited to the Columbian White-Tailed Deer National Wildlife Refuge.[8,9] Parts of this refuge were actually created from material that the Army Corps of Engineers dredged out of the Columbia River.

New reservoirs may disrupt, bisect, or eliminate big game migration routes. These developments also inundate food and cover used by game year round. In 1965 preconstruction surveys for the High Mountain Sheep Project on the Snake River, the Oregon State Game Commission estimated that the reservoir would inundate habitat that supported 850 deer and 300 elk during the winter.[10]

Riparian areas provide game birds such as quails, pheasants, chukar partridges, and doves with nesting, feeding, and brood-rearing cover all year. Riparian woodlands provide interlocking tree canopies, which are used by squirrels for food and escape routes and by other small mammals for resting and thermal cover. Destruction of this vegetation results in loss of animals. Water level fluctuations in reservoirs create mud flats that small animals must cross in order to drink from the river; thus, they are exposed to increased risk of predation. Extensive erosion, like that encountered at Grand Coulee Dam, is caused largely by wave action and fluctuation of the reservoir's shoreline. Such erosion reduces upland as well as riparian habitat.

Waterfowl suffer from loss of nesting and brooding areas on banks and islands. Drawdowns in reservoirs often create land bridges for terrestrial predators such as skunks and coyotes, enabling them to cross over to island nesting areas and feed on waterfowl adults, young, and eggs. In his study of Columbia River riparian habitat, McKern noted that water levels in McNary Reservoir dropped to a minimum during the critical incubation period for Canada geese (March through mid-April). As a result of the drawdown, coyotes destroyed all the nests and killed four adult geese on three of the five Hat Rock islands in the reservoir. Waterfowl are more susceptible to predation during the first year after inundation of their habitat, probably because they are searching for new areas in which to loaf (rest and preen) and construct nests.[11] Migrant waterfowl resting beside reservoirs are forced to relocate many times each day as water levels rise.[12] This activity reduces their fitness for migration.

Hydroelectric dams and reservoirs destroy den sites and may create an unsuitable environment for beavers, muskrats, otters, minks, and nutria. Food resources for beavers and muskrats, which depend entirely on shoreline vegetation, may be completely eliminated by inundation and water level fluctuations, and while traversing the mud flats in search of food, the animals are quite vulnerable to predation. Flooding of dens forces aquatic mammals into environments where they are exposed to predators, and the floodwaters often drown helpless young. In addition, drawdowns in reservoirs directly expose these animals' dens to entry by predators.

Otters and minks are adversely affected when carp, a major item in their diet, decline as a result of water level fluctuations in hydropower reservoirs. Carp eggs attach to submerged vegetation and require 3 to 6 days of incubation; the eggs will die if they are exposed to dry air during this time. Most submerged vegetation in the Columbia River reservoirs is above minimum operating water levels, and fluctuations approaching the minimum and maximum levels are expected on the Columbia on a daily basis in the future.[13] McKern found that aquatic furbearers were more numerous and diverse along mildly fluctuating or nonfluctuating portions of the Columbia River.[14] Terrestrial furbearers such as raccoons, opossums, striped and spotted skunks, and red and gray foxes suffer from the loss of their small mammal prey base when riparian areas are disturbed.[15] Trees and shrubs that provide nesting sites for passerine birds (songbirds) in riparian habitat are permanently lost when reservoirs are created. Bald eagles and ospreys depend on riparian habitats to provide perches for hunting, resting, and nesting. McKern implied in 1976 that the lack of nesting trees was already limiting osprey nesting and eagle use along the Columbia and Snake rivers.[16] Those songbirds and birds of prey that nest elsewhere but feed in riparian zones lose a large proportion of their food base when populations of insects and small mammals decrease in response to decreased riparian vegetation. Reservoirs eliminate thermal cover used by birds as well as island nesting sites for gulls, terns, herons, killdeers, and other shorebirds. Colony-nesting gulls and terns are particularly vulnerable to fluctuating water levels, as they prefer to nest on the ground near the water's edge. Water level increases can eliminate entire colonies built at low water levels.

Reptiles and amphibians are largely limited to inhabiting those backwaters and embayments with little or no water level fluctuation.[17] Fielder and co-workers stated that when Chief Joseph Pool on the Columbia River in northern Washington filled with water, it flooded many yellow-bellied marmot burrows while the marmots were still hibernating. Many voles were stranded on emergent vegetation and floating debris by the rising water. These animals died within three minutes of being stranded.[18]

The Northwest Power Planning Act of 1980 contains provisions to rectify the damage done to fish and wildlife by construction of the

Hungry Horse Dam on the Flathead River inundated the habitat of from two to four grizzly bears. (Sketch by author)

Columbia River basin hydroelectric system, as long as the mitigation program does not jeopardize the Northwest's cheap electrical supply. The first plan to mitigate damages to terrestrial wildlife was advanced in 1987, more than two generations after the first injuries were inflicted. This plan proposes to charge ratepayers for easements on critical wildlife range to compensate for wildlife habitat affected by two of the smaller dams in the system—Libby Dam on the Kootenai River and Hungry Horse Dam on the Flathead River. The Northwest Power Planning Commission estimates that construction of Libby Dam resulted in the loss of about 1,340 white-tailed deer (8,745 acres of winter habitat), 485 mule deer (10,586 acres of habitat), 66 bighorn sheep (3,190 acres of habitat), 2,462 acres of habitat used by the Columbian short-tailed grouse, and 10,460 acres of waterfowl habitat. Hungry Horse resulted in an estimated loss of 133 elk (6,650 acres of winter range), 27 to 34 black bears (8,590 acres of critical habitat), 2 to 4 grizzly bears (8,590 acres of habitat), and 11,050 acres of habitat used by terrestrial furbearers. Effects on wildlife of hydroelectric development and operation at other dam sites throughout the basin are still being studied.[19]

Although the Northwest Power Planning Act will never fully compensate for the intensive alteration of natural habitat that accompanied the harnessing of the region's phenomenal rivers, it will do what no law has accomplished before: mitigate damages that occurred half a century before—mitigation not needed to justify the projects from an environmental point of view.

The Story of the Lower Snake

The Snake River begins in Yellowstone National Park and the Teton wilderness and is augmented by the lakes bordering Jackson Hole, Wyoming. The valley floor of the Snake in Idaho is made up of a series of lava beds that degrade into highly fertile soils. Between some of these lava beds are deposits of clay and coarser waterborne materials laid down along stream courses and in ponded areas during the long intervals between lava flows. Rather than forming surface channels, the water percolated into crevices between layers of basaltic lava; large portions of the Snake River's basin are therefore devoid of streams, which increases the value of valleys equipped with water.

The Snake flows westward across the entire southern part of Idaho defining much of the Idaho-Oregon border and forming the southeastern corner of the Idaho-Washington border as it turns north. By the time it joins the Columbia River in southeastern Washington, the Snake has traveled 1,078 miles. The Lower Snake River Project area lies in the Snake River Canyon between Ice Harbor Lock and Dam and Lewiston, Idaho.

The Snake River's discovery was the result of a famous excursion. In 1803, President Thomas Jefferson ordered two army riflemen, Captain Meriwether Lewis and Lieutenant William Clark, to secure a trade route up the Missouri River and across the continent and to explore the newly acquired Louisiana Territory. Political motives played a part in the organization of this voyage as well: the French, under Napoleon Bonaparte, desired to reclaim Louisiana, which they had previously ceded to Spain. Were this to occur, the French empire would then border the United States from the Gulf Coast up along the Mississippi frontier country, placing it in a position to cut off trade with the western territories at New Orleans. Additionally, in Canada, the British navy would be in a position to blockade the Atlantic Coast. The United States, under the squeeze of these potentially hostile neighbors, wished to establish a trade route to the Northwest and expand westward.

Captain Lewis, a diplomat and commercial wizard, and Lieutenant Clark, a riverman and negotiator, executed their duties with astounding success. At one point in their journey, however, it looked as though all might be lost. In 1805, the explorers had reached the source of the Missouri River and were stranded at the foot of the Rocky Mountains with their crew, a translator named Toussaint Charbonneau, his Indian wife, Sacajawea, and their tiny papoose. The voyagers had very little time before snow would block any possible passage through the mountains and no means by which to cross. A band of Indians suddenly appeared in the hills; by a strange twist of fate, it was the same band from which Sacajawea had been kidnapped years before and of which her brother was now the leader. The travelers purchased pack horses from the Indians and safely crossed over to the Pacific side of the Rockies, where they encountered Clearwater River, a tributary of the Snake, and, eventually, the Columbia. The reservoir later created by Ice Harbor Dam on the lower Snake was named for the Indian squaw.

The Snake River basin was extensively settled following the gold rush in the late 1800s. During the nineteenth and early twentieth centuries, settlers used the Snake for irrigation and began to channelize it for navigation. In 1902, Congress adopted the first formal proposal for development of the lower Snake. In 1935, the Senate Commerce Committee requested a review report on the Columbia and Snake rivers. The resulting report included provisions for construction of four dams on the Snake, supplemented by open-channel work to obtain specific navigation depths. The general plans drawn up for Snake River development recommended the eventual construction of ten low dams with locks to provide slack water navigation from the Pacific Ocean to Lewiston, Idaho. The dams were also to contain powerhouses for the generation of hydroelectricity. The basis for construction of the Lower Snake River Project and much of the other modern water development on the Snake and Columbia rivers was a congressional report produced in 1950. The first four projects on the Snake — Ice Harbor, Lower Monumental, Little Goose, and Lower Granite dams — were completed in 1962, 1969, 1970, and 1975, respectively.

These dams flooded salmon and steelhead spawning grounds, covered river islands that geese used for nesting, and eliminated gently sloping bottomlands and sparse, discontinuous riparian vegetation that were critical winter habitat for the region's wildlife. In April 1966, the Army Corps of Engineers' Walla Walla District requested the Bureau of Sport Fisheries and Wildlife (the predecessor of the Fish and Wildlife Service) to prepare a wildlife compensation plan that regarded the four lower Snake dams as one project.[20] No development of wildlife mitigation measures occurred on the lower Snake for many years, however, because sufficient funds were unavailable within the Washington Department of Game and a disagreement existed over which agency should fund the mitigation efforts. The first draft of the report by the Bureau of Sport Fisheries and Wildlife was not submitted to the corps until 1971. In October 1976, Congress authorized the final compensation plan, which had been produced over a decade of meetings, consultation, and data collection. The plan received its first appropriation in 1978. By then, the estimate of costs for on-project wildlife developments had increased from $2.6 million to $7 million.[21] The bulk of this money was earmarked to purchase hunting easements on and fee title to lands in Washington along the Snake. In 1979, the corps held a meeting to discuss wildlife mitigation plans in each of five counties slated for mitigation. Most of the people attending these meetings opposed the wildlife compensation plan for various reasons, including disbelief that the wildlife losses had actually occurred, concern about vandalism, and opposition to selling hunting rights in perpetuity. Ironically, one common reason for opposition to the compensation plan was that many of those whose lands were suitable for wildlife compensation had previously had lands taken for the development of the Lower Snake River Project and, in the process, had developed an animosity toward the corps.

By 1984, only 12 acres of land had been acquired to implement mitigation on the lower Snake. This land was purchased to provide fishing access to the public.[22]

Ice Harbor Lock and Dam

Ice Harbor Dam, located in the state of Washington just above the Snake's confluence with the Columbia, is 2,822 feet long and 100 feet high. It is a concrete gravity structure that contains fish passage facilities, a six-unit powerhouse, a ten-bay spillway section, and a navigation lock. The dam's instantaneous generating capacity is 603,000 kilowatts. Ice Harbor Dam impounds Lake Sacajawea at an elevation of 440 feet, mean sea level, at normal pool (the ordinary high water level of a reservior when no drawdown is occurring). The lake inundates a total of 9,200 acres and extends 32 miles up the Snake River to Lower Monumental Dam.

The operation of Ice Harbor Dam results in significant pool level fluctuations in the upper reservoir. Fluctuations usually are greatest in the period from September through March and result in a 5-foot maximum drawdown. Water level fluctuations depend on power demand, but the normal daily and weekly fluctuation is about 3 feet.[23] Ice Harbor Dam is typical of the facilities constructed by the Army Corps of Engineers on navigable waterways in the Columbia River basin. The Sport Fishing Institute, the Washington Department of Game, and the Fish and Wildlife Service conducted studies of the environmental impacts of this project.

The impoundment of Lake Sacajawea inundated about 3,253 acres of terrestrial wildlife habitat consisting of high brush, trees, and orchards in narrow shoreline strips.[24] Although small patches of native vegetation such as white alder, Russian olive, and shrub willows still exist in the project area, almost half of the reservoir shoreline now consists of rock riprap, installed to reduce shoreline erosion. Another 28 percent of the shoreline has been taken over by rubber rabbitbrush, a low-forage-value exotic species that was probably encouraged by overgrazing of livestock on reservoir banks.[25,26] This loss of native riparian habitat severely affected wildlife populations.

Before construction began, the Lake Sacajawea area had supported a moderate number of resident mule deer, along with migrants from adjacent upland areas, which were especially numerous during severe winters. Comprehensive four-dam impact surveys conducted from

1964 through 1966 indicated that about 100 deer had occupied an 8,337-hectare corridor in the Ice Harbor Project area.[27] After the reservoir was filled, no deer were harvested in the project area. The Washington Department of Game concluded that no deer remained.[28] Upland game species (pheasants, quails, Hungarian partridges, cottontail rabbits, chukar partridges, and mourning doves) had depended on the vegetated riparian habitat that existed prior to inundation for cover and nesting. Vegetated banks had also provided safe travel corridors to adjacent agricultural areas where these animals could feed. Mourning doves used riparian habitat in this area for nesting, producing about 900 young per year for a total annual population of about 1,500 birds, and quail coveys occupied vegetated shorelines and grass-covered islands. Field observations made before construction led to a population estimate of 700 valley quails. All told, filling of the reservoir resulted in the loss of about 20,350 upland game animals.[29]

The average numbers of Canada geese and ducks using the Ice Harbor Project area per year from 1956 to 1959 were 9,284 and 19,935, respectively. Waterfowl had used thirteen river islands for nesting prior to impoundment (islands greatly improve waterfowl nesting success by prohibiting entry by terrestrial predators). When Lake Sacajawea filled, twelve of the thirteen existing river islands were covered with water. Goose nesting activity declined almost 100 percent following impoundment.[30] According to a habitat biologist and a game protector from the Washington Department of Game, sustained annual harvest of furbearers in the Ice Harbor Project area prior to construction was as follows: 100 beavers, 10 muskrats, 20 minks, 20 raccoons, 10 weasels, and 10 skunks. Censuses and scent station data collected in 1974 and 1975 indicated that of these animals, only beavers and striped skunks still occurred in the study area.[31] The decline of these animals is attributable to loss of the vegetative food base and riprapping of their bank habitat.

The Lower Snake River Project as a whole inundated 140.2 square miles of land. The project's reservoir area totals 33,890 acres, of which 14,400 were previously bottomlands and canyon walls. Forty-eight river islands were inundated, and seven were formed, for an overall loss of 1,225 acres of island habitat, and the project destroyed an estimated 1,123 acres of riparian vegetation. Riprap embankments replaced 40 percent of the shoreline along the lower Snake due to railroad and roadway reconstruction. Riprap created hazards to wildlife, especially deer, in gaining access to water; the mechanical stabilization of the banks also precluded reestablishment of vegetation.[32] The Lower Snake River Project destroyed over 3,100 acres of important nongame habitat. An estimated 33,400 breeding and

92,500 wintering nongame birds were lost, along with an unquantified number of reptiles and amphibians. Upland game populations decreased by about 120,800 animals because of the loss of riparian habitat. Bobcat, skunk, and coyote populations plummeted also as their nongame and upland-game prey base declined.[33] This is typical of the environmental destruction associated with normal construction and operation of dams for the generation of hydroelectricity and other uses.

The Change to Peak Power Operations

In the late 1960s and early 1970s, the BPA's strategy regarding hydropower changed and the agency developed the first stage of its "hydrothermal power plan." This plan envisioned twenty nuclear plants and two coal facilities to provide base energy in addition to the hydroelectric plants, which can fluctuate power output more easily in providing peak energy needs.[34] "Peak power" refers to increases in energy output that become necessary during certain times of the day and year to satisfy the energy demands of residential and commercial consumers. The highest daily peaks in the Northwest occur in December and January, when lighting, heating, and other demands are greatest. Transmission lines connect the Pacific Northwest to the Southwest, allowing summer peak power to be transferred from facilities on the Columbia and Snake rivers to that region to meet cooling needs. The BPA intended to have most of its hydroelectric facilities operating on a "power-peaking" basis by the mid-1980s. Development of peak power was to be accomplished by the installation of additional generating units in some hydroelectric plants, and new powerhouses in others, the raising of some dams, and possibly the construction of new projects. Operations of all projects were to be closely coordinated to get maximum use of all the water in the system for power production. This would mean more frequent and severe fluctuations of river and reservoir levels than occur under normal, base-level operations.[35] When the dams on the Columbia and its tributaries are operated to supply peak power needs, flows below the dams decrease, tailwaters are reduced to a minimum, and pool levels are raised between peak periods. When peak power is desired, water flows through the turbines at near-maximum capacity, tailwaters increase to maximum levels, and the level of the forebay (the water directly behind the dam) drops.[36]

Environmental Impacts of Peak Power Operations

The impacts of intensified peak power operations on the Columbia River would be similar in type to those of normal hydropower operations but dramatically magnified due to increased frequency and magnitude of water level fluctuations. Biologists can only speculate about the increases in erosion, bank denudation, vegetation inundation, and losses of fish and wildlife habitat that would result from peak power operations in full swing on the Columbia.

Reptiles and amphibians are the classes most threatened by power-peaking operations in the Columbia River basin. Amphibians generally lay their eggs in the shallows of ponds and streams, where the eggs adhere to submerged vegetation until they hatch; reptiles often lay their eggs on shores adjacent to the water. Under power-peaking operations, increased water levels could dislodge amphibian eggs and wash them out of nursery areas; drops in water levels could strand the eggs and allow them to dry out. Many reptile eggs would be inundated. McKern speculated that without protection of vital habitats, power-peaking operations would doom the western toad in Hells Canyon Reservoir; the Pacific tree frog and long-toed salamander in John Day Reservoir; and the Woodhouse toad, the Great Basin spadefoot toad, the bullfrog, and the painted turtle in McNary Reservoir.[37]

The BPA saw an opportunity to achieve its goals through the development of coal and nuclear power plants to be financed and managed by a municipal corporation, the Washington Public Power and Supply System (WPPSS—pronounced "whoops" by critics of the plan). The BPA was legally prohibited from owning the plants itself, but it arranged to own most of the electricity that the plants would generate. The BPA lobbied each of its utility clients to support plant construction, believing that by mixing expensive nuclear power with cheap hydroelectric power, the utilities would ultimately benefit from a "blended" rate.[38] In 1969, the BPA pushed for construction of first three, then five, WPPSS nuclear power plants in the Columbia River basin. The agency's utility clients approved construction of the first three plants immediately; the final two were approved by 88 utilities in 1974. The BPA's projected cost for the project was $4.1 billion. That year, 100 of the utilities pledged revenue from their energy sales for repayment of the first three plants' construction debts.[39]

Construction began in the 1970s. During that decade, because of regulatory delays, construction snags, management problems, and soaring inflation, costs increased by a factor of five, to $23 billion. In 1975, Don Hodel, administrator of the BPA and future secretary of the interior, addressed the City Club of Portland in an attempt to bolster waning public confidence in the Washington Public Power and Supply System. He admitted that erratic federal funding, labor disputes, shortages, and technical problems had created substantial delays in bringing the plants on line. He predicted, however, that regional power demand would continue to grow and that "by 1990—just 15 years from now—loads will increase nearly 3 times to about 250 billion kilowatt-hours a year."[40] Over the next decade; however, ill fortune assailed the BPA and WPPSS. Construction of two of the nuclear plants was canceled, and two others may never be completed. The BPA raised utility rates three times to cover its losses. Rates rose from $.005 to $.0156 per kilowatt-hour (adjusted for inflation) for a total compounded increase of 478 percent.[41] From 1973 to 1983, the wholesale cost of electricity to BPA customers climbed. Industries that had originally planned to take advantage of cheap power rates in the Pacific Northwest, such as Alamax, Inc., which had hoped to build a $660 million aluminum reduction plant in Oregon, changed their plans.

Thirteen utilities filed two lawsuits in the U.S. Court of Claims, charging that the BPA had coerced them into investing in the plants.[42] Each year since 1975, the long-range forecasts by Pacific Northwest utilities for future power demands have dropped, increasing the risks surrounding power planning by billions of dollars.[43]

Other factors further thwarted plans for conversion to intensified peak power operations. In 1982, high water flows, mild weather, and a sluggish regional economy combined to increase supply of and decrease demand for hydropower. The BPA shut down some thermal units to save money.

In addition, in January 1976, the BPA contracted with Skidmore, Owings and Merrill to study conservation potential, devise strategies to conserve energy, and project the effect of these strategies on the Pacific Northwest. The study concluded that conservation could reduce the need for energy in an amount equal to the output of eleven thermal plants by 1995 and that energy made available through conservation is six times less expensive than energy delivered by investment in new thermal plants.[44]

The BPA first denounced the findings of the study.[45] Then, in 1980, Congress authorized creation of the Northwest Power Planning Council to encourage conservation and development of renewable resources in the Northwest and to "prepare, adopt and promptly transmit to the Administrator [of BPA] a regional conservation and electric power plan."[46] The plan released by the council in 1983 emphasized conservation as the cheapest resource for the region and one that should play a major role in meeting future electrical energy demands.

The Bonneville Lock and Dam: Expansion
on the Columbia

Bonneville Dam was the first Columbia River dam built by the Army Corps of Engineers. Construction began in 1933 as part of the federal government's effort to reverse the economic deterioration caused by the Great Depression. Congress passed the Bonneville Project Act in 1937 and gave the BPA responsibility for the distribution and marketing of power from the dam. The act was later amended to give the BPA authority over other projects in the area.

Bonneville Dam, completed in 1938, contained facilities for producing hydroelectric energy, fish passage structures, and a navigation lock. During World War II, the powerhouse in the dam was enlarged and additional generators were added. The powerhouse extending across Bradford Slough to the Oregon shore accommodates ten generating units. Two of these units produce 43,200 kilowatts each, and eight produce 54,000 kilowatts each, for a total instantaneous capacity of 518,400 kilowatts. Bonneville Pool covers 20,400 surface acres and provides a 15-foot deep navigation channel for 47 miles between Bonneville and The Dalles dams. The navigation lock is 76 feet wide, 500 feet long, and 24 feet deep.

Bonneville Pool, situated in the heart of the Columbia River gorge, lies in one of the principal migratory waterfowl lanes of the Pacific flyway.[47] Although reservoir inundation, industrial development, construction of a railroad line, and two highway rights-of-way in the river valley decreased the project area's value as waterfowl nesting habitat, the Oregon Department of Fish and Wildlife has reported 2,000 to 3,000 waterfowl using the reservoir at peak migration times. The department has also estimated that an average of ninety-four pairs of Canada geese breed in the Bonneville Pool area.

The Columbia River gorge had been a major botanical migration route between eastern and western Oregon. In its natural condition, the floodplain supports black cottonwood, willow, Oregon ash, and scattered stands of conifers. On the Bonneville project grounds, construction and landscaping activities have altered the natural vegetation patterns.[48]

Species of reptiles and amphibians within the project area include the western toad, the Pacific tree frog, the common garter snake, and the northwestern garter snake. The red-legged frog is found in forested areas, while the northwestern salamander inhabits lowlands. The endemic (native) Larch Mountain salamander evolved under the unique environmental conditions of the gorge.[49]

The Columbia River gorge also serves as an important wintering area for bald eagles and other raptors. Fifteen to twenty eagles are

Bonneville Lock and Dam. (Courtesy Portland District, U.S. Army Corps of Engineers)

regularly seen where Hamilton Creek empties into the Columbia. Ospreys, as well as hawks, owls, and vultures, frequent the area.[50]

A stand of cottonwoods downstream from Pierce Island supports a great blue heron rookery, where Oregon Department of Fish and Wildlife biologists counted thirty-one nests in March of 1975. By spring of 1978, the rookery had expanded to sixty-four nests.

All vegetation zones in the vicinity of Bonneville Dam include voles, moles, mice, opossums, striped skunks, short-tailed weasels, and black-tailed deer among the mammalian fauna. At high elevations, in coniferous and mixed deciduous-coniferous zones, porcupines, black bears, and bobcats are common. Red foxes occur in the area but are rare. One herd of Rocky Mountain elk is often present on the Washington side of the gorge. These animals summer at high elevations but drop down into the river valley during the winter, seeking food and thermal cover.

In lowland brush and pasture areas, eastern cottontail rabbits and snowshoe hares are common. Coyotes inhabit both sides of the gorge. Raccoons, river otters, minks, muskrats, and beavers occur in stream, marsh, pond, and riparian habitats in the gorge.[51] In 1977, the Washington Department of Game found 155 species of birds and 29 species of mammals in the Bonneville Pool area. Tabor reported 104 species of birds below and 94 species of birds above Bonneville Dam.[52] He found 3 species of bats below and 10 above the dam.

The environmental repercussions of the initial construction of Bonneville Dam and the filling of Bonneville Pool were not documented at the time. We do know that after the reservoir was filled few islands remained in the pool and that those that did remain were primarily outcroppings of volcanic rock.[53] Water levels, though fluctuating, were permanently raised, creating a new shoreline.

Newton stated that many of the oak trees that are valuable to wildlife as food and cover in the Sauvie Island area (and possibly in other areas) were killed by changing water levels caused by the dam.[54] Water levels higher than natural for prolonged periods in the spring have raised the water table in the project area, precluding the establishment of young oak trees.

Wildlife agencies suspect that goose nesting and rearing areas have disappeared as a result of initial inundation by the reservoir and that many waterfowl ground nests have been lost because of water level fluctuations over time.[55] Oregon Department of Fish and Wildlife personnel have observed broods of goslings caught in currents, swept against the dam, pulled under water, and killed. Newton estimated that fifty goslings per year are lost in this manner.[56]

Phase II

In 1971, while the BPA was still anticipating growing power demands through the end of the century, the Army Corps of Engineers issued an environmental impact statement recommending construction of a second powerhouse at Bonneville Dam to facilitate peak power operations, increase reservoir storage capacity, and increase operating flexibility.[57] Construction costs of the new powerhouse were estimated to be over $250 million.

Building a second powerhouse at Bonneville necessitated relocating a town. North Bonneville, Washington, a community containing a school, a rest home, 53 commercial enterprises, 3 churches, 2 sets of farm buildings, and 153 residential and miscellaneous structures, was moved onto land purchased by the federal government so that an additional 562 megawatts of energy could be generated on the lower Columbia River.[58] The Washington Department of Game estimated in 1977 that the town relocation and powerhouse construction would impact 998 acres of fish and wildlife habitat, resulting in a loss of 8,798,036 animal unit years (the amount of forage consumed by a large animal, such as a cow or an elk, in 1 year) over the life of the project.[59]

Losses of habitat resulting from construction of the second powerhouse include 20 acres of riverbank vegetation, composed of black cottonwood, willow, red alder, birch, and some aquatic plants, as well as big-leaf maple and grass and shrub communities. This may cause the wildlife population in the relocation area to shift to more urban-adapted species.[60]

In addition, about 18 million cubic yards of soil and rock were excavated from a goose nesting island and deposited on a 500-acre site that contained some tree growth. The forested land used for disposal was "inhabited either permanently or occasionally by a wide variety of animal life. . . ."[61] Twenty-five acres of wetlands were filled and became dry land, with this eulogy by the corps: "Wetlands are scarce and are becoming scarcer because man is eliminating them. They are biologically productive and their availability is usually the limiting factor to waterfowl population size."[62] The second powerhouse at Bonneville was operating by 1981, ready to provide peak power, though the demand never developed.

In 1977, the corps issued a feasibility study on construction of a new navigation lock at Bonneville Dam. The existing lock, the oldest lock on the Columbia River navigation system, has the capacity to pass 12.9 million tons of commerce per year.[63] Although traffic through the lock in recent years has not reached this capacity (figures for 1980, 1981, and 1982 are 8.9, 9.7, and 8.3 million tons, respectively),[64] the corps is concerned because long delays and double lockages at the dam are creating economic hardships for the government-subsidized barge industry. The agency is also expecting increases in barge traffic by 1990 that would surpass the current capacity of the lock.[65]

The corps is again planning a major construction effort based on speculation. An addendum report on the new lock, issued in 1981, predicts a total increase in congestion per tow of 2,600 percent as annual tonnage increases from 8.4 to 13.4 million tons. However, the performance monitoring system of the corps's Portland district shows that actual congestion per tow is increasing much more slowly than these projections indicate.[66] The federal government may still expend $170 million to construct this lock.

The taxpayers of the Columbia River basin subsidize navigation on the Columbia and Snake twice if they purchase energy from the BPA. Lock use by traffic on these rivers allows the spillage of water that would otherwise be used to generate hydroelectricity. Culver and Millham estimated that recreational lockages resulted in a loss of more than 34.2 million kilowatt-hours (worth $1,369,000) and that commercial lockages accounted for the indirect loss of 127.5 million kilowatt-hours (worth $5,104,000) in the basin in 1979. No charge is assessed for tows moving along these rivers, though a trip from Portland, Oregon, to Lewiston, Idaho, and back, which requires at least one lockage at each of eight dams, will cause the loss of 77,000 kilowatt-hours.[67]

A 1981 study by Martin and Arthur pointed out that the justification for the new lock project contained in the corps's 1977 feasibility report was seriously flawed. Among the problems identified were a lack of documentation of estimation procedures so that estimates could be replicated and verified, estimates based on questionable assumptions (the feasibility study assumes that the price of hydro-electric power will remain constant throughout the life of the project, for example), and questionable techniques used in arriving at the projected benefit-cost ratio. One of the inconsistencies in the benefit-cost analysis is the expectation of increased shipments of agricultural products from Idaho, which would necessitate more lockage capacity at the Bonneville site. The corps's estimates are based on a projected increase in use of fertilizer and new irrigation works. In Idaho, however, fertilizer dealers estimated that their production was "nearly at optimum levels," and there are no new irrigation projects in progress or planned.[68]

The construction of a new lock at Bonneville would, of course, contribute to the slow death of riparian communities in the area. On the shorelines of Ives and Pierce islands, riparian plant communities would probably be lost as the low areas of the islands are raised and new communities take over. Although revegetation work might re-establish some plant life on the islands, the new growth probably would not be as dense or diverse as the native riparian flora. Wind erosion, lack of organic matter in the soil, poor soil fertility, soil desiccation, and other factors could combine to retard the revegetation effort. Additionally, nesting and fawning success could be reduced by disturbances occurring during the construction phase. Noise from construction has recently been identified as a cause of reduced goose nesting success along the Snake River.[69] The cumulative result of all construction activity at Bonneville could mean the depletion or elimination of the great blue heron rookery on Pierce Island.[70]

excavation and disposal of 4.7 million cubic yards of spoil; some excavation would be from Bradford Island and Eagle Point. The Bradford Island excavation plan includes removal of most of a reed canary grass flat that typically harbors three or four goose nests per year. The resulting loss of goslings would be between ten and twenty per year. Geese also use the flat for breeding, feeding, and loafing throughout the year.[71] The Eagle Point habitat that the new lock construction would destroy is composed mostly of Douglas-fir and contains high densities of small mammals and game birds.

Proposed disposal areas include Ross Island in the Willamette River, which supports a riparian woodland composed of cottonwood and Oregon ash. The lagoon and river shore on the island comprise important habitat for beavers, river otters, muskrats, minks, nutria, raccoons, waterfowl, wading birds, gulls, kingfishers, ospreys, and bald eagles. About 4.7 million cubic yards of spoil would be deposited in the lagoon, reducing this habitat by 35 acres.[72]

The Franz and Arthur Lake disposal area contains a grassy pasture used by geese for winter feeding and probably for brooding. These lakes seasonally support several hundred waterfowl, including Canada geese, tundra swans, and various ducks. About 50,000 cubic yards of material would bury 9 acres of habitat, with additional habitat destroyed by the construction of an access road.[73]

These are merely examples of the piecemeal destruction of vital riparian habitats in the Columbia and Snake rivers. Certainly, society must make trade-offs in order to harness the inexpensive, safe, clean power produced by hydroelectric dams. Perhaps more concessions are necessary to provide inexpensive water transportation for agricultural products and other goods. But society often ignores the value of living things, which cannot be easily measured in monetary terms and, before we realize it, can be forever lost to us.

The Supreme Court heard a case concerning the development of hydropower in Hells Canyon on the Snake River in 1967. The case was remanded to the Federal Power Commission on the grounds that the commission had not adequately considered whether development of the canyon was in the public's interest. Justice Douglas wrote the following opinion for the court:

> The grant of authority to the Commission to alienate federal water resources does not, of course, turn simply on whether the project will be beneficial to the licensee. Nor is the test solely whether the region will be able to use the additional power. The test is whether the project will be in the public interest. And that determination can be made only after an exploration of all issues relevant to the "public interest," including future power demand and supply, alternate sources of power, the public interest in preserving reaches of wild rivers and wilderness areas, the preservation of anadromous fish for commercial and recreational purposes, and the protection of wildlife.
>
> The need to destroy the river as a waterway, the desirability of its demise, the choices available to satisfy future demands for energy—these are all relevant to a decision under Section 7 and Section 10 but they are largely untouched by the Commission.[74]

The decisions to alter riparian habitats in the Columbia River basin were never explicitly made. The benefits of power production, irrigation, and navigation were not weighed against the associated environmental costs until most of the system had been constructed. Complete evaluation of the public interest in water resources projects must encompass a full range of concerns—including ecological integrity.

NOTES

1. J. Howerton, Personal communication, 1985.
2. C. Komanoff, H. Miller, and S. Noyes, *The Price of Power: Electric Utilities and the Environment* (Cambridge, MA: The MIT Press, 1972), 64.
3. Department of the Interior, Bureau of Reclamation, *Final Environmental Impact Statement: Proposed Columbia River Basin Project,* (Washington, DC: Government Printing Office, 1976).
4. Northwest Power Planning Council, *Northwest Conservation and Electric Power Plan* (Portland, OR: Northwest Power Planning Council, 1983).
5. Ibid.
6. S. P. Cross, "Responses of Small Mammals to Forest Riparian Perturbations," *Riparian Ecosystems and Their Management: Reconciling Conflicting Uses.* (Forest Service publication GTR RM-120), ed. R. R. Johnson et al. (Washington, DC: Government Printing Office, 1985), 271.
7. International Union for the Conservation of Nature and Natural Resources, *Red Data Book* (Gland, Switzerland: IUCN, 1976).
8. Army Corps of Engineers, *Lower Granite Lock and Dam, Environmental Impact Statement* (Walla Walla, WA: Army Corps of Engineers, North Pacific Division, 1971).

9. J.L. McKern, *Inventory of Riparian Habitats and Associated Wildlife along the Columbia and Snake Rivers* (Walla Walla, WA: Army Corps of Engineers, North Pacific Division, 1976).
10. Pacific Northwest Power Company and Washington Public Power Supply System, initial reply brief of Oregon State Game Commission staff council, 1970.
11. Fish and Wildlife Service, *Status Report on Wildlife Mitigation, Bonneville Lock and Dam Project* (Washington, DC: Government Printing Office, 1984).
12. McKern, *Inventory of Riparian Habitats and Associated Wildlife.*
13. J. Tabor et al., *Study of the Impacts of Project Modification and River Regulation on Riparian Habitats and Associated Wildlife along the Columbia River* (Olympia, WA: Washington Department of Game, Habitat Management Division, 1980).
14. McKern, *Inventory of Riparian Habitats and Associated Wildlife.*
15. Ibid.
16. Ibid.
17. Tabor et al., *Impacts of Project Modification and River Regulation.*
18. P. C. Fielder and B. Perleberg, "Power Peaking and Wildlife Impacts along the mid-Columbia River, Washington," unpublished report (Olympia, WA: Washington Department of Game, 1981).
19. P. M. Walker, "Help for Montana Wildlife," *Northwest Energy News* 6, no. 3 (1987):12–13.
20. D. R. Holzworth, "Managing Wildlife Compensation Efforts on the Lower Snake River Project," in *Strategies for Protection and Management of Floodplain Wetlands and Other Riparian Ecosystems,* Forest Service general technical report WO-12 (Washington, DC: Government Printing Office, 1978), 388.
21. Ibid.
22. J. Howerton, et al., *Status Review of Wildlife Mitigation, Columbia Basin Hydroelectric Projects, Columbia River Mainstem Facilities* (Washington, DC: Government Printing Office, 1984).
23. Department of the Interior, Sport Fishing Institute, *Evaluation of Planning for Fish and Wildlife: Ice Harbor Lock and Dam Project,* (Washington, DC: Government Printing Office, 1977).
24. Howerton et al., *Status Review of Wildlife Mitigation.*
25. D. A. Asherin and J. J. Clear, *Inventory of Riparian Habitats and Associated Wildlife Along the Columbia River* (Moscow, ID: University of Idaho Press, 1976).
26. Howerton et al., *Status Review of Wildlife Mitigation.*
27. Department of the Interior, Sport Fishing Institute, *Evaluation of Planning for Fish and Wildlife.*
28. Ibid.
29. Ibid.
30. Ibid.
31. Army Corps of Engineers, Office of the Chief of Engineers, *Final Environmental Impact Statement: Lower Snake River Fish and Wildlife Compensation,* (Washington, DC: Government Printing Office, 1976).
32. Howerton et al., *Status Review of Wildlife Mitigation.*
33. Howerton et al., *Status Review of Wildlife Mitigation.*
34. Northwest Power Planning Council, *Northwest Conservation and Electric Power Plan.*
35. Northwest Power Planning Council, *Northwest Conservation and Electric Power Plan.*
36. Tabor et al., *Impacts of Project Modification and River Regulation.*
37. McKern, *Inventory of Riparian Habitats and Associated Wildlife.*

38. N. Thorpe, "Bonneville Power Is Criticized for Its Role in Planning Nuclear Plants for Northwest," *The Wall Street Journal*, 1980.
39. Ibid.
40. "Remarks by Don Hodel, Bonneville Power Administrator, Before the City Club of Portland," *BPA News*, 11 July 1975.
41. Northwest Power Planning Council, *Northwest Conservation and Electric Power Plan*.
42. Thorpe, "Bonneville Power Criticized for Planning Nuclear Plants."
43. Northwest Power Planning Council, *Northwest Conservation and Electric Power Plan*.
44. Skidmore, Owings and Merrill. *Bonneville Power Administration Electric Energy Conservation Study* (Seattle, WA: Skidmore, Owings and Merrill, 1976).
45. National Wildlife Federation, unpublished briefing paper, 1980.
46. Northwest Power Planning Council, *Northwest Conservation and Electric Power Plan*.
47. Fish and Wildlife Service, *Status Report on Wildlife Mitigation*.
48. Army Corps of Engineers, *Bonneville Lock and Dam, Oregon and Washington: Feasibility Study for Modified Lock* (Portland, OR: Army Corps of Engineers, 1977).
49. Ibid.
50. Ibid.
51. Ibid.
52. McKern, *Inventory of Riparian Habitats and Associated Wildlife*.
53. Army Corps of Engineers, *Lower Granite Lock and Dam, Environmental Impact Statement*.
54. L. Newton, "Managing Oregon's Nongame Wildlife," *Oregon Wildlife* 36, no. 7 (1981).
55. Fish and Wildlife Service, *Status Report on Wildlife Mitigation*.
56. Newton, "Managing Oregon's Nongame Wildlife."
57. Army Corps of Engineers, *Lower Granite Lock and Dam, Environmental Impact Statement*.
58. Ibid.
59. Howerton et al., *Status Review of Wildlife Mitigation*.
60. Ibid.
61. Army Corps of Engineers, *Lower Granite Lock and Dam, Environmental Impact Statement*.
62. Ibid.
63. Army Corps of Engineers, *Bonneville Lock and Dam, Oregon and Washington*.
64. T. McNamara, "A New Lock at Bonneville: Whether It Should Be Built and Who Should Pay. Draft." (Washington, DC: Association of American Railroads, 1983).
65. Army Corps of Engineers, *Bonneville Lock and Dam, Oregon and Washington: Feasibility Report, Addendum*. (Portland, OR: Army Corps of Engineers, 1981).
66. McNamara, "A New Lock at Bonneville."
67. C. F. Culver and C. B. Millham, "Hydropower Losses from Navigation in the Snake-Columbia Rivers: 1978-1979," *Water Resources Bulletin* 17, no. 3 (1981): 501-2.
68. M. V. Martin and L. M. Arthur, "Evaluating Inland Waterway Navigation Improvement Projects: The Case of the Bonneville Lock," *Water Resources Bulletin* 18, no. 3 (1981): 481-83.
69. Army Corps of Engineers, *Bonneville Lock and Dam, Oregon and Washington*.
70. Ibid.

71. Army Corps of Engineers, *Draft Environmental Impact Statement Supplement #1: Navigation Development, Bonneville Lock and Dam* (Walla Walla, WA: Army Corps of Engineers, 1985).

72. Ibid.

73. Ibid.

74. *Udall, Secretary of the Interior* v. *Federal Power Commission et al.* (387 U.S. 463).

4

Riparian Ecosystems in the Lower Colorado River Basin: The Wasted Oases

The Colorado River is probably the subject of more books, journal articles, legislation, litigation, and engineering blueprints than any other river in the world. Divided for water allocation purposes into an upper basin (including parts of Utah, Colorado, and Wyoming), where it derives the majority of its flow from the Rocky Mountains, and a lower basin (including parts of Arizona, California, New Mexico, and Mexico), where the river now shrivels into nothingness before it can rejoin the sea, the Colorado River may receive the devoted attention of more political characters than do the Geneva arms negotiations.

Floodplain immigrants on the lower Colorado River, be they man or beast, are caught in the midst of a battle over dams and water. On the one hand, the Colorado can have dry years in which crops will shrivel and die if no store of water exists in man-made reservoirs. On the other hand, one deep, snowy Rocky Mountain winter can cause torrents of water to rush down the river the following spring, and if there is no room in the reservoirs to capture these flows, a flood will devastate floodplain property. The federal government, by providing subsidies to farmers in the form of irrigation projects and crop deficiency payments, encourages water-dependent agriculture. Therefore, the government increases the potential harm that can result

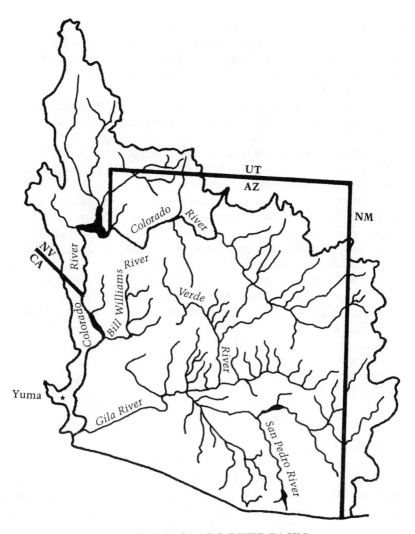

LOWER COLORADO RIVER BASIN

from having an inadequate reservoir water supply. The federal government, by providing subsidized flood insurance and flood control features, also encourages human development of floodplains, thereby increasing the potential danger of having inadequate reservoir storage available.

The consequences of irrigation and floodplain settlement are devastating to riparian communities and wildlife. The use of river water for irrigation increases soil salinity and changes the flood regime of riparian communities, thus weakening them so that they are easily overtaken by invading species of plants and animals. Invasion by salt cedar and starlings, for example, degrades conditions for native plants and animals such as cottonwoods and summer tanagers. The latter slowly die off.

Floodplain development destroys riparian communities both directly, by necessitating clearing of floodplains for the placement of homes and businesses, and indirectly, by triggering proposals for the construction of new dams (such as the recently deceased Cliff Dam, proposed for construction on the Verde River in Arizona) to protect human communities from high flows.

In some instances, affected biological communities are not directly destroyed but are replaced, component by component, by less diverse, more common, and hardier species. This replacement, though more subtle than inundation or real estate development, is equally impoverishing for the environment as a whole. The southwestern riparian communities, for example, are a unique, fragile treasure, and in their diversity lies their value. Interspersed with other living communities, these habitats create a quilt that blankets the earth. Like the parts of a human body, every living creature plays a role in maintaining the health of the earth. When parts are rendered nonfunctional, the body, or the biosphere, is certain to weaken and likely to die.

Life on the Floodplain

In 1983, the river was rough on those homo sapiens who had built their homes in the floodplain of the Colorado River. An angry desert dweller gave the following testimony before Congress:

> I wade in from the highway to my home; it's a foot deep in the
> living room and what a mess!! I press on to the barn, it's on lower
> ground so the water comes to the bottom of my work bench,
> maybe 30 inches deep. I climb on the bench to get out of the brown
> sewer water; warned by the National Guard (hepatitis danger).
> Damn!! Look at my place, it's a lake of fetid muck.[1]

High water releases from dams on the Colorado River in 1983 contributed to a flood that left over $100 million in damages to property and flood control structures. In the Yuma, Arizona, area the inundation of septic tanks and cesspools caused groundwater and sewage to mix. A population of 37,000 people was subject to water supply contamination. Like a proud lion mauling its trainer, the "tamed" Colorado River seemed to have struck a blow for its freedom.

The Bureau of Reclamation, which had constructed nine main-stem dams on the lower Colorado River, was swept up in the currents of controversy that flowed with the flood. The bureau had released the flows that damaged dikes and inundated homes and businesses on the floodplain, but they were merely responding to high water flows in a manner consistent with their current inflexible reservoir operating plans.

When those plans were formulated in 1970, the Colorado River had been experiencing several years of below normal runoff. Reservoir storage was well below the levels needed to contain excess water for flood prevention, and general concern existed that sufficient water would not be available for the Central Arizona Project (a massive canal system scheduled to become operative in late 1985) and for future development in the upper basin.[2] Because of the apparent lack of sufficient flows for water development in the lower Colorado River basin, the bureau's 1970 operating criteria were geared to conserving flows in reservoirs rather than to maintaining low water levels, in order to accommodate high flows should they occur. The secretary of the interior asked the basin states in 1975, and again in 1980, whether they desired a formal review of the operating criteria, which could result in changes in those criteria to reflect changing conditions in the basin. On both occasions, the consensus was that no changes were necessary and that a formal review was not needed.[3] Flows began to increase prior to 1983, however. In 1979 and 1980, runoff from the Colorado watershed was above normal. Extra releases into the river from storage reservoirs in 1979 were sufficient to prevent damage to main-stem dams and downstream developments. The next year also provided above-average flows, but Robert Broadbent, then commissioner of the Bureau of Reclamation, testified that he was optimistic that the bureau's operating plan would keep enough storage space available in the reservoirs to make large flood control releases unnecessary.[4]

The Bureau of Reclamation releases water from main-stem Colorado River reservoirs in proportion to estimates of the current river flow by the Colorado Basin Weather Forecasting Center. This center is staffed by representatives from the National Weather Service, the Bureau of Reclamation, the Geological Survey, the Soil Conservation Service, and the Army Corps of Engineers. The 1970 regulations required that space sufficient to store 5.35 million acre-feet of water be retained in the Colorado River reservoirs. Robert Broadbent recalled the bureau's 1983 operations in the following testimony before the House Committee on Interior and Insular Affairs:

> On January 1, we had 6.6 million acre-feet of available storage. The Weather Service Forecasting Center said there was about 112 percent of average flow; therefore, our releases at that time were mandated to be at a certain level. We met that level. We released a little over 19,000 cubic feet per second starting January 1.
>
> On February 1 our estimate from the Weather Service again was 102 percent; March 1 it was 96 percent, April 1 — these dates are approximate, they are usually a couple of days later than that — 114 percent; on May 1, 117; on June 1, 131.
>
> In all these cases, we felt there was no serious problem in the operation of the Colorado River System. We believed we had adequate storage to take care of the problem.
>
> All of a sudden, on June 14, the estimate went up to 163 percent. We knew that we were going to have to make high releases and our challenge then as we looked at it in the Bureau of Reclamation was to manage the system in such a way that we kept those releases at as low a possible level out of Hoover Dam and subsequently out of Davis and Parker Dams.[5]

Clearly, this disaster came as a shock to the agency, which had believed that it could predict and control the fickle moods of the mighty Colorado River.

The issue of Colorado River flooding extends well beyond the operation of Bureau of Reclamation dams. Floods are natural occurrences; to some life forms they are essential. They become disasters only when they threaten human life or property.

Despite escalating annual damages, people continue to construct homes and businesses on the floodplains of temperamental rivers. The United States incurs costs of $3 to $4 billion per year in flood damages.[6] Yet people still insist on building on floodplains, depending on some benevolent federal wizard to protect them from the consequences and balking at any restrictions on development their benefactors may seek to impose.

In fact, the citizens of Yuma had stalled their application for admission into the National Flood Insurance Program in 1983 so that they might persuade the Federal Emergency Management Agency (FEMA) to adjust their floodplain maps. According to regulations for the flood insurance program, any party that places structures within a 100-year floodplain as depicted on FEMA maps must purchase federal flood insurance or lose all federal aid for construction, structural improvements, and flood damage compensation. The maps, Yuma complained, did not take a new Bureau of Reclamation levee system

into account and were therefore too restrictive of floodplain development. Resentful of federal regulation, yet unwilling to restrict its own
development, the town of Yuma nevertheless went before the Committee on Interior and Insular Affairs that September and asked that
FEMA provide them with compensation for their flood-related losses.

The Colorado River's Natural History

The Colorado River rises from its headwaters in the Rocky Mountain
National Park in Colorado, about 70 miles northwest of Denver. The
river is 1,400 miles long and drains about 244,000 square miles
of Colorado, Wyoming, Utah, Nevada, Arizona, California, New Mexico, and Mexico. The Colorado's major tributaries are the Green,
Gunnison, San Juan, Little Colorado, Virgin, and Gila rivers.

The river's name was derived from the Spanish *colorado*, which
means "red." In late spring, the river would swell with snowmelt,
carving and carrying off the red soils of the Rocky Mountains and
badlands that cradled it. Spring floods scoured many areas and often
destroyed large tracts of cottonwood and willow forests, but they also
prepared seedbeds for future plant regeneration.

Before diversions for irrigation, industry, and cities shriveled the
Colorado's southern end, the river emptied into the Gulf of California. Aldo Leopold explored the Colorado's delta with his brother in
1922 and described it as follows:

> A verdant wall of mesquite and willow separated the channel from
> the thorny desert beyond. At each bend we saw egrets standing in
> the pools ahead, each white statue matched by its white reflection.
> Fleets of cormorants drove their black prows in quest of skittering
> mullets; avocets, willets, and yellowlegs dozed one-legged on the
> bars; mallards, widgeons, and teal sprang skyward in alarm. As the
> birds took the air, they accumulated in a small cloud ahead, there
> to settle, or to break back to our rear. When a troop of egrets
> settled on a far green willow, they looked like a premature
> snowstorm.[7]

The Colorado River has carved canyons of unique and spectacular
beauty. Differential uplift and erosion of segments of the earth's crust
created broad, horizontal segments in the upper basin and narrow,
tilted segments in the lower basin. The rate and manner of erosion by
the river is controlled by the composition and position of the rocks.
Weak formations are easily chiseled away; strong formations are
undermined. This persistent cutting by the river results in layer-cake

canyons of pink and golden history, often garnished with glistening snow frosting and candles of pine.

The land that the river removed from banks and canyon walls was gently laid to rest elsewhere, forming alluvial soils on which young trees could sprout and grow. The riparian groves that developed on these fresh soils are the veins of life in the desert; nowhere else is the growth lush enough and the floral diversity great enough to support the rich animal life these groves contain.

The Cottonwood-Willow Association

Cottonwood-willow galleries may be the most valuable habitat types in the desert Southwest, and they may also be the most endangered. At elevations below 3,500 feet, associations of Fremont cottonwood and various willow species are found on fine soil and rock deposits. These communities depend on spring floods caused by snowmelts in the mountains and flash floods triggered by summer thunderstorms. Where water flows are stabilized, however, stands become decadent and trees fail to reproduce.[8]

Cottonwood and willow, which often form galleries 100 feet high, are commonly the tallest floodplain trees and provide a mosaic of open space and vegetation under their canopies. The horizontal and vertical habitat diversity provided by the structure of these plants allows colonization by a wide variety of breeding and migratory bird species.

Honey Mesquite

Honey mesquite, which provides an open understory and a food source, is also very valuable to wildlife. Honey mesquite forms a subtropical habitat type below elevations of 3,500 feet. Mesquite bosque (open woodland) reaches its maximum development on the alluvium of old, dessicated floodplains laid down between the intersections of major watercourses and their larger tributaries. The deep roots of a mesquite tree enable it to tap water sources far below the soil surface. Mesquite is a legume and therefore enriches the soil by transforming atmospheric nitrogen into a form that can be used by plants. Like many other legumes, mesquite produces beans, which are eaten by various animals.

Mesquite woodlands are vital colonial nesting sites for mourning and white-winged doves.[9] Gambel's quails reach their highest spring breeding and wintering densities in stands of honey mesquite, where they feed on mesquite seeds and abundant annuals.[10] Stands of honey mesquite are dominated by permanent resident insectivores (insect eaters) such as Crissal thrashers, cactus wrens, verdins, and black-tailed gnatcatchers. Frugivorous (fruit-eating) species also frequent honey mesquite bosques to feed on the mistletoe that parasitizes the trees.

Salt Cedar

Salt cedar is a shrubby species that rarely exceeds 30 feet in height. Common salt cedar (*Tamarisk chinensis*) has a dense understory, making it poor habitat for resting or hunting birds and virtually unusable by large mammals. This plant was introduced by the Department of Agriculture to create a windbreak and provide bank stabilization on the Gila River in the late 1800s. It spread to the Colorado River valley between 1910 and 1920.[11] By the 1940s, salt cedar had become the dominant species along most desert rivers in the Southwest. In 1983, 40 percent of all riparian vegetation along the lower Colorado River was salt cedar, 43 percent was native vegetation mixed with salt cedar, and only .77 percent was native cottonwood and willow.[12]

Salt cedar has many properties that have allowed it to overwhelm native riparian species. While cottonwoods produce seeds once a year, in synchrony with spring floods, salt cedar produces seeds from April until October. One plant may produce 600,000 seeds per year.[13] Salt cedar is deciduous and will cover the ground beneath it with dead foliage. Fires therefore occur frequently in stands of salt cedar,[14] which is fire tolerant and regenerates rapidly. Cottonwoods are killed by fire, as are mesquite trees under 5 years of age and some willows. All of these native trees regenerate less rapidly than does salt cedar. Salt cedar also has a high tolerance for prolonged flooding, such as that caused by the 1983 reservoir releases, and for high soil salinity. Salinity levels have risen drastically in the water and soils of the Colorado River since the development of dams and irrigated agriculture, to the detriment of native species and to the benefit of salt cedar.[15] Salt cedar has dense foliage and a high transpiration rate. It sustains the lowest density and variety of birds of any riparian habitat type except for arrowweed, a treeless biological community.[16] Bird populations will probably continue to decrease in number and variety as cottonwood-willow and mesquite stands are replaced by salt cedar.

History of Irrigation on the Colorado

Indians were the first irrigators in the Southwest. The Hohokams, centered around what is now the Phoenix metropolitan area, used primitive dams in about 200 B.C. to create small water impoundments on streams. By the time their civilization fell, in the middle of the fifteenth century, the Hohokams had constructed 200 to 250 miles of canals diverting water from the Salt and Gila rivers. Irrigation of crops caused increased soil salinity and high water tables, which stunted the growth of the Hohokams' crops, causing the tribe's decline. The Pima Indians reoccupied Hohokam land, encountered salinity problems, and addressed these problems by applying more water to leach accumulated salts out of the soil.[17] This wasteful technique is used by modern irrigators today.

Spaniards from Mexico were the first nonnative people to travel along the Lower Colorado. Hernando de Alarcón discovered the Colorado in 1540 as he traveled north from the Gulf of Mexico. Spanish settlement followed. Between 1768 and 1822, irrigation structures were built along the Santa Cruz River, near missions and the Spanish presidios of Tubac and Tucson.

Indians destroyed the Spanish missions built on the lower river in 1781, and Spanish activity in the region subsided. Until the middle of the next century, only a few trappers, explorers, and pioneers visited the river.

The United States purchased the Colorado River valley from Mexico in 1848, and large-scale settlement and irrigation took root in Arizona.

Thomas H. Blythe filed the first claim on Colorado River water in California in 1877. At about the same time, the first modern irrigation works were being constructed in Wyoming, Utah, and Colorado. The federal government first attempted to "reclaim" arid lands on the Colorado River Indian Reservation in 1867. The first diversion from the main stem of the Colorado River to the Imperial Valley in California occurred in 1901. By 1904, the California Development Company had developed 700 miles of irrigation ditches in southern California and put 75,000 acres into cultivation.

The Colorado River near Yuma, Arizona, was swollen with floodwaters, mostly contributed by the Gila River, for 16 months in 1905. The river broke through a headgate on a California Development Company canal and filled the Salton Sink in California with water, creating the Salton Sea, which still collects saline irrigation runoff from the Imperial Valley. Before the break was closed, 30,000 acres of arable land were inundated, farms and homes were destroyed, and highways and railroad tracks were washed away. The frontier spirit of the settlers remained undaunted, however. Determined to break this belligerent bronco of a river, they called in the federal government. Enter the Bureau of Reclamation.

The "Taming" of the River

Before federal construction of large dams on the Colorado, the river waters deposited enormous amounts of silt on the floodplain and in deltas. Near the Colorado's mouth at the Gulf of California, freshly deposited mud flats and banks quickly became covered with seedling willows.[18] The Bureau of Reclamation estimated that in the early 1900s, the Colorado River was depositing more than 100,000 acre-feet of silt per year in the delta region.[19] The Imperial Irrigation District was spending more than $500,000 per year in 1923 and 1924 to remove silt from its canal systems.

During the 1920s, irrigated agriculture began to dominate the economy of the basin. The river remained in near-natural condition at this time, still experiencing flooding when Rocky Mountain snows began to melt. Along the valleys of the lower river, cottonwood, willow, and mesquite bosques still regenerated on the annually deposited mud flats. These river woodlands resounded with the songs of Bell's vireos, Lucy's and yellow warblers, and summer tanagers. Local populations of flickers, willow flycatchers, and Bewick's wrens lived in pockets along the river.

The Colorado River, though long, is not large in terms of volume; the Colorado is not even one of the United States' thirty most voluminous rivers. Yet every drop belongs to somebody — the river is overallocated. Current interstate compacts appropriating water to the upper and lower river basins and to Mexico are based on an average annual flow of 14.9 million acre-feet, measured during a period of unusually high flows. The actual average annual flow is between 11 and 13.8 million acre-feet. Still, both upper and lower basin states are planning to construct more huge dams and reservoirs to store and protect their legal share of the wrung-out river.

The combination of king-sized dams and overappropriation of flows creates a double jeopardy for riparian ecosystems. The reservoirs behind the dams destroy vegetation through prolonged inundation and unnatural fluctuation; river dewatering promotes deadly dessication of plants and harmful alteration of fish habitat. The continued existence of healthy river and riparian communities depends in part on the availability of in-stream flows.

Hoover Dam, completed in 1935, changed forever the character of the Colorado River. From a temperamental, and at times quite muddy, river, the Colorado became a steady, clear-flowing stream that no longer annually overflowed its banks. Hoover Dam created Lake Mead, with 32 million acre-feet of storage, then the country's largest reservoir.

Between 1950 and 1960, the population of Arizona increased by 74 percent. By 1967, thirty reservoirs in the entire river basin were capable of storing 72.5 million acre-feet of water, or five times the average annual flow of the river.[20] In the lower basin, eight dams had been completed, including the controversial Glen Canyon Dam, which inundated a breathtaking desert canyon just south of the Arizona-Utah border in 1963. Edward Abbey, in *Desert Solitaire*, wrote of this dam with appropriate reverence:

> To grasp the nature of the crime that was committed imagine the Taj Mahal or Chartres Cathedral buried in mud until only the spires remain visible. With this difference: those man-made celebrations of human aspirations could conceivably be reconstructed while Glen Canyon was a living thing, irreplaceable, which can never be recovered by any human agency.[21]

Glen Canyon Dam permits control of almost all flows leaving the upper Colorado River basin. Flows in the lower basin are mostly controlled by a series of storage and diversion dams.

Davis Dam's reservoir, Lake Mojave, backs up the river 67 miles at high water to the tailwaters of Hoover Dam. The construction of Parker Dam created Lake Havasu, which covers 25,000 acres and is 45 miles long when full. Headgate Rock Dam, Palo Verde Diversion Dam, and Laguna Dam were all built primarily to divert water into irrigation canals, so they have no storage facilities. Imperial Dam is the last major dam on the Colorado River and is the major diversion structure for irrigation projects in the Imperial and Coachella valleys of California and for Yuma, Arizona. Water not diverted from Imperial Dam flows southwest for about 20 miles to Mexico's Morelos Dam, near Yuma. Morelos Dam diverts most of the river's remaining flow into the Mexicali Valley for irrigation. The river only reaches its natural outlet in the Gulf of California during years of extremely high flow.

Since the turn of the century, the most productive land in the Colorado River valley has been either inundated by reservoirs or developed for agriculture. During the 1940s and 1950s, wide portions of the floodplain near Yuma, Blythe, and Parker were cleared; large remnant tracts of vegetation were left only on national wildlife refuges and Indian reservations. In the 1950s and 1960s, the Indians followed suit and began to develop modern irrigation works on their lands. Brown noted that the continued clearing of mesquite bosques along the Gila and Colorado rivers has resulted in their replacement by agriculture and other conversions.[22] According to Dr. R. Roy Johnson,

> Today, less than one half of the more than 1,000 miles of river are not impeded by major dams. Even along this half are located diversion structures for local irrigation projects, mining and other uses. The remaining half of the system consists of dry stream bed and more than 100 miles of storage reservoirs and large diversion structures.[23]

Arizona is guaranteed 2.8 million acre-feet per year of Colorado River water under the 1928 Boulder Canyon Project Act. Of the almost 2 million acre-feet that Arizona was diverting before the Central Arizona Project became fully operational, 89 percent was used for agricultural irrigation and a tiny .8 percent was allocated to fish and wildlife.[24] According to the Bureau of Reclamation, in 1946 crop production in the basin depended almost wholly on irrigation. Livestock raising was the basin's principal agricultural pursuit, but the numerous herds of cattle and sheep that grazed the vast ranges and forests depended on supplemental feed from irrigated farms. By 1984, 300,000 acres along the Colorado River had been put to the plow. Most of this land is now used for the production of alfalfa, cotton, and winter wheat. All of these plants consume large quantities of water, and alfalfa and cotton have low market values. In fact, according to the Department of Agriculture, 45 percent of the acreage irrigated by the Bureau of Reclamation produces crops that are already in surplus in the United States. The Department of the Interior estimates that taxpayers subsidize 85 percent of the cost of the water that the Bureau of Reclamation delivers to western farmers.[25]

Irrigation has been a boon in building populations of the sun-drenched Southwest, but not enough attention has been paid to the environmental and economic costs of this development. In 1959, income from farming accounted for only 7.9 percent of all personal income in Arizona. By 1971, farm earnings had increased but had failed to keep pace with the rest of the state's economy, and they had actually declined to 3.7 percent of total personal income. The Department of Agriculture sets a target price for certain crops as part of a pseudo-insurance program for farmers. If the market price of these crops falls below the target price, the federal government will compensate the farmers for the difference in what are known as "deficiency payments." In 1984, the Department of Agriculture gave Arizona farmers a total of $46.8 million in deficiency payments, an

average of $29,348 per farmer. Forty-four million dollars of these
deficiency payments, or 94 percent, were for cotton crops.[26] In 1985,
139 million acres of Arizona cotton farmland, 77 percent of the land
eligible for federal cotton price support payments, did not produce
crops.[27]

The Decline of the Natural River

While artificial lacustrine (lakelike) environments have expanded
considerably along the lower Colorado, native riparian communities
have declined drastically. The lower part of the Colorado River supported more than 8,000 acres of cottonwood communities in the
1600s. By 1977, only 2,800 acres of cottonwood-willow communities
and fewer than 500 acres of pure cottonwood communities
remained.[28] One of the original causes of riparian decline was the
cutting of trees to fuel steamboats in the late 1800s. Overgrazing by
livestock has stunted regeneration of native trees as well, but these
problems are almost trivial compared with the complete dismantling
of ecological processes on the river. Approximately 85 percent of all
native riparian vegetation in Arizona has been destroyed by the
interruption of natural stream flows for irrigation.[29] Ohmart, Deason,
and Burke concluded that "the demise of cottonwoods on the lower
Colorado River has been related to the implementation of dams and
the data indicates that dams expedited the natural loss by stopping
annual overflow."[30] Natural, periodic overflow of banks by the river
releases nutrients from detritus on the stream banks, lays sediment
beds for tree regeneration, and prevents frequent fires in established
groves.

The side effects of controlling the Colorado River waters for flood
damage reduction and for irrigation have accelerated the decline of
riparian habitats. Among the causes of riparian degradation are prolonged flooding, phreatophyte (water-loving plant) control, and
increased soil salinity.

Longer Floods in Fewer Years

Although native riparian species depend on seasonal bank overflow
for regeneration, prolonged flooding kills native trees.

In 1974 through 1978, a study plot in the floodplain of the Bill
Williams River, one of the last remaining thickly forested portions of
the lower basin contained within the Havasu National Wildlife
Refuge, was dominated by cottonwoods and willows more than 30
feet tall with a patchy understory of salt cedar, cattail, and bulrush.[31]

From 1978 through 1981, the Army Corps of Engineers released excess springtime floodwaters from Alamo Dam on the Bill Williams River, a tributary to the Colorado. Before the floods, 40 percent of all the trees in the study area were cottonwoods. After the floods, 99 percent of these died. Willows, considered an ecological equivalent to cottonwoods in terms of bird use, declined by 64 percent as a result of the floods. Therefore, the combined loss of cottonwood-willow habitat on the study plot was 75 percent. Snags (dead trees), which are valuable to cavity-nesting birds, increased temporarily after the floods but quickly rotted and fell between 1981 and 1982. By 1983, 70 percent of the cottonwood snags that had been present in 1981 had fallen. Willow snags declined by 35 percent between 1981 and 1983.[32]

Populations of two bird species in the study area increased after the floods. These were brown-headed cowbirds and European starlings; both parasitize the nests of native cavity-nesting birds.[33]

Many riparian dependent bird species declined following the floods: Abert's towhees, yellow-billed cuckoos, summer tanagers, northern orioles, gila woodpeckers, brown-crested flycatchers, winter wrens, and hermit thrushes. Marsh-dependent birds, such as marsh wrens, red-winged blackbirds, and various rail species, increased after the floods.[34] These trends in species density reflect an ecosystem completely transformed by prolonged high flows released from man-made reservoirs.

As for the lower river flooding of 1983, Rosenberg and co-workers speculated that "high flows during 1983 and 1984 may result in the death of most of the remaining cottonwoods that were completely inundated.... Long term effects of flooding in 1983 through 1984 will not be known completely for several years."[35]

Hazards from Phreatophyte Control

Expansion of human populations in the lower river valley and a low-flow trend in the mid-1960s made water conservation desirable and influenced the Bureau of Reclamation's decision to commence a "phreatophyte control" program. The bureau's goal was to eradicate 140,000 acres of riparian trees along the lower Colorado in order to salvage 411,000 acre-feet of water per year. Only part of this project has been accomplished to date.[36]

Campbell predicted that soil erosion would increase as a result of phreatophyte control, as water moving down the river channel cut into soil banks that had previously been protected by deep-rooted vegetation. Water evaporation from the soil would increase because of increased soil temperatures and shallower water tables. Stream temperature would increase due to loss of the shading effect of the trees, and the additional light on the water would enhance algal growth and stagnation in quiet, still pools. Campbell warned that because of this reduction in shade and resulting thermal pollution, fish habitat and fish populations could be degraded or destroyed.[37]

When phreatophyte eradication was put into practice, few of the predicted benefits were realized. Graf noted that clearing phreatophytic vegetation from stream banks did little to ease evapotranspirative losses of water (losses of water through a combination of evaporation and plant respiration) for any length of time. The cleared banks, which still received moisture from the adjacent river, were perfect seedbeds for salt cedar to colonize. Dense growth of this species occurred within 18 to 24 months of clearing.[38]

Evaporation, Irrigation, and Increased Salinity

In addition to the detrimental effects of eradicating woody riparian vegetation on the watershed, the bureau was defeating its purpose of storing water in its reservoirs. By 1968, 650,000 acre-feet of water had been lost through evaporation from Lake Mead. An additional 300,000 acre-feet were lost through evaporation between Lake Mead and the Mexican border—principally from the reservoirs created by the Bureau of Reclamation.[39] Current evaporative losses from reservoirs average 1,369 acre-feet per year.[40] Additionally, evaporation of water from reservoirs concentrates salts in the remaining water and contributes greatly to salinization of the river and surrounding soils.

Irrigation also concentrates salts and accounts for about one-third of all salts delivered into the Colorado River.[41] Between 1941 and 1972, Colorado River water flows ranged from 5,615,000 acre-feet to 14,714,000 acre-feet, and salinity ranged from 649 parts per million to 918 parts per million. Diversion of water in the basin is increasing; therefore, river flows are decreasing. From 1964 until the 1983–1984 floods, flows arriving at Imperial Dam had consistently been below 6 million acre-feet on a yearly average. As a consequence, salinity levels were rising during that period. At Imperial Dam, water salinities averaged 835 parts per million in 1974, and studies predict that an annual average of 950 parts per million could be reached by 1993.[42]

Because the bed of the Colorado River is perched (raised by sediment deposition above the groundwater table), surrounding banks derive their moisture largely from the river. The salinity of the river water causes salt levels in floodplain soils to increase, making survival difficult for native vegetation.

In order for water to pass readily from the soil into the roots of a plant, the osmotic pressure of the solution inside the root cells must be considerably greater than that of the solution outside. When the concentration of salt in solution in the soil is greater than that inside the plant root cells, water passes "backward" from the roots into the soil.[43] The plant dries up and is either stunted or killed. This phenomenon has decreased the success rate of efforts to revegetate banks of the Colorado River with native riparian trees.[44]

Soil salinity has other consequences besides its effect on native flora. High concentrations of salt corrode most metals, causing mechanical damage to pipes and other appurtenances with which the solution comes in contact. Saline water caused between $75 million and $104 million in damages in 1980 and will cause between $122 million and $165 million worth in 2000 if no control measures are taken. Most of these damages are incurred by industrial and municipal water users, although agricultural users face declining crop yields, increasing water requirements for leaching toxic substances from soils, and higher management costs.[45]

Perhaps the most difficult problem created by increased water salinity in the Colorado River basin is the violation of the United States-Mexico Treaty for Utilization of Waters of the Colorado and Tijuana Rivers and of the Rio Grande. This treaty, signed in 1944, guarantees delivery to Mexico of 1.5 million acre-feet of Colorado River water each year. Until 1961, excess flows diluted saline return flows from cultivated fields. In 1961, pumping of water from the Wellton-Mohawk Irrigation District on the Gila River began and the availability of excess flows came to an end. Water salinity increased that year from 800 parts per million to 1500 parts per million. In November of that year, the Mexican government protested that "the delivery of water that is harmful for the purposes stated in the Treaty constitutes a violation of the Treaty."[46]

The Irrigation Merry-Go-Round

The Wellton-Mohawk Irrigation District receives water from the Bureau of Reclamation's Gila Project in southwestern Arizona. Originally, water for the irrigation project, which lies alongside the Gila River, was diverted from the river. Then, beginning in the 1940s, the bureau began to dam the upper Gila, reducing the lower Gila to a mere intermittent trickle. To supply the Wellton-Mohawk Irrigation District, the bureau began to pump groundwater out of the aquifer. The pumping sustained agricultural production until it caused the water table to drop, the crops to dry out, and the district's agricultural economy to decline. Water for the project is now diverted from the Colorado River at Imperial Dam and travels through as much as 94 miles of canals before irrigating the district's 65,000 acres along the

Gila River and in bordering mesa areas. The water is used to grow
cotton, alfalfa, and flax, along with small quantities of more valuable
crops, before it is mechanically pumped out of the soil into the
Wellton-Mohawk conveyance channel.

The pumping system was installed by the Bureau of Reclamation
in 1961 because a natural basaltic "dam" at the head of the valley
prevented the water from returning to the Colorado River. Earlier, the
underground water table had risen, inundating croplands and, at one
point, a state highway. The briny water, seasoned by the surfacing of
salts accumulated in the soil over many years of irrigation, sucked the
moisture out of crops and caused the failure of thousands of cultivated
acres. The pumps, along with the conveyance channel and 109 wells,
made possible the return of the poisoned groundwater to the Colorado
River.[47]

The Mexican government complained when this liquid herbicide
began to reach their fields. Unlike the United States, Mexico did not
have the financial means to construct a complex, subsidized drainage
system. They protested at the American consulate in Mexico, hinted
that they might withdraw their support for President Kennedy's
Alliance for Progress, and threatened to take the problem to the World
Court. The United States has taken interim measures since 1961 to
alleviate the salinity problem. In 1974, Congress passed the Colorado
River Basin Salinity Control Act, which authorized construction of a
desalting unit on the lower Colorado River; federal acquisition of
10,000 acres of the Wellton-Mohawk Irrigation District, which were
then taken out of agricultural production; education and technical
assistance for irrigators by the Soil Conservation Service; and other
measures. Construction involved in implementing the salinity control project will destroy an estimated 1,000 acres of terrestrial habitat
and 400 acres of aquatic wildlife habitat. The total federal cost will be
almost $.5 billion. This amounts to more than $7 thousand per acre to
keep the Wellton-Mohawk producing excess crops.

The Loss of the Singing Spirits

The music of a bird-filled woodland and the sight of a soaring hawk or
colorful songbird bring joy to many human hearts. Beyond the
aesthetic pleasure birds impart, they are important indicators of
ecosystem health and stability or metamorphosis. If a full and diverse
complement of avian life is present in an ecosystem, the components
of that ecosystem are probably functioning well and performing the
ecological service for which nature designed them. If, however, the
native bird species are declining, chances are that the ecosystem has

been drastically disturbed and that more severe consequences, such as loss of other floral and faunal components and the sterilization, pollution, and wasting of land and water will follow if balance is not restored.

On the Colorado River, the in-stream ecosystem has already exhibited symptoms of chronic illness. Three fish species, including the Colorado squawfish, which, until 1910, was sufficiently abundant to sustain commercial harvesting, are now federally listed as endangered. These fish no longer reproduce in the lower Colorado River; they now depend largely on hatchery rearing for their continued survival. Their decline was caused by the construction of dams and resulting transformation of their native habitat.

The birds in terrestrial habitats bordering the river are following suit. In the past 50 years, mature cottonwood-willow forests have declined to almost nothing while agricultural acreage has steadfastly increased. Conine and co-workers studied streamside ecology on the Colorado and found that agricultural communities did not support bird populations as large as those found in native riparian communities.[48] In fact, several species of riparian-dependent birds have suffered drastic population declines during the past century. Although most of these species are not yet on the federal endangered species list, their Colorado River populations are close to being extirpated. As similar trends toward destruction of native riparian habitats continue in other areas, these species could be eliminated from the planet.

Species Decreasing Along the Colorado

Harris' Hawks   These dark buteos bear chestnut-colored patches on their thighs and shoulders. The immature bird is light and streaked on the underside and has rusty shoulders. Harris' hawks inhabit woodlands and generally hunt in mesquite bosques.[49] They were common breeders along the Colorado River until 1959, when their population experienced a sudden drop-off.[50,51] The bird is now virtually extirpated from the lower Colorado River.[52]

Vermilion Flycatchers   These birds reach the northern edge of their range in the southwestern United States. The male has a scarlet crown and a dark brown streak on the side of his head. The female is somewhat paler. Vermilion flycatchers, which depend on cottonwood-willow woodlands for breeding, were common from Yuma, Arizona, to the Gulf of Mexico in the late 1800s. In 1983, only one breeding pair was found.[53]

Sonoran Yellow Warblers   These cheery-looking, all-yellow birds have equally cheery songs. Abundant in cottonwood-willow groves in the early 1900s, their Colorado River population underwent a drastic decline in 1955. By 1960, they were considered extirpated from the valley.[54]

Cooper's Hawks   These hawks are smaller than crows. They have short wings, long tails, rusty breasts, and blue-grey backs. Once common breeders along the Colorado, their population steadily declined from the early 1950s through the early 1960s. During the mid-1960s, the birds stabilized at population levels below their 1950s numbers.[55] As breeders, they are now considered eliminated from the Colorado River.[56]

Summer Tanagers   Like the tropical members of their subfamily (the *Piranga* tanagers), summer tanagers keep their bright red color all year. These insectivores grab insects in midair and open wasps' nests to eat the larvae and pupae. These tanagers need high canopies to construct their nests.

Summer tanagers were common in cottonwood-willow habitats along the Colorado River in the late 1800s and early 1900s. Now they are in danger of complete extirpation from the river.[57]

Yellow-Billed Cuckoos   These cuckoos have green backs, rusty wings, and white spots on the undersides of their tails. Unlike their parasitic relatives, yellow-billed cuckoos construct their own nests, in which they lay two to five blue-green eggs. Yellow-billed cuckoos frequently sing at night. They hunt by waiting for katydids or caterpillars to reveal their presence through movement, then striking quickly and mashing the insects with their bills. These birds, also dependent on the high canopies of cottonwood-willow groves, have been proposed for the federal endangered species list since 1982.

Arizona Bell's Vireos   Bell's vireos are small migratory songbirds that feed mostly on insects and nest in dense willow- or mesquite-dominated riparian thickets. Vireos obtain all their survival needs within the riparian zone. The California subspecies of Bell's vireo (*Vireo bellii pusillus*) was proposed for the federal endangered species list in May 1985. The Arizona subspecies (*Vireo bellii arizona*) is rapidly declining along the Colorado River, but it was not proposed for listing because its status is relatively stable in other parts of its range.

Northern Gilded Flickers   The males of this species sport red mustaches and yellow wing and tail linings. These woodpeckers excavate cavities in saguaro cacti or cottonwood snags for nesting and often inhabit cottonwood-willow groves, in which they feed almost exclusively year round.[58] They prefer vegetative communities of high foliage diversity and density. Northern gilded flickers reach their northern and western ranges at the Colorado River, but the Colorado River population is declining, due primarily to the loss of cotton-wood-willow habitat. Woodpeckers demonstrate less flexibility than other birds in adapting to salt cedar communities, possibly because their body size is large in relation to salt cedar limbs and trunks, making excavation of suitable nesting cavities difficult or impossible.[59]

Other bird species are increasing along the Colorado River. Some of these are cosmopolitan species that take advantage of the native birds' ecological misfortunes and crowd the natives out of the river corridors. Others are birds that are well adapted for habitats other than riparian, such as open fields and lakes, and that increase as these habitats become more common.

Species Increasing Along the Colorado

Brown-Headed Cowbirds   These parasitic blackbirds have brown heads and feed with their tails pointed upwards. The grey females lay eggs in the nests of other birds, often destroying the eggs of their host. This behavior has added to the decline of many native birds along the lower Colorado River, including the Arizona Bell's vireos and Sonoran yellow warblers.

Populations of cowbirds have been steadily increasing as riparian habitat becomes fragmented and agricultural areas increase. Cowbirds are primarily agricultural-riparian "edge" species; therefore, as riparian habitat patches are diminished by growing agricultural use of the floodplain and surrounding uplands, cowbird populations expand.

European Starlings   These introduced birds are dedicated opportunists and, at times, parasitize the cavity nests of other birds. Starlings have forced Gila woodpeckers, another declining Colorado River species, from their nests during the breeding season, disposed of the eggs, and frustrated the woodpeckers' breeding attempts. Starlings are well adapted to human habitations and thrive on agricultural lands.

Yuma Clapper Rails   These large, heavy, grey-brown rails are federally listed as endangered. They breed in freshwater marshes along the Colorado River from the Nevada-California border south to the Colorado River delta in Mexico. Yuma clapper rails have expanded their range northward with the creation of suitable marsh habitat associated with dam development. Regulated water releases in the lower Colorado have slowed and stabilized river flow sufficiently to allow sedimentation and the development of cattail and bulrush marshes.[60]

Deep-Water Birds   Rare ducks, such as scoters and oldsquaws, as well as Sabine's gulls and other species associated with the formation of huge lakes and deep channels, now occur along the Colorado River.[61]

Agricultural development creates habitat as well for such migratory and wintering birds as geese, ducks, hawks, sandhill cranes, shorebirds, horned larks, pipits, and meadowlarks. These temporary feeding habitats exist at the expense of rare riparian breeding habitats for native birds.

Human harnessing of natural forces decreases biological diversity and, therefore, ecosystem stability in many instances. Incidental benefits accrue to some wildlife species, as not all habitat is sterilized; some is merely transformed. This habitat alteration allows colonization by previously absent species when the habitat can no longer support the natives.

Biologists do not pass judgment on individual life forms. The present task for conservationists is to maintain the diversity of life forms and habitats that exist on earth in the face of increasing sterilization and monoculture resulting from human manipulation and exploitation of natural resources.

The lakes, fields, and marshes created by the development of dams on the Colorado River are not completely devoid of wildlife, but they are increasingly replacing valuable native communities of plants and animals. Every new dam, each freshly plowed field, increases the value of the remaining native riparian habitat. As Hunter succinctly stated,

> The bird species considered . . . are reported on as separate entities, but it is important to consider all of these declining or rare species as components of a single bird community. With the dramatic loss of cottonwood-willow habitat during the 20th century, we are witnessing the loss of an entire ecological community with all its plants and animals.[62]

The Verde: Saving a River

The Verde River is a tributary to the Salt River, flowing into the Gila River, which once joined the Colorado. The Verde is 178 miles long and drains a 6,600-square-mile watershed. The headwaters are located at Del Rio Springs in the Chino Valley of Arizona (elevation 4,348 feet), but many of the Verde's tributaries drain from higher elevations of the Colorado Plateau. Portions of the Verde are eligible for inclusion in the federal wild and scenic rivers program.

Stands of sycamore, ash, and walnut, intermixed with cottonwood and willow, occur along cobble and gravel alluvium benches upstream of Horseshoe Dam on the Verde. One of Arizona's largest cottonwood-willow stands is near Horseshoe Dam. Downstream, by the Verde's confluence with the Salt River, is a large mesquite bosque (about 6,000 acres), which varies from dense woodland near the river to open savanna adjacent to the desert. Bosques along the Verde frequently contain large stands of pure mesquite that reach heights of over 50 feet. Often the mesquite is intermixed with other trees, such as cottonwood, willow, and salt cedar. The mature mesquite bosques are carpeted with thick red brome in the spring. These riparian communities are frequented by bald eagles, black hawks, ospreys, snowy egrets, great egrets, javalinas, and raccoons, along with many other wildlife species. According to J. W. Byrkit,

> Prehistoric people channeled the [Verde's] water to grow irrigated crops. Modern newcomers felt that they could do the same. And so they set about transforming nature by "taming" the "raging" floods and by "harnessing" the "fitful" streams and rivers, forgetting that nature did not design Arizona to support farms and fountains, cities and subdivisions, smelters, and swimming pools.[63]

The Verde River valley was inhabited by the Hohokam Indians until the 1400s. Spaniards entered the valley in 1583. In 1878, the Willard brothers became the first Anglo settlers to build irrigation systems to grow food for their livestock. In the 1880s, the Willards helped to organize the group that built the Cottonwood Ditch, one of the largest irrigation projects in the valley. Descendants of the Willards now own the utility that sprang from that ditch: the Cottonwood Waterworks.

Throughout the 1880s and 1890s, the canal structure in central Arizona expanded. Between 1905 and 1911, the Bureau of Reclamation built Roosevelt Dam and Granite Reef Diversion Dam on the Salt River, paving the way for extensive irrigated agriculture near Phoenix.[64]

Modern irrigation was born on the Verde with construction of Bartlett Dam in 1939. Bartlett impounds a lake 12 miles long and 88.5 feet deep with 178,000 acre-feet storage capacity. The second largest dam on the Verde is Horseshoe Dam, completed in 1946. Horseshoe Reservoir extends 5 miles behind the dam and has a storage capacity of 142,830 acre-feet.

The massive Central Arizona Project (CAP) emerged from studies initiated in 1944, and by 1947, the Bureau of Reclamation had completed a report detailing the individual elements of the program. The CAP is designed to divert about 1.2 million acre-feet of water per year from the Colorado River using high-lift pumping plants and an open, concrete-lined aqueduct into Central Arizona.

The CAP's system of pumps and canals is truly impressive. Marc Reisner compared the 1,200-foot *minimum* lift that would be necessary to move Colorado River water to Phoenix and Tucson to taking water "out of the Hudson River and lifting it over the World Trade Center in order to water lawns on Long Island."[65] Hundreds of miles of canals are necessary to transport the water to its final destinations.

The canals pose a threat to large animals such as deer and javalina. Bureau of Reclamation staff described the fate of deer that stumble into canals in Arizona:

> Once in the canal, reactions vary with the individual deer. Generally, they will make one or two attempts to escape near the point of entry. Failing this, they tend to swim against the current, attempting to escape where brushes and grass overhang the canal. Tiring rapidly, but still swimming, they allow the current to carry them while pawing at the lining on both sides of the canal trying to escape. Upon reaching a drop structure, they either drown or are forced through and killed. Those that come upon a check structure thrash around until exhaustion causes drowning or, in the case of large bucks, the overhang of the structure pins their antlers down, forcing their heads underwater.[66]

Initially, more than 70 percent of the water diverted by the CAP will be allocated to irrigation of croplands. Eventually, municipal and industrial uses will receive a larger share. Because there was no binding agreement between California and Arizona for the allocation of Colorado River flows, the CAP was not authorized until 1964.[67] In 1968, Congress authorized $832 million, plus normal cost escalation, for construction of the CAP. By September 1984, over $1 billion had been appropriated and made available for the project. The average annual amount appropriated since 1981 is $165 million.[68] The total cost of the CAP, including Cliff Dam, would have been more than $3.7 billion.

The CAP is an immense and complex program that is divided into eleven separate but interrelated components for purposes of planning and construction. One of these functions is the Regulatory Storage Division, which was investigated under the Central Arizona Water Control Study. The Regulatory Storage Division includes pumps that lift Colorado River water 824 feet from Lake Havasu into the Granite Reef Aqueduct for delivery to Phoenix. The Granite Reef Aqueduct, which began carrying water in 1985, will be linked to the 58-mile-long Salt-Gila Aqueduct and the 90-mile-long Tucson Aqueduct. These conveyance channels are scheduled for completion in 1991. Power for the pumps is provided by the Navajo coal plant near Page, Arizona. The choice of power source is the result of a compromise between the Bureau of Reclamation, which had planned to build hydroelectric dams in the Grand Canyon for this purpose, and conservationists, who vehemently opposed that idea.

The purposes of the Regulatory Storage Division are to conserve the flows of the Salt, Verde, and Agua Fria rivers; to regulate delivery of Colorado River waters from the Granite Reef Aqueduct; to reduce potential for flood damage; and to provide for the structural safety of existing Bureau of Reclamation dams on the Salt and Verde rivers.[69]

The Bureau of Reclamation prepared seven alternative plans to satisfy the purposes of the CAP Regulatory Storage Division. An eighth plan, the "no action" alternative, was included in the original environmental impact statement. The agency chose Plan 6, which includes construction of New Waddell Dam (this dam would replace an existing structure) and Cliff Dam, along with modifications of Roosevelt and Stewart Mountain dams, as its preferred alternative. Because of public opposition to construction of Cliff Dam, however, the bureau formulated a ninth alternative that was equivalent to Plan 6 without Cliff Dam. By the end of 1985, the public had not been given an opportunity to comment on Plan 9. On April 3, 1984, Secretary of the Interior Don Hodel approved Plan 6 with the condition that final approval of Cliff Dam be contingent on a further analysis and report of the impact of Cliff on the endangered desert-nesting bald eagle.[70]

The Cliff Calamity

Cliff Dam would have been a 338-foot-high earthen flood control and water supply structure built about 6 miles downstream from the existing Horseshoe Dam. The reservoir created by Cliff Dam, which was to have an active conservation storage volume of 332,740 acre-feet, would have risen to breach Horseshoe Dam. When filled to this volume, Cliff Reservoir would have backed up the Verde River 13 miles, and the water would have reached an elevation of 2,001 feet.

On April 12, 1984, however, biologists discovered an active bald eagle nest site on a cliff approximately 5 miles below Horseshoe Dam at an elevation of 1,967 feet. The planned reservoir behind Cliff Dam would have inundated this nest; thus the dam posed jeopardy to an endangered species.

Conservationists objected to Cliff Dam for a number of reasons. Cliff, which would have cost $385 million and been funded primarily by taxpayers, was unnecessary for flood damage reduction. Data contained in a study by a nationally recognized engineering firm indicated that dam safety on the Verde could be had for $11 million.[71] Frank Welsh, an author and civil engineer, believes that Salt River flood protection could be achieved simply by improving Stewart Mountain Dam on the Salt at the expense of the Salt River Project, a private utility.[72] Seventy percent of the estimated reduction in flood damages is attributed to the projected increase in real estate value of the Salt River floodplain had Cliff been completed. Cliff Dam would have lowered the flood volume from 200,000 cubic feet per second to 55,000 cubic feet per second. Once this was accomplished, real estate developers intended to build a billion-dollar Rio Salado Parkway, consisting of hotels, homes, and businesses for 36,000 people, in the middle of the floodplain. The wisdom of such a development, in the shadow of the recent floods near Yuma, is questionable.

The water storage benefits of the dam were also questionable. Cliff Dam would have contributed only 10 percent of the total water storage capacity of the CAP,[73] and the Rio Salado development would have used more water for its ornamental lakes and bermuda grass than the dam could store.[74]

Conservationists were further concerned that because Rio Salado was to be built in a presently vacant floodplain, new dams would be required on the Verde as upstream dams silted in. These would destroy any wild, scenic, wilderness, or free-flowing options on the Verde for future generations.

The plans for Cliff Dam prevented 10 miles of the Verde from being included in the federal wild and scenic rivers program. The reservoir would have submerged about 8,700 acres of the Tonto National Forest, along with some of the last remaining cottonwood-willow habitat in the Southwest.

When their habitat is threatened, the eagles soar into the picture. Cliff Dam's reservoir would have inundated one bald eagle nesting site and adversely affected other eagle breeding and foraging habitat. The conversion of the majority of the existing riverine fishery to a reservoir-based fishery might have altered the eagles' prey base and diminished the availability of such prey during the breeding season.[75] The Fish and Wildlife Service, instead of merely stating that the dam would jeopardize an endangered species and therefore should not be built, offered the Bureau of Reclamation several "reasonable and prudent alternatives," all of which were to be complied with before the dam could be built. One of these alternatives was that the bureau must provide habitat mitigation in the old bed of Horseshoe Reservoir, which would be drained. Restoration of high-quality riparian habitat in the old Horseshoe Reservoir bed was unlikely, though. In 6 of the past 7 wet years, virtually all of the proposed mitigation habitat would have been inundated by reservoir waters if Cliff Dam had been in place.[76]

A more promising alternative would have required the bureau to support, fund, and complete in-stream flow studies within 2 years so the Arizona Game and Fish Department could determine the amount of water necessary to maintain the bald eagles' forage fish base on the Verde and East Verde rivers above the reservoir. Once the requisite flows were determined, mechanisms could have been developed and implemented to ensure the availability of such flows. In light of the fattening of thirsty human populations in Arizona towns, this alternative, if acted on in good faith, would have meant a continued supply of water to riparian communities along these rivers. Conservationists would have had to decide whether they were willing to accept a $385 million, environmentally unsound earthen real estate subsidy in exchange for potentially valuable in-stream water rights.

Ultimately, however, it was not concern for eagles, in-stream flows, or riparian habitat that caused the Cliff's untimely collapse. The Department of the Interior's Office of the Inspector General issued an audit report in April 1986 pinpointing some flaws in the financing scheme that undercut the dam at its unstable foundations. The Bureau of Reclamation had intended to appropriate funds for Plan 6 under the authorization for Orme Dam. (Orme Dam was the original "preferred alternative" for CAP regulatory storage near Phoenix, but the plans were abandoned because of Orme's anticipated impacts on bald eagles and on the Fort McDowell Indian Reservation.) In 1986 dollars, Orme Dam would have cost $166 million. Plan 6, including Cliff Dam, would have cost about $1.1 billion, a difference of over 500 percent. The inspector general's office considered a 500 percent price increase "a significant departure from the authorized project."[77] In other words, Plan 6 technically would require a brand-new authorization from Congress before it could be built with federal funds.

The time was not right for a Plan 6 authorization. A coalition of environmental groups, including the National Wildlife Federation, the Sierra Club, the National Audubon Society, and Friends of the Earth, filed a lawsuit against the Bureau of Reclamation in 1986 for noncompliance with the National Environmental Protection Act (NEPA) and the Endangered Species Act. The administration proposed a 1987 funding increase of 34 percent over the 1986 level for Plan 6. These funds would have had to be cut from other Bureau of Reclamation projects throughout the West, such as the Garrison Diversion Project in North Dakota, which had tremendous congressional support. Republican congressman Larry Coughlin of Pennsylvania promised to offer an amendment to the House appropriations bill to kill funding for the entire CAP if the Arizona delegation refused to drop Cliff Dam. Such an amendment would guarantee a floor fight, one that Arizona had little hope of winning. The 1986 elections had weakened Arizona's congressional clout. Senator Barry Goldwater, who held a fistful of power as chairman of the Armed Services Committee and had 30 years of seniority, had just retired. So had Congressman Eldon Rudd, with 10 years of seniority and a seat on the Appropriations Committee. *The Phoenix Gazette* accused congressmen Jon Kyle and Jim Kolbe, both conservative Arizona republicans, of "refusing to go along and get along in the old horsetrading tradition of Congress" and of "challenging spending proposals often categorized as pork barrel."[78]

The Arizona delegation was clearly over a barrel. Finally, the delegation signed off on an agreement drafted by the conservation groups. In exchange for the delegation's dropping its support for Cliff Dam, the conservationists would drop their lawsuit and allow other features of Plan 6 to proceed unopposed. In a letter to Arizona congressman Morris Udall, chairman of the House Committee on Interior and Insular Affairs, Dr. Jay Hair, the National Wildlife Federation's executive vice president, made the following statement:

> The essence of the dispute over Cliff Dam relates to the loss of unspoiled riparian habitat along the Verde River that would result from construction of the dam and the storage of water for supply purposes.
> We believe that the natural values of the remaining, unspoiled portions of the Verde River warrant permanent protection and national recognition. We look forward to working with the delegation in the future on appropriate legislation to accomplish this purpose.[79]

The response from *The Phoenix Gazette* was one of bemusement. "This must be some sort of record," opened a June 1987 editorial. "Cliff Dam on the Verde River collapsed years before it was built."[80]

The battle over Cliff Dam serves to illustrate how complex water resource politics can become. The resource at stake on the Verde is not a single species. It is an entire biological community: an amorphous, nonmobile, infinitely valuable organism with no legislative program or vast public appeal to shelter it.

The San Pedro — Another Win

The shores of the San Pedro River comprise one of America's richest wildlife habitats, containing several riparian community types; nesting, migratory, or wintering habitat for 20 raptor species and a total of 210 bird species; and essential habitat for many wildlife species, possibly including the ocelot, which travels between the United States and South America.[81] The San Pedro is very highly ranked nationally under the Fish and Wildlife Service's unique ecosystems program.

The 120-mile-long San Pedro River originates in Sonora, Mexico, about 25 miles south of the U.S.-Mexico border, and flows northwest until it joins the Gila River. It drains 4,487 square miles of land entirely within the Basin and Range geological province. This province is characterized by broad, arid valleys separated by sharply carved mountains that rise abruptly above the plains.

Because the basins in the province drain poorly, erosion and runoff have filled them with sediment, creating a porous, alluvial substrate through which the San Pedro has cut its channel. These sediments comprise the major aquifer of the San Pedro River basin, from which local farms and towns have been pumping their water for more than a hundred years. The river itself underwent several changes during the nineteenth and twentieth centuries. Originally, the wooded floodplain was dotted with many marshes and swamps, a result of the river basin's high water table.

In the late 1800s, following the introduction of cattle into the area, overgrazing severely depressed ground cover. Scrub species such as whitethorn, tarbrush, and mesquite overtook much of the grassland along the river. In addition, removal of the ground cover allowed the sun to bake the soils. Mesquite, which often occurs as a low-growing invader of disturbed uplands, crowded out many of the oak woodlands that had grown above the riparian corridor. Livestock overgrazing and trampling eliminated the water-spreading effects of sacaton, a large bunchgrass that grew on the heavy clay floodplain soils. Once the sacaton was eliminated, the river waters began to scour and channelize the streambed.

The first recorded series of floods on the San Pedro occurred in 1885. The banks, largely denuded of their vegetation by livestock, could not bear the otherwise normal stress exerted by the floodwaters.

Rapid runoff tore a trench into the riverbed and lowered the water table. The worn-down condition of the river channel contributed to a high load of suspended sediment in the river.

Withdrawals of water from the aquifer for irrigation and municipal use contributed to the drop in groundwater levels. Even now, the groundwater supply is being withdrawn at a rate in excess of recharge capacity.

The combined decline in groundwater levels, soil moisture, water quality, and soil stability resulted in large-scale changes in riparian habitat. Riparian woodlands increased at the expense of grassy meadows and marsh habitats. As a consequence, the extensive riparian woodlands that the San Pedro River valley boasts today are partially the result of human exploitation.

Raptors of the River

All classes of fauna are well represented along the San Pedro River, but perhaps the most remarkable delegation is from the birds of prey, or raptors.

Mississippi Kites   These kites are graceful, grey, falcon-shaped birds with white heads. They nest in cottonwoods and reach the western edge of their range in Arizona.

Sharp-Shinned Hawks   The sharp-shinneds are woodland hawks with about a 2-foot wingspan, which allows them to maneuver between trees when hunting. The adults have blue-grey backs and rusty, barred breasts. They are common in cottonwood forests during migration but are rare in the winter.

Red-Tailed Hawks   These soaring buteos, common in the Southwest, are easily recognized in flight by their bright, rust-red tails. Along the San Pedro, they prefer to nest in cottonwoods or on cliffs.

Swainson's Hawks   Swainson's hawks are buteos, proportioned like the red-taileds but with more sharply pointed wings. They hold their wings horizontally when they fly, and the adults may be recognized by their dark breast bands. They are common along the San Pedro during migration seasons.

Zone-Tailed Hawks   Zone-taileds are black buteos with white stripes on their tails. They nest along the San Pedro River and in tributary canyons in cottonwoods and sycamores.

The zone-tailed hawk (left) can be recognized in flight by its narrow, two-toned wings. It has several white tailbands and is frequently confused with the black hawk. The black-tailed hawk (right) is a resident of desert riparian habitats, particularly cottonwood galleries. Its thick-set black wings and single white tail stripe distinguish it from the zone-tailed hawk. (Courtesy of National Wildlife Federation)

Ferruginous Hawks   These hawks are large, with wingspans approaching 4 feet. The adults are rufous above and pale beneath, with a red V formed by the feathers of their legs that is visible from the ground. They are common along the San Pedro in the fall and winter.

Gray Hawks   Gray hawks are small grey buteos with white, barred underparts, a white rump, and a broadly banded tail. Approximately one-third of their entire U.S. population occurs along the San Pedro River, where they depend on cottonwood trees for nesting.

Birds such as Cooper's hawks, Harris' hawks, and American kestrels maintain high nesting densities in the cottonwood and mesquite groves along the river. They are among the many species of raptors and other birds that crowd the native riparian groves along the San Pedro.

The Struggle for Ownership

The 1968 plan for the Central Arizona Project included the construction of Charleston Dam and Reservoir on the San Pedro River, from which water would be piped to the city of Tucson. Anticipating the opportunity to develop lakeside chalets and boat ramps for affluent vacationers, Tenneco West, Inc., purchased two land grants on the river, the San Rafael del Valle Grant and the San Juan de las Boquillas y Nogales Grant, referred to collectively as Little Boquillas Ranch. Charleston Dam, though authorized by Congress, was never built, however, because local residents voiced concern over the threatened drowning of natural and historic resources. Tenneco was left with rich land and no way to make money with it.

The Fish and Wildlife Service considered purchasing the land for the creation of a national wildlife refuge in 1978. The agency had originally planned to use the Land and Water Conservation Fund to purchase land along the San Pedro. This fund, established by Congress in 1965 to enable the government to purchase recreational lands and important wildlife habitat, had grown to more than $70 million by 1979. But Robert Jantzen, then director of the Fish and Wildlife Service, was encountering resistance to the service's proposed acquisition of the land from local ranchers and so did not move immediately to acquire it.[82]

Because of a Reagan administration policy discouraging federal land acquisition, federal funds for national wildlife refuges dried up while the service was negotiating with Tenneco in 1981. The service had formulated a bargain with Tenneco by the spring of 1985, but the chilly political climate on Capitol Hill gave the agency cold feet. It never sought an appropriation to purchase Little Boquillas Ranch.

If the proposed acquisition had been for a water project and not a refuge, the task of rolling an appropriations bill through Congress would not have been impossible. But a new refuge bill for Arizona was not likely to be backed by a strong consensus in either the Senate or the House. Arizona congressmen had been chastised by constituents earlier that year regarding federal purchase of a refuge for the endangered masked bobwhite in the southern part of the state. Because of the federal deficit and the potential for cuts in public programs, conservation had paled in comparison with programs that seemed essential at the time, such as western water projects and space-based defense systems.

State conservationists changed their strategy, and the Bureau of Land Management (BLM) entered the scene. The BLM offered Tenneco a choice of several federal land tracts, ranging in value from $400 to $12,000 per acre, in exchange for the Spanish land grant. The value of the 57,000-acre Little Boquillas Ranch was estimated at $20 million.[83,84]

In short, a land swap with the BLM would allow some of the valuable San Pedro riparian habitat to pass into federal hands without a bloody battle on Capitol Hill. Whether in Treasury dollars or lost land use options, the public would still foot the acquisition bill.

The acquisition of Little Boquillas drove a small wedge into the conservation community. Many people believed that the quickest way to remove the land from private hands was the best; they feared the blighting of the corridor by subdivisions. In addition, Dean Bibles, the

BLM's Arizona state office director, had attracted some conservation group support for the agency when he helped to establish the Birds of Prey natural area in Idaho. BLM supporters had faith in local BLM personnel and felt that the agency should be given a chance to change its current image as a broker for excessive resource extraction on public lands.

Other conservationists were apprehensive of the BLM's ability to properly protect a riparian corridor. The BLM has a mandate under the Federal Land Policy and Management Act of 1976 to manage its land for multiple uses, including grazing and recreation. Unfortunately, these two uses have great destructive potential for the San Pedro ecosystem. If grazing and recreational use were allowed, the invasion of delicate river corridors by all-terrain vehicles could proceed virtually unregulated and destroy any seedlings that had not already become a bovine brunch. The conservation faction opposed to BLM management of the San Pedro corridor believed that designation of the area as a national wildlife refuge, with the primary purpose of protecting wildlife, was the only sure way to keep the ecosystem intact for any substantial length of time.

The BLM did acquire the land in 1986, amid rumors that the Fish and Wildlife Service intended to try to persuade Congress that it was the appropriate agency to manage the area. At present, the fate of the San Pedro River valley is still somewhat uncertain. Even federal ownership per se will not prevent the infusion of the corridor's aqueous lifeblood into anemic desert towns. If riparian communities along the river are to be maintained, the application of western water law, which tends to channel river flows toward development, must be reversed. This means that either the governor of Arizona must make some provision to keep San Pedro waters in the stream or the Arizona Game and Fish Department must struggle with the state's growth-oriented legislature to gain in-stream water rights on the river.

The protection of this little piece of paradise will set a precedent for future acquisitions. Not only will acquisition of Little Boquillas Ranch demand the evaluation of conservation strategies, but it may also expand the role of the BLM, allowing the agency to become a conservator of natural habitats rather than a mere overseer of resource extraction from the national wastelands. Whichever way the cloth is woven, the tapestry is the goal. An enduring San Pedro riparian corridor, rich in design, color, and texture, would give every nature lover cause for celebration and hope for the future.

Even so, the San Pedro, now protected by the federal government, will become nothing more than a museum-piece demonstration of what desert riparian habitat once looked like unless the Colorado

River and others like her are more prudently managed in the future. Floodplain development must be halted, agricultural subsidies must be eliminated, in-stream flows must be provided, and revegetation of floodplains must be undertaken. The immediate preservation and restoration of desert riparian ecosystems is essential if America's biological richness is to be maintained.

Many management tools are being put to use to help restore and preserve riparian habitat along the rivers and streams of the lower Colorado River basin. The Bureau of Reclamation is funding habitat restoration work; the Colorado River Floodway Protection Act of 1986 will discourage foolish development in flood-prone areas; and in-stream water rights are finding a place within the structure of western water law.

In spite of recent advances, however, the legal structure in the United States is not sufficient in itself to provide for a healthy environment. Riparian habitats and other endangered ecosystems will not be adequately protected until the public at large recognizes nature as the whole and itself as a part of that whole.

NOTES

1. House Committee on Interior and Insular Affairs, *Oversight Hearings on Colorado River Management,* 98th Cong., 2d sess., 1983, 603.
2. Ibid., 13–26.
3. Ibid.
4. Ibid., 10–11.
5. Ibid.
6. D. Fisher, Personal communication, 1985.
7. A. Leopold, *A Sand County Almanac* (New York: Sierra Club and Ballantine Books, 1949), 151.
8. D. E. Brown, C. H. Lowe, and J. F. Hausler, "Southwestern Riparian Communities: Their Biotic Importance and Management in Arizona," in *Importance, Preservation and Management of Riparian Habitat,* Forest Service general technical report RM-43 (Washington, DC: Government Printing Office, 1977), 201–11.
9. Ibid.
10. K. V. Rosenberg et al., "Birds of the Lower Colorado River Valley," unpublished paper (Tempe, AZ: Arizona State University, Center for Environmental Studies).
11. B. W. Anderson, A. Higgins, and R. D. Ohmart, "Avian Use of Salt Cedar Communities in the Lower Colorado River Valley," in *Importance, Preservation and Management of Floodplain Wetlands and other Riparian Ecosystems,* Forest Service general technical report RM-43 (Washington, DC: Government Printing Office, 1977).
12. Rosenberg et al., "Birds of the Lower Colorado River Valley."
13. J. S. Horton, F. C. Mounts, and J. M. Kraft, *Seed Germination and Establishment of Phreatophyte Species,* technical report 48 (Fort Collins, CO: Forest Service, 1960).
14. Anderson, Higgins, and Ohmart, "Avian Use of Salt Cedar Communities."

15. Rosenberg et al., "Birds of the Lower Colorado River Valley."

16. D. R. Cohen, B. W. Anderson, and R. D. Ohmart, "Avian Population Response to Salt Cedar along the Lower Colorado River," in *Strategies for Protection and Management of Floodplain Wetlands and Other Riparian Ecosystems,* Forest Service general technical report WO-12, ed. R. R. Johnson and J. F. McCormick (Washington, DC: Government Printing Office, 1978), 373.

17. P. L. Fradkin, *A River No More* (New York: Alfred A. Knopf, 1981), 23.

18. R. D. Ohmart, *Past and Present Biotic Communities of the Lower Colorado Mainstem and Selected Tributaries,* vol. 1 (Boulder City, NV: Department of the Interior, Bureau of Reclamation, 1982).

19. Department of the Interior, Bureau of Reclamation, *The Colorado—"A Natural Menace Becomes a National Resource."* (Washington, DC: Government Printing Office, 1946).

20. Committee on Water of the National Research Council, *Water and Choice in the Colorado River Basin* (Washington, DC: National Academy of Sciences, 1968).

21. E. Abbey, *Desert Solitaire* (New York: McGraw-Hill, 1968).

22. Brown, Lowe, and Hausler, "Southwestern Riparian Communities."

23. R. R. Johnson, "The Lower Colorado River: A Western System," in *Strategies for Protection and Management of Floodplain Wetlands and Other Riparian Ecosystems,* Forest Service general technical report WO-12, ed. R. R. Johnson and J. F. McCormick (Washington, DC: Government Printing Office, 1978), 46.

24. Ibid.

25. *Congressional Record,* 100th Cong., 1st sess., 1987, vol. 133, no. 34.

26. C. Arvidson, "Easterners Balk at Subsidy for Western Water Projects," *Tempe Daily News,* 14 July 1985.

27. G. Webster, "77% of Upland-Cotton Acreage to Be Idle," *Arizona Republic,* 16 April 1985.

28. R. D. Ohmart, W. O. Deason, and C. Burke, "A Riparian Case History: The Colorado River," in *Importance, Preservation and Management of Riparian Habitat: A Symposium,* Forest Service general technical report RM-43, (Washington, DC: Government Printing Office, 1977), 35–47.

29. D. E. Brown, et al., "Inventory of Riparian Habitats," in *Importance, Preservation, and Management of Riparian Habitat: A Symposium,* Forest Service general technical report RM-43 (Washington, DC: Government Printing Office, 1977).

30. Ibid.

31. J. G. Deane and D. Holling, "Ravage the Rivers, Banish the Birds," *Defenders* (May/ June 1985)

32. C. Hunter, B. W. Anderson, and R. D. Ohmart, "Changes in Avian Community Structure after Extensive Flooding through a Mature Floodplain Forest," unpublished paper (Tempe, AZ: Arizona State University, Center for Environmental Studies, 1984).

33. Ibid.

34. Ibid.

35. Rosenberg, et al., "Birds of the Lower Colorado River Valley."

36. Ohmart, *Past and Present Biotic Communities of the Lower Colorado.*

37. C. J. Campbell, "Ecological Implications of Riparian Vegetation Management," *Journal of Soil and Water Conservation* 25, no. 2 (1970): 52.

38. W. L. Graf, *The Colorado River: Instability and Basin Management* (Washington, DC: Association of American Geographers, 1985).

39. R. Dunbier, *The Sonoran Desert: Its Geography, Economy, and People* (Tucson, AZ: University of Arizona Press 1968).

40. California Department of Water Resources, *Water Conservation in California*, Department of Water Resources bulletin 198-84 (Sacramento, CA: California Department of Water Resources, 1983).

41. K. D. Frederick and J. C. Hanson, *Water for Western Agriculture* (Washington, DC: Resources for the Future, 1982).

42. Department of the Interior, Bureau of Reclamation, *Colorado River Basin Salinity Control Project* (Boulder City, NV: Bureau of Reclamation, 1979).

43. A. Howard, *The Soil and Health: A Study of Organic Agriculture* (New York: Schocken Books, 1947).

44. R. D. Ohmart, personal communication, 1985.

45. Frederick and Hanson, *Water for Western Agriculture*.

46. Department of the Interior, Bureau of Reclamation, *Colorado River Basin Salinity Control Project*.

47. Fradkin, *A River No More*, 303.

48. K. H. Conine et al., "Responses of Species to Argicultural Habitat Conversions," in *Strategies for Protection and Management of Floodplain Wetlands and Other Riparian Ecosystems*, ed. R. R. Johnson and J. F. McCormick (Washington, DC: Government Printing Office, 1978), 257.

49. R. T. Peterson, *A Field Guide to Western Birds* (Boston, MA: Houghton Mifflin Company, 1967), 855.

50. Deane and Holling, "Ravage the Rivers, Banish the Birds."

51. J. V. Remsen, Jr., *Bird Species of Special Concern in California: An Annotated List of Declining or Vulnerable Bird Species* (Sacramento, CA: California Department of Fish and Game, 1978).

52. R. Todd, personal communication, 1985.

53. Hunter, Anderson, and Ohmart, "Changes in Avian Community Structure."

54. Ibid.

55. Remsen, *Bird Species of Special Concern in California*.

56. Deane and Holling, "Ravage the Rivers, Banish the Birds."

57. Hunter, Anderson, and Ohmart, "Changes in Avian Community Structure."

58. Rosenberg et al., "Birds of the Lower Colorado River Valley."

59. Anderson, Higgins, and Ohmart, "Avian Use of Salt Cedar Communities."

60. Fish and Wildlife Service, "Yuma Clapper Rail," *Endangered Species Technical Bulletin* 8, no. 7 (1983): 7.

61. Rosenberg et al., "Birds of the Lower Colorado River Valley."

62. Hunter, Anderson, and Ohmart, "Changes in Avian Community Structure."

63. J. W. Byrkit, "A Log of the Verde: the 'Taming' of an Arizona River," *Journal of Arizona History* 19, no. 1 (1978): 31.

64. Department of the Interior, Bureau of Reclamation, *Final Environmental Impact Statement: Regulatory Storage Division of the Central Arizona Project*, vol. 2 (Boulder City, NV: Bureau of Reclamation, 1983).

65. M. Reisner, *Cadillac Desert: The American West and Its Disappearing Water* (New York: Viking Penguin, 1986), 282.

66. H. R. Guenther, F. P. Sharpe, and P. Strauss, "Mule Deer Losses — Mohawk Canal, Arizona: A Problem Identified, A Solution Sought," in *The Mitigation Symposium: A National Workshop on Mitigating Losses of Fish and Wildlife Habitat*, ed. G. A. Swanson (Fort Collins, CO: Forest Service, 1979), 642.

67. Committee on Water of the National Research Council, *Water and Choice in the Colorado River Basin* (Washington, DC: National Academy of Sciences, 1968).

68. Arizona Department of Water Resources, *Options for Funding Plan 6: A Report to the Arizona Congressional Delegation* (Phoenix, AZ: Arizona Department of Water Resources, 1985).

69. Department of the Interior, Bureau of Reclamation, *Final Environmental Impact Statement.*
70. M. Spear, memorandum to the director of the Bureau of Reclamation, Boulder City, NV, 15 August 1985.
71. H. Fibel, R. Witzeman, and A. Williams, *The Bureau Strikes Back,* informational leaflet, 1985.
72. K. Bagwell, "County Delays Action on Dam Proposal," *Scottsdale Daily Progress,* 3 July 1985.
73. National Coalition to Stop Cliff Dam, "Fact Sheet: Cliff Dam, Arizona," unpublished document (Phoenix, AZ: National Coalition to Stop Cliff Dam, 1985).
74. R. Witzeman, "Building in a River Bed—Update on Rio Salado," *The Cactus Wrendition* 33, no.2 (1985), Maricopa Audubon Society, Phoenix, AZ.
75. Spear, memorandum to the director of the Bureau of Reclamation.
76. National Coalition to Stop Cliff Dam, "Fact Sheet."
77. Department of the Interior, Office of the Inspector General, *Review of the Status of the Central Arizona Project, Bureau of Reclamation* (Washington, DC: Government Printing Office, 1986), 9.
78. "Cliff Dam Crumbles" (editorial), *The Phoenix Gazette,* 19 June 1987.
79. J. Hair, letter to Congressman Morris Udall, 24 June 1987.
80. "Cliff Dam Crumbles."
81. R. McNatt, "Possible Strategies for Preservation of the San Pedro River Riparian Community," in *Strategies for Protection and Management of Floodplain Wetlands and Other Riparian Ecosystems,* Forest Service general technical report WO-12, ed. R. R. Johnson and J. F. McCormick (Washington, DC: Government Printing Office, 1978), 201–6.
82. M. Spear, presentation to conservation group representatives gathered at the office of The Wilderness Society, Washington, DC, 5 November 1985.
83. M. Shaffer, "BLM Pushes Swap to Transfer Control of Sensitive Land," *Arizona Republic,* 1985.
84. D. Dale, "BLM, Property Owner Shop for Land to Swap," *Arizona Daily Star,* 14 August 1985.

5

Water and the Law
of the West in the
Upper Colorado River Basin

The Colorado River, bled dry at the mouth by the concrete leeches of desert irrigators and cities, receives much of its flows from the Wind River Range in Wyoming, where the Green River begins. The Green meanders 750 miles until it reaches its confluence with the upper Colorado. The upper Colorado, formerly called the Grand River, begins in Rocky Mountain National Park. Above the Colorado's confluence with the Green, the rivers sink into the mysterious canyons whose painted cliffs have colored the dreams of Americans for many centuries. The rivers and riparian ribbons in this arid sagebrush world of endless blue skies have received praise in prose, though their poetic aspects seem to elude water developers.

The first settlement of the upper Colorado River basin began in 1854 with the establishment of Fort Supply on the Emigrant Trail in Wyoming. Miners and prospectors leaving old mining districts on the eastern slopes of the Continental Divide settled Breckenridge, Colorado, in 1859. In the 1860s, other mining camps sprung up around the basin. Unsuccessful miners often turned to irrigated farming and supplied the foodstuffs that fueled the settlements.[1] Conflicts with Indians triggered the establishment of forts, such as Fort Bridger in the

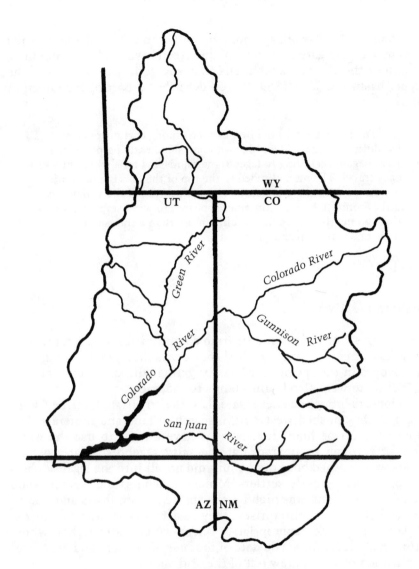

UPPER COLORADO RIVER BASIN

Green River valley, which Mark Twain described as follows in the mid-1800s:

> The fort is a beautiful location on Black's Fork of Green River, receiving fine fresh water from the snow on the Uinta Range. The streams are alive with mountain trout. It passes the fort in several channels, each lined with trees, kept alive by the moisture of the soil.[2]

John Wesley Powell, a major who fought in the Civil War, was the first man to navigate the waters of the Green River and float the entire length of the Grand Canyon. His first voyage in the canyons of the upper basin began in 1869. Powell described a part of the Green in 1869:

> The party entered the first canyon among cottonwoods backed by bluffs 12 hundred feet high—on one side nearly perpendicular. Here began, according to legend, the rapids and falls which blocked easy travel. The men climbed to the top of the flaming red bluffs, entranced with the grandeur of the sculpturing of the valleys and hills. From the heights, the river appeared to wind serpent-like through nearly perpendicular cliffs more than a thousand feet high, and was deep and calm as a lake.[3]

Right to the Rivers

In the upper Colorado basin, riparian communities were not the only entities competing for the melted snowdrifts that rolled down mountain slopes in the spring. Settlers struggling with an often inhospitable climate were also laying claims to the streams.

Pioneers brought eastern water law, the "riparian doctrine," with them as they pushed westward in search of land and minerals. The riparian doctrine holds that persons have a right to use the water flowing through their land, but the salty sagebrush states, where rivers were washed bone dry by July, did not fit into the legal satchels brought west by early settlers. Miners, ranchers, and farmers soon found that demand was high for the sparse stream flows and that to serve their upland enterprises, they had to divert water from the streams. Thus the "appropriative doctrine" of water rights, which prioritizes claims based on date of first use, diversion, and beneficial application of water, grew out of the arid plains.

Private organizations accomplished much of the early irrigation work and aided evolution of the appropriative doctrine. The American Indians and Spaniards were the original western irrigators, but the Mormons irrigated Utah on a much larger scale. These pious pioneers had irrigated and cultivated 263,000 acres by 1890, more than a decade before Congress created the Bureau of Reclamation. Cooperative colonies, the predecessors of modern irrigation districts, also reclaimed considerable tracts of dry land. The Greeley Colony, founded in 1870, brought 32,000 acres under irrigation and triggered a development trend in Colorado. By 1910, over 13 million acres in the West were irrigated by private organizations.[4]

Mark Twain once said of the West that "whiskey is for drinking and water for fighting." Powell echoed Twain's sentiments in noting that

> in the whole region, land as mere land is of no value; what is really valuable is the water privilege. Rich men and stock companies have appropriated all the streams and they charge for the use of the water.[5]

Major Powell witnessed water grabs that resulted in a haphazard development of diversion works. He believed that all the water in the West was capable of irrigating only 2 or 3 percent of the land and that therefore, the river basins should be surveyed, basin plans should be devised, and impoundment sites should be carefully selected. Powell feared that control of water by private enterprise would not be in the best public interest, and he encouraged the federal government to become involved in strategic development of the resource. As the first director of the Geological Survey, Powell requested a moratorium on western water development until the agency completed basin surveys and drew up systematic plans.

Drought hit the West in the late 1800s, killing cattle and rousing ranchers. Congress was assailed by political pressure favoring immediate construction of water storage facilities to protect against future drought, and it responded by cutting the funding for Powell's surveys.

Powell's dream of public water management was partially realized in the creation of the Bureau of Reclamation in 1902. As the bureau developed water programs, however, it built partnerships with the private irrigation districts that sponsored and lobbied for bureau projects.

Major federal development of the upper Colorado and its largest tributaries began in 1956 when Congress passed the Colorado River Storage Project Act. The act authorized construction of four storage units and eleven participating units intended to temper the erratic Colorado flows and make the river more usable by irrigators and cities. By the end of 1956, the bureau had broken ground on Glen Canyon and Flaming Gorge dams. By the 1960s, nine major dams and other developments in the upper Colorado basin had reduced flows by 35 percent. It is predicted that by 1990, only 300,000 acre-feet, or 5 percent of the 5.5 million acre-feet of water available for appropriation, will be left unappropriated.[6]

Riparian Ravage

Phillip Fradkin, a student of Colorado River history, visited the Green River in the 1960s and praised "the cottonwoods, huge yet wraithlike and fluttering, always indicating the presence of water in what is frequently an otherwise lifeless terrain."[7] But these welcome strips of vegetation had already decreased greatly from their natural occurrence.

The tributaries of the upper Colorado, meeker than the main-stream and granting more breadth to floodplains, still bear patches of cottonwood-willow gallery. The main stem is less fortunate—one estimate states that 90 percent of the native riparian habitat along the Colorado portion of the river has disappeared.[8] Other areas in the basin have also lost large portions of their original riparian habitat. In southwestern Wyoming, for example, only 17 percent of the region's riparian meadow habitat still exists.[9] Written records of the upper river tell little of the decline of riparian ecosystems, but a variety of factors, including the construction and operation of major water storage and diversion projects, play major roles in changes of flood-plain ecology.

To date, the Bureau of Reclamation has begun or completed twenty-five projects in the upper basin. Development of storage projects has inundated at least 6,960 acres of riparian habitat. The Dallas Creek and Dolores projects are two examples of undertakings that have submerged valuable habitat.

Dallas Creek

Dallas Creek flows into the Uncompahgre River, a tributary of the Gunnison, which is a major tributary of the Colorado. Most of the large streams in the project area originate in the San Juan Mountains, in canyons cut by glaciers from volcanic rock. Relatively smooth alluvial terraces as much as a mile in width parallel the Uncompahgre and Dallas Creek. The terraces rise 5 to 50 feet above the stream channel.

Cottonwood-willow communities comprise less than 1 percent of the total vegetation in the Uncompahgre River basin. These riparian stands, contrasting sharply with upland vegetation, provide critical winter range for deer and elk. The Uncompahgre River valley offers little nesting habitat for waterfowl, but approximately 24,000 ducks winter in western Colorado along the Uncompahgre, Gunnison, and Colorado rivers.

Denver's Tri-County Water Conservation District sponsored and actively supported the Dallas Creek Project, which is part of the

Colorado River Storage Project (CRSP). The project consists of two reservoirs: Ridgeway Reservoir on the Uncompahgre and Dallas Divide on Pleasant Valley Creek. The project reduces flows into the Gunnison and Colorado rivers, diminishes seasonal flow fluctuations, and inundates valuable riparian habitat.

Water depletions by the Dallas Creek Project average 17,200 acre-feet per year, about 19 percent of the total 90,000 acre-feet depleted from the Gunnison by Bureau of Reclamation projects. The Gunnison has historically contributed 41 to 53 percent of the Colorado's flows at the Colorado-Utah border. In reviewing the plans for the Dallas Creek Project, the Fish and Wildlife Service claimed that because of the cumulative adverse effects of flow reductions on the endangered Colorado squawfish and humpback chub, the Project would jeopardize the continued existence of these fishes and thus violate the Endangered Species Act. The Fish and Wildlife Service offered the bureau the "reasonable and prudent alternative" of providing guaranteed in-stream flows to conserve the endangered fishes. The service was to determine the amount and timing of the necessary flows, in studies scheduled for completion in 1981. By 1981, however, the service still had inadequate data to determine the flows, and deliberations over in-stream flows on the upper Colorado were escalating.

The plans for Dallas Creek did include some provisions for maintaining in-stream flows, but these were intended to preserve recreational fisheries on the Uncompahgre. The bureau set minimum flows at 75 cubic feet per second for half the year and 45 cubic feet per second for the other half on one stretch; flows were to remain at 30 cubic feet per second year round on another stretch. However, these flows may not be adequate to maintain riparian wetlands, which serve as nurseries for fish, or riparian forests. If depletions or drought were to draw river flows down to these levels, the natural rhythm of river fluctuations under which fisheries and riparian communities have evolved would be completely disrupted, and the over-bank flows that provide nursery habitat for fish and regenerate riparian communities probably would not occur.

Inundation and induced clearing (removal of native trees to make room for crop cultivation) were the only impacts on riparian communities specifically addressed in the Dallas Creek environmental impact statement:

> Mule deer winter range is now decreasing as a result of agriculture and residential development, and the trend shows no sign of abatement. Effects of development on other wildlife species are not significant at this time except for species inhabiting riparian areas.

Riparian habitat is often lost during construction and clearing
activities and these activities can be expected to continue.[10]

The document anticipated a 3,800-acre reduction in critical deer
winter range as a result of the project and the induced conversion of
3,880 acres of woodland to irrigated cropland.

The Dolores Project

The Dolores River rises in the San Miguel Mountains northeast of the
La Plata River, flows southwest until it reaches the town of Dolores,
Colorado, then heads northwest until it joins the Colorado River near
Cisco, Utah. North of the river, the basin land rises gradually and then
drops abruptly into the Dolores River canyon, adorned with wooded
slopes, rock outcroppings, scattered bottomland pasture, and dense
riparian vegetation. The zone of riparian vegetation parallel to the
Dolores River is composed primarily of cottonwood, box elder, willow, alder, and hawthorne, with an understory of forbs and shrubs.

The Dolores Project is an interbasin diversion, as are several other
Bureau of Reclamation endeavors in the upper Colorado River basin.
The project transfers Dolores River water to the San Juan River,
resulting in a 24,300-acre-foot increase in the San Juan's average
annual flows, a 105,200-acre-foot decrease in the Dolores River's
annual flows, and an overall annual decrease of 80,900 acre-feet in the
Colorado River as the water is depleted for irrigation. Within 100 years
of project life, the Dolores Project is expected to cause a salinity
increase in the Colorado at Imperial Dam of approximately 8.4 milli-
grams per liter as a result of the depletions.

Inundation caused by the Dolores Project has reduced wildlife
habitat by 4,850 acres. As in the Dallas Creek Project, the greatest
habitat losses have occurred in riparian areas. In addition, migration
routes and winter habitat for deer and elk in the Dolores River canyon
have been disrupted by project construction. Most deer move out of
the national forest in the winter, dropping directly into the canyon.
McPhee Reservoir, the major storage facility for the Dolores Project,
destroyed winter habitat for about 600 deer and 300 elk and created a
10-mile long barrier to the animals' traditional migration route along
the Dolores River.

An environmental impact statement for the Dolores Project,
issued while the project was still in the planning stages, stated that

the riparian woodlands [habitat type] along the Dolores River and
other Colorado waterways, which is probably the most limited in

extent, is utilized by the greatest number of species [of nongame birds].[11]

The canyon also supports concentrations of mountain lions, black bears, spotted skunks, muskrats, minks, raccoons, bobcats, and rock squirrels.

The Dolores Project is similar to the Dallas Creek Project in that it eliminated spring floods, posed jeopardy to endangered Colorado River fishes, and induced the conversion of wildlands to croplands. Both projects also reduced river water quality.

Water Quality and Riparian Systems

The Uncompahgre River contained mildly contaminated water before construction began on Dallas Creek. The river receives runoff from mines, cultivated fields, construction projects, and the leaching of highly mineralized soils; heavy metals and toxic chemicals such as copper, iron, manganese, arsenic, selenium, silver, lead, chromium, and cyanide flow slowly into the river. Below Ridgeway Reservoir, increased human habitation and agriculture cause increased turbidity and increased concentrations of coliform bacteria, indicating fecal contamination. Levels of nitrogen and phosphorus also increase in proportion to agricultural land use. Concentrations of magnesium, selenium, silver, iron, and manganese occasionally exceed limits recommended as safe for drinking water by the Public Health Service.

Above the town of Dolores, the Dolores River receives mine runoff containing heavy metals as well as runoff from urban areas containing nutrients and coliform bacteria. Downstream from the town, withdrawals by the Montezuma Valley Irrigation Company, which sometimes diverts the entire flow of the river, increase water temperatures, salinity, and susceptibility of soils to erosion. Upstream sewage discharges often result in high levels of phosphorus and coliform bacteria.

Riparian woodlands and wetlands are able to assimilate large quantities of pollutants from upland runoff and over-bank flows from streams, thus preventing them from being transported downstream. Special physiographic features of a riparian ecosystem—such as a thin aerobic soil zone layered on top of a water-saturated anaerobic zone, complex topography, and a layer of decomposing organic debris on the forest floor—enable it to clean runoff and stream flow more efficiently than would an upland ecosystem. Riparian corridors clean runoff from agricultural and urban areas as it passes over the floodplain; riparian forests and wetlands purify stream waters when over-bank flooding occurs.

Rhodes and co-workers found that "the riparian meadows and other wetlands that support populations of denitrifying bacteria . . . seem to be critical natural controls in the transport of nitrate."[12] Kibby found that "mixed hardwood swamps have been shown to remove up to 99 percent of the nitrogen in sewage effluent."[13] Kibby also presented data that showed high assimilation rates of heavy metals, including chromium, copper, iron, manganese, and zinc, in a floodplain sedge community. In studying nutrient uptake in a riparian ecosystem, Brinson and co-workers found that "input to the ecosystem, mostly from upstream inflows, exceeded outputs by 3.15 and 7.30 kilograms of phosphorus per hectare per year for each of the 2 years of study which characterizes the floodplain as a phosphorus sink . . . ." They concluded that

> in the absence of a complex floodplain ecosystem . . . there would be little opportunity for phosphorus recycling and sedimentation. . . . Measures to control flooding or speed the conveyance of water downstream tend to deprive riparian ecosystems of the influx of materials that sustain their nutrient-rich properties. When drained and deprived of flooding by streams, it is likely that disrupted riparian ecosystems will become sources, rather than sinks, of nutrients and sediments for ecosystems downstream due to the elimination of specialized nutrient transformations that depend on the "aquatic" phase.[14]

Riparian ecosystems are therefore important maintainers of water quality, especially in areas where farmers apply nitrogen and phosphorus to cultivated fields and where irrigation water leaches large amounts of heavy metals from soils. Riparian corridors also purify runoff from mines and urban areas, an important function in the upper Colorado River basin. To conserve the water-cleansing properties of riparian ecosystems, water project managers must ensure the continuation of periodic over-bank flows and in-stream flows sufficient to maintain riparian vegetation.

Keeping the Water Flowing

Under traditional western water law, a valid claim to water requires diversion and application of the water to a "beneficial" use. According to *The Wall Street Journal,*

> legal rights to water in the West depend on the chronological order of claims, and the governing principle is "use it or lose it." . . .

> Although the Colorado River compacts reserve water rights for each of the seven states, some Coloradans think California and Arizona could acquire permanent use of the water if Colorado doesn't develop its own uses.[15]

Fear of losing some of the 7.5 million acre-feet of water per year guaranteed to the upper basin under the Colorado River Compact has provided a major incentive for the construction of new impoundments, the sale of water from old impoundments, and interbasin transfers of water.

Colorado–Big Thompson, an interbasin diversion project, was designed to bring water from the cool creeks of western Colorado across the Continental Divide and through an underground tunnel to the parched eastern slopes of the Rocky Mountains. One feature of Colorado–Big Thompson is Green Mountain Reservoir, located on the Blue River, a Colorado tributary. Green Mountain has a storage capacity of more than 153,000 acre-feet; 52,000 acre-feet of this is made available to replace the water that Colorado–Big Thompson diverts from western Colorado. The other 100,000-plus acre-feet produces power as it passes through Green Mountain Dam on its way to the Colorado River. Operating policy allocates 66,000 acre-feet of the power pool water to "historic" agricultural and municipal beneficiaries, leaving about 28,800 acre-feet available for sale under long-term contracts. The Colorado River Conservation District, a political subdivision of the state of Colorado, negotiated with the Bureau of Reclamation to market this water.

The Colorado River Conservation District issued a request for potential contractors for Green Mountain Reservoir water in 1984. Twenty-nine potential contractors responded, representing a demand for about 22,700 acre-feet of water. Of this amount, 53 percent would be used to produce oil shale and 20 percent would be transformed into artificial snow for Colorado's ski resorts.[16]

These sales of water from the Colorado River system might have a relatively small impact on riverine and riparian ecology if they represented an isolated event, but the Bureau of Reclamation has a number of other water sales and storage projects in the planning stage or under construction. Private developers have another set of water depletions targeted for the river system, most of which require a permit from the Army Corps of Engineers. Projected monthly depletions for fifteen of these projects, including Dolores, Dallas Creek, and the Green Mountain water sales, would range from 210 cubic feet per second in October to 957 cubic feet per second in June.[17] The cumulative effects of these diversions are unknown.

People such as Doyle G. Berry have even more incredible plans for Colorado River water. Berry wants to build the biggest reservoir in the state of Colorado on the Yampa River, one of the last free-flowing Colorado River tributaries, and sell the water to San Diego County in southern California. The county currently receives much of its water from the lower Colorado River via a 242-mile aqueduct. Now that the Central Arizona Project is in operation, and Arizona's demands on lower Colorado River have skyrocketed, the San Diego County Water Authority is considering paying $10,000 for an option to buy what is now luxuriant white water from the Yampa. The water would bring Berry's corporation, the Galloway Group, Inc., a 17 to 18 percent return on a $200 million investment for 30 years.[18]

The ecological ramifications of cumulative depletions on the upper Colorado have come into focus as a result of the Endangered Species Act. Depletions have already altered the hydrology, chemistry, and temperature of the river to the point of endangering the existence of several fish species, yet developers are planning more diversions.

From 1977, when Congress established the consultation process under the Endangered Species Act, until 1985, the Fish and Wildlife Service completed consultations on eighty-one water project plans in the upper Colorado River basin. The service found that the projects, if constructed, would jeopardize an endangered species in only nine cases. In thirty-two of the "no jeopardy" cases, the service required project planners to undertake certain conservation measures to preclude jeopardy to endangered Colorado River fish. These measures included the provision of sufficient funds for a study of the habitat needs of, and impacts of flow depletions on, the Colorado squawfish, the humpback chub, and the bonytail chub. In total, these thirty-two projects are depleting or will deplete 415,200 acre-feet of water from the upper basin, yet as of 1985 the service still had not accumulated adequate data to target in-stream flows for conservation of the fishes. Meanwhile, twenty-eight more water projects in the upper basin were awaiting biological opinions from the Fish and Wildlife Service.

The tension between water development interests and the endangered fishes threatened to culminate in a moratorium on the former or a mortuary for the latter. Fearing a no-win situation, concerned parties gathered for a peaceful powwow on management of the basin, and in 1984, the Fish and Wildlife Service, the Bureau of Reclamation, and the states of Colorado, Wyoming, and Utah established the Upper Colorado River Basin Coordinating Committee. The committee appointed a task group to forge a plan that would recover the endangered fishes without disrupting state water rights systems, interstate compacts, or court decrees that allocate rights among the states to use Colorado River water.

The recovery plan includes several components; one of these is a provision for maintaining in-stream flows in the Colorado and its tributaries. The plan requests Congress to establish a fund to implement the plan. Other funding sources will include the Fish and Wildlife Service; the Bureau of Reclamation; the states of Colorado, Utah, and Wyoming; and the water project proponents. A portion of these funds will be used to purchase water rights; other means of providing flows include changes in the operations of federal reservoirs, purchase or lease of agricultural water for use during dry years, water conservation and the conversion of conserved water to in-stream flows, conversion of existing consumptive rights to in-stream flow rights, changing of the point of diversion for senior rights to downstream locations, filing of permits to pump groundwater into streams, and appropriation of unclaimed surface flows or surface flows that have not yet been applied to a beneficial use.[19]

The squawfish and friends must be relieved to have this western cavalry galloping to their rescue just when their demise seemed imminent. The cooperation of states, conservation groups, water developers, and federal agencies in designating in-stream flows sets an admirable, almost astonishing, precedent for the dusty West. Riparian communities, a mere half step from the thirsty fish, will gain only indirect benefits from these actions, however.

The upper Colorado River basin riparian communities have not inspired much research. John Hamil, a biologist with the Fish and Wildlife Service, postulated that under the proposed carefully managed flow regime, over-bank flows that have traditionally sustained cottonwood-willow galleries will be rare.[20]

The potential impacts of carefully calculated low flows on Colorado River riparian habitat are unknown. Possible long-term trends include narrowing of the riparian zone; replacement of phreatophytes with species adapted to dryland habitat; and increased colonization by salt cedar, which has already crept up from the lower valley and severely constricted the river's channel in places. Riparian habitat is not protected under the Endangered Species Act; therefore, riparian preservation was not discussed during the upper Colorado deliberations. The Wild and Scenic Rivers Act can protect riparian zones from development, but it is quite sensitive to political squabbles; designation of wild and scenic rivers can be stalled or prevented if water project developers exert sufficient pressure on Congress. The Yampa, Green, Elk, Gunnison, and Dolores rivers, and Westwater Canyon on the Colorado River, have all been studied and found eligible for inclusion in the federal wild and scenic rivers system but have not yet begun to move through the designation process, largely because of the delay in reaching a compromise on water management.[21] Thus, riparian habitat has gained little from the victory of the fishes; the instream flows may not be sufficient to support riparian forests and wetlands.

Indians . . .

Adding to the current conflicts over established water uses in the Colorado River basin are the still largely unquantified rights of native Americans to water.

Indian water rights date from an 1898 Supreme Court decision in the case of *United States* v. *Rio Grande Dam and Irrigation Company,* in which the court ruled that state laws could not prevent the federal government from using water bordering its property to achieve federal purposes. (Such federal purposes included nudging native Americans into an agrarian life-style — a feat the could not be accomplished in the arid West without granting rights to divert water.)

The 1898 ruling set the stage for a 1908 court decision in *Winters* v. *the United States,* wherein American Indians were granted reservedrights to water, now known as "Winters rights." In this court case, a non-Indian diversion of water for irrigation from the Milk River in Montana upstream from the Fort Belknap Indian Reservation was depleting flows used for irrigation on the reservation. The non-Indians had established their water rights in accordance with Montana's prior appropriation doctrine. Since the Indians had not "legitimately" claimed their water under the state system, the white irrigators believed they had no right to continued use of the river. The Supreme Court ruled that when Congress had established the reservation, it had implicitly reserved rights to fulfill the purpose for which the reservation had been established — to encourage the Indians to adopt the white agrarian culture.

The 1963 case of *Arizona* v. *California* extended the reserved water rights principle to all federal reservations. For the Indians, this decision meant that each reservation owned the rights, effective on the date the reservation was established, to as many acre-feet of water as would be necessary to supply all the "practicably irrigable acreage" on the reservation. The "practicably irrigable acreage" standard, though obviously biased toward inflicting a white life-style on the Indians, did not limit legitimate use of the water to agriculture. Several reservations exist on land completely unsuitable for agriculture; these reservations were established largely to sustain the hunting and fishing traditions of the tribes.

The development of case law supporting Indian rights to unappropriated water has paralleled the boom in federal water project construction throughout this century. Federal water projects have helped non-Indians to store and divert water that may be subject to unquantified Indian rights. The secretary of the interior is faced with two competing interests when conflicts arise; as the agent responsible for the Bureau of Indian Affairs he must look after the interests of native Americans, and as the agent responsible for the Bureau of Reclamation he is under pressure to supply non-Indian farms and towns with water projects. The tension created over such conflicts tends to resolve itself through litigation. Meanwhile, pressure grows for more water projects in the Colorado River basin to increase the supply of water available to satisfy thirsty claimants.[22]

Indian water rights represent more than additional demands on the nation's rivers. They represent a long chain of attempts to remake the Indian in the image of the Anglo settler. Indians do not have a strong tradition of private property ownership; if they are to become reflections of Anglo-American culture, they must learn not only to quantify their rights to their land and water but to respect the rights of Anglo settlers to the land and water that the American government has taken from them. The Ute tribe is an example of the failure of Indian remake recipes.

The Ute Indians were originally a Colorado Rocky Mountain tribe that pastured their ponies on the prairie and lived on the wild game, fruits, and nuts generously brought forth by the land. They were a fierce and free people who moved about as unpredictably as the shifting wind.

In 1863, the governor of the Colorado Territory signed a treaty with the Utes giving white people control over all of the territory east of the Continental Divide. The Utes sold the mineral rights to the land on the western slope of the divide for 10 thousand dollars' worth of goods and 10 thousand dollars' worth of possessions, to be distributed annually for 10 years. By 1868, white miners on the western slope were complaining that the Indians were wandering too frequently into their camps, and the governor decided he had given the Indians too much land. A new treaty was drawn up, restricting the Utes to 16 million acres of land on the western slope of the divide. This treaty stipulated that no white men would be allowed to pass through or settle on the Indian lands.

White miners did trespass on this land, however, and a coalition of wealthy miners wanted to add a quarter of the Indian lands to the

Colorado Territory. A government agent informed the Utes that a war would result if the federal government attempted to remove the white miners from the Indian lands and that such a war would result in the Utes' losing the land, with no compensation. The Utes finally sold 4 million acres of their territory to the United States.

In 1878, a government agent by the name of Nathan Meeker came into the remaining Ute territory to convert the Indians from their hunter-gatherer life-style to an agricultural community. The Indians were not enthusiastic about this prospect, so Meeker instructed his men to plow the fields where the Indians pastured their horses. Hostilities evolved from this intervention in the affairs of the tribe, the hostilities led to warfare, and the fighting led to the removal in 1881 of most of the Utes from their fruitful Colorado homeland to the Uintah and Ouray Indian Reservation in Utah, established on lands that had been rejected by the Mormons. According to Dee Brown, the white government's purpose in moving the Utes was "to push them off of those twelve million acres of land waiting to be dug up, dammed up, and properly deforested so that fortunes could be made in the process."[23]

In the twentieth century, the state of Utah has become involved in the skirmishes of the Colorado River basin states to store their shares of Colorado River water. The Central Utah Project (CUP), for which planning began in the 1950s, is a major project designed to divert water from the western slope of the Continental Divide, which contains the drainage basin of the Colorado River, to the eastern slope, which contains most of the population of the basin states. The CUP, incidentally, is largely financed by sales of power from Glen Canyon Dam.

The Bureau of Reclamation and the state of Utah began negotiating with the Utes in order to quantify the Indians' rights to water from the Duchesne River, a tributary of the Green. The parties involved in the deliberations formulated the Deferral Agreement of 1965, which directed the Indians to defer their rights to irrigate their lands with Duchesne water until completion of the Ute Indian Unit of the CUP. The agreement called for mitigation of impacts on fish and wildlife and allowed Indian use of water for purposes other than irrigation, but it did not make clear when that water would be made available to the Indians, since the Ute Indian Unit would be constructed as the last phase of this gigantic project.

Funding for the CUP came in irregular trickles, and construction was sluggish. The Utes became discouraged in the early 1970s and requested renegotiation of the deferral agreement. The resulting compact recognized the Utes' right to 248,943 acre-feet of Duchesne

River water per year, an amount that would be considered part of Utah's share of Colorado River water, but it provided no funding for the tribe or the federal government to construct irrigation facilities for the Indians' use. Utah ratified the new compact in 1980, but not enough Indians voted in a referendum to legitimate the compact. No new referendums were scheduled. By 1985, the tunnel that will carry CUP water under the Continental Divide was completed, and the Deferral Agreement of 1965 was still in effect.[24]

Other tribes are using rights like poker chips to cash in on the capitalistic game that they know they will lose by default if they do not play. In 1957, for example, the Navajos waived the early priority date on their water rights to the San Juan River in exchange for congressional approval of the Navajo Indian Irrigation Project. In 1968, the Navajos agreed not to divert more than 50,000 acre-feet of water for 50 years in the upper Colorado River basin, where more than half of their reservation lies, in exchange for construction of a coal-burning power plant on their reservation, which brought them jobs and income.[25] This power plant, incidentally, is the source of power for the Central Arizona Project water pumps.

... And Cowboys

The millions of acre-feet of water dammed and siphoned from the upper Colorado River basin support a critical component of the western ambience — cattle ranching. In 1984, approximately 63 percent of the more than 1.5 million acres that the Bureau of Reclamation irrigated in Colorado, Utah, and Wyoming was used to grow alfalfa and other forage crops, primarily for cattle. Impoundments and diversions produce only supplemental feed for these hungry ungulates, however; the main course is wild vegetation.

Livestock overgrazing is a major cause of riparian habitat degradation in the West. When left to wander as they will, cattle concentrate in river valleys, where the water flows and the most succulent vegetation grows. Cattle loitering in riparian zones severely injure land and stream by gorging on greenery and stomping on soils. Overgrazing removes the vegetative cover from an area, decreasing the soil's ability to absorb heavy rains. Thus, the erosive action of rain increases, as does the amplitude of peak runoffs. More voluminous run-off results in increased flood peaks. Increased flooding trenches land and rivers with pliable substrates so that gullies form; if the substrate is bedrock, flood energy dissipates through stream spreading and braiding (channel separation). The formation of gullies lowers the water table of the stream, narrowing the riparian zone so that upland plant species, which are relatively unpalatable and under-productive, replace lush and lovely riparian plants. Behnke and Raleigh found accounts of several impacts of overgrazing on riparian lands repeated throughout the relevant scientific literature. These include widening and shallowing of the streambed, trenching or braiding of the stream channel, siltation of spawning and invertebrate food-producing areas, loss of streamside and in-stream cover, in-creases in water temperatures and velocities, decreases in input of organic matter, such as leaves and insect carcasses, and threefold and fourfold decreases of trout biomass in grazed versus ungrazed stream sections.[26]

Riparian areas can withstand gentle grazing of short duration, but much of the western rangeland is overstocked and under intense grazing pressure. Part of the reason for this situation is federally subsidized grazing.

The Bureau of Land Management manages 170 million acres of public rangelands in the western United States, excluding Alaska. Of this vast holding, only 860,000 acres are in riparian zones. The bureau charges $1.35 per AUM (animal unit month—the quantity of forage consumed by one cow in one month) for grazing rights on public lands. The Forest Service and the Bureau of Land Management estimate that comparable rights on private lands cost about $8.55 per AUM. The Appropriations Committee of the House of Representatives found that in 1984, 880 ranchers sublet their public grazing rights for amounts ranging from $4 to $12 per AUM.[27] Thus, low grazing fees encourage not only overstocking but profiteering at public expense. If the federal government exacted grazing fees comparable to private rates, the pressure on public rangelands in general and riparian areas in particular would ease. Perhaps some of the grazing revenues could be used to heal riparian lands that careless cattle grazing has wounded.

A Happy Ending?

There is hope for upper Colorado River basin riparian habitats. The Sierra Club won water rights for all of Colorado's wilderness areas in a district court case (*Sierra Club* v. *Block*) in 1985; these rights were supported on appeal in 1987. Colorado state water law allows appro-priation of water for in-stream uses. Utah's Department of Natural Resources has formed a riparian task force to effect the restoration, preservation, and proper management of riparian systems in that state. In 1986, the Utah state legislature enacted a bill permitting the

Department of Wildlife Resources to acquire water, with legislative approval, for in-stream flow protection. The Wyoming Water Center sponsored the state's first riparian conference in April 1986, and Wyoming's state legislature simultaneously enacted a law protecting in-stream flows under the state's water rights system.

Gradually, the western states are learning to share their water with nature rather than store it all for oil shale production, maintenance of artificial snow at ski resorts, cattle raising, and future auction. If the states allocate flows for riparian habitats, if grazing is controlled in riverside zones, and lost if habitat is restored, the stability, diversity, and quality of western river systems will be well served.

NOTES

1. Department of the Interior, Bureau of Reclamation, *Colorado River Storage Project: Arizona, New Mexico, Colorado, Utah and Wyoming; Upper Colorado Region* (Washington, DC: Government Printing Office, 1983).
2. M. Twain, *Roughing It* (New York: The New American Library, 1962).
3. W. C. Darrah, *Powell of the Colorado* (Princeton, NJ: Princeton University Press, 1951).
4. T. L. Anderson, *Water Crisis — Ending the Policy Drought* (Washington, DC: Cato Institute, 1983).
5. Darrah, *Powell of the Colorado.*
6. Senate Committee on Environment and Public Works, Subcommittee on Environmental Pollution, statement on the Endangered Species Act by R.P. Davison of the National Wildlife Federation, 99th Cong., 1st sess., 1985.
7. P. Fradkin, *A River No More* (New York: Alfred A. Knopf, 1981).
8. M. Leccese, "Life on the Margin: Destruction of Western Stream Zones Threatens Fish and Wildlife," *Outdoor America*, (Summer 1985): 24–27.
9. W. E. Schmidt, "U.S. Puts Beavers to Work Restoring Creeks," *The New York Times*, 15 August 1983.
10. Department of the Interior, Bureau of Reclamation, *Dallas Creek Project, Colorado: Draft Environmental Impact Statement* (Washington, DC: Government Printing Office, 1976).
11. Department of the Interior, Bureau of Reclamation, *Dolores Project, Colorado — Draft Environmental Impact Statement* (Washington, DC: Government Printing Office, n.d.).
12. J. Rhodes et al., "Quantification of Nitrate Uptake by Riparian Forests and Wetlands in an Undistrubed Headwaters Watershed," in *Riparian Ecosystems and Their Management: Reconciling Conflicting Uses. First North American Riparian Conference* (Fort Collins, CO: Forest Service, Rocky Mountain Forest and Range Experiment Station, 1985), 177.
13. H. V. Kibby, "Effects of Wetlands on Water Quality," in *Strategies for Protection and Management of Floodplain Wetlands and Other Riparian Ecosystems: Proceedings of the Symposium*, Forest Service general technical report WO-12 (Washington, DC: Government Printing Office, 1978), 289–97.

14. M. M. Brinson et al., *Riparian Ecosystems: Their Ecology and Status* (Kearneysville, WV: Fish and Wildlife Service, Eastern Energy and Food Use Team, 1981), 42.

15. R. L. Simpson, "Debate Is Growing over a Proposal to Sell Water from the Colorado River," *The Wall Street Journal*, 19 November 1984.

16. Resource Consultants, Inc., and Bio/West, Inc., *Colorado–Big Thompson, Windy Gap Projects, Green Mountain Reservoir, Colorado Water Marketing Program: Draft Supplement to the Final Environmental Impact Statement* (Fort Collins, CO: Bureau of Reclamation, 1985).

17. Resource Consultants, Inc., and Bio/West, Inc., *Biological Assessment — Green Mountain Reservoir Water Marketing Program* (Denver, CO: Bureau of Reclamation, 1985).

18. Simison, "Debate over a Proposal to Sell Water from the Colorado River."

19. Recovery Implementation Task Group, "Recovery Program for Endangered Fish Species in the Upper Colorado River Basin: Draft," report prepared at the request of the Upper Colorado Coordinating Committee, 1986.

20. John Hamil, personal communication, 1985.

21. P. Carlson, "The Colorado Basin — Workshop Summary," in *Winning Strategies for Rivers: Proceedings of the 10th Annual National Conference on Rivers*, ed. C. B. Brown, P. Carlson, and R. Emeritz (Washington, DC: American Rivers Conservation Council, 1985), 80–83.

22. J. R. Folk-Williams, *What Indian Water Means to the West*, vol. 1 of *Water in the West* (Santa Fe, NM: Western Network, 1982).

23. D. Brown, *Bury My Heart at Wounded Knee*. (New York: Bantam Books, 1970).

24. J. R. Folk-Williams, *The Use of Negotiated Agreements to Resolve Water Disputes Involving Indian Rights* (Santa Fe, NM: Western Network, n.d.).

25. G. D. Weatherford and F. L. Brown, eds., *New Courses for the Colorado River* (Albuquerque, NM: University of New Mexico Press, 1986).

26. R. J. Behnke and R. F. Raleigh, "Grazing and the Riparian Zone: Impact and Management Perspectives," in *Proceedings of the Symposium for Strategies for Protection and Management of Floodplain Wetlands and Other Riparian Ecosystems* (Washington, DC: Government Printing Office, 1978), 263–67.

27. "Rates for Grazing Public Lands Should Match Private Prices" (editorial), *Rocky Mountain News*, 1 January 1986.

6

The Missouri's Misery

On the lower Colorado River, the sweet, green blanket of riparian communities stands out as abruptly from the subtle beiges of the desert uplands as yin from yang. Many riparian corridors are far from being monochromatic strips, however. Instead, they appear as patchwork quilts fashioned with scraps of multicolored cloth, all of different sizes and shapes and occurring at varying intervals. Nature has carefully created these heirlooms, thousands of years of evolution going into each scrap, each stitch. The Missouri River and its tributaries contain within their floodplains biological treasure chests of diversity. Yet diversity is difficult to manage in human terms; monoculture is much more convenient. The more potentially useful to human society a river is, the more likely it is that the river and its associated habitats will be altered, stripped of their diversity, and put to work as cultivators of crops, conduits of commerce, and purveyors of power.

The Missouri River and its tributaries are useful to man and beast, and like other American rivers, their benefits to human society have turned into their greatest vulnerabilities. The main-stem Missouri became a midwestern corridor for travel to the West a century and a half ago. Since then, the Army Corps of Engineers and the Bureau of Reclamation have been partners in the carving and straightening of the Missouri for navigation. While the river has attained a useful symmetry, it has lost the diversity that made it the home of throngs of songbirds, waterfowl, and mammals. The Platte River, a major tributary to the Missouri, has also suffered severe environmental degradation, mainly as a result of stream dewatering. Habitat losses on the Platte have triggered a western water courtroom brawl.

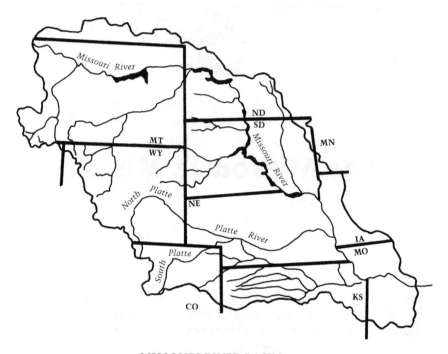

MISSOURI RIVER BASIN

Continued guardianship of this river by American society will be necessary in order to make secure the living quarters of its wild inhabitants. It may also be necessary to set precedents for in-stream flow preservation that could influence western water allocation for many years to come.

The Missouri River's Natural History

The Missouri River once freely swung from side to side, busily eroding old banks and depositing material in new locations to form bars, shoals, and new banks. Before substantial human alteration occurred, the river's channel occupied about 300,000 acres consisting of numerous islands, channels, chutes, sandbars, and slack water that supported vegetation in various stages of succession. The meander belt, the soft soil through which the river coiled in its perpetual dance, occupied about 606,000 acres adjacent to the channel.

The Missouri River flows through the Great Plains, lands once carpeted with mixed-grass prairie, churned and trampled by earth-quake herds of buffalos and pronghorns. The headwaters of the stream in this part of the country originated in unbroken sod. Downstream from the first trickles of river water, dry prairie grasses give way to more mesic, or water-tolerant, grasses, such as big bluestem and forbs. Farther down, the streams remain intermittent but are strong enough to cut into the sod and form a channel. Along the first few miles of the streams' courses, the channels widen and expose fresh soil. As the new rivers continue to carve their way toward the ocean, they are joined by other streams, develop perennial flows, and cut banks on either side of their channels.

When rain or snow increased the depth of the Missouri River before the river was channelized, dammed, and leveed, the river would overflow its banks. Having lost the velocity of the main channel, the overflow water would drop its sediment load on the banks, eventually building natural levees that could grow to heights of 4 to 14 feet. As tributaries joined the Missouri they created cross levees, and the resulting matrix trapped overflow waters. In this manner, swamps were formed adjacent to the main channel. Eventually, water running off hills or overflowing the levees would silt in these swamps so that they became marshes and, eventually, dry land.

Often, in apparent boredom with its course, the Missouri would cut through one of its levees. Following flows were similarly diverted and a new channel would form. This process occurred often across the necks of large meanders. The river would take a shortcut, slicing the loop of a meander from its course and depositing silt on the sides of its chosen channel to lock in a new oxbow lake. Like the swamps and marshes, these lakes also gradually silted in to become dry land; meanwhile, the river was creating new meanders, both upstream and down.

Like a child in a sandbox, the Missouri built islands and sandbars at one moment only to wipe them away in the next. Uninhibited creativity kept the river in a dynamic flux, with braided channels shifting under the feet of trees and shrubs and occasional scouring flows flushing infant forests from the floodplain. Because the Missouri was perpetually creating and destroying its streamside communities, a lavish complement of habitat types was always present within the meander belt.

On newly deposited or exposed soils, the seeds of willows and cottonwoods would alight and take root. Sandbar willow, a shrub-tree that rarely exceeds 20 feet in height and 2 or 3 inches in girth, grew in dense thickets on sandy deposits. Sand is shifted easily by a restless river, but in spots along the Missouri the fibrous roots of the willow bound it to one spot. The shrub willows, if they survived their first season of growth, imparted some permanence to new floodplain deposits and sandbars. Sediment would continue to accumulate around their roots and the newly formed land would expand, allowing colonization by the more squeamish tree willows, shade-intolerant willow species that may become 40 feet high and 8 to 20 inches thick. Farther upland on the growing island or bank, cottonwoods would begin to sprout. In the Missouri River valley, this queen of trees reaches 70 feet in height and may reach 3 to 6 feet in diameter.

This stair-step floodplain forest occurred on new soils: porous, sandy soils with little organic matter or nitrogen content. The cottonwoods and willows that bravely rooted on them were frequently drowned by high summer flows or scoured away by winter ice. Therefore, the bottommost land in the Missouri River valley consistently supported bare banks and sandbars, small islands and bank areas covered with sandbar willow thickets, and more developed groves of cottonwood and willow.

On soils with a higher content of silt and clay, water drained less easily, so wetlands formed instead of forests. Bottomlands not barren or covered with trees were spattered with combinations of marshes, swamps, lakes, and some growth of coarse grasses and shrubs. Of all habitat types, these wetlands are the most generous suppliers of nutrients to river systems.

Deep marshes are the wettest of the Missouri River valley backwater habitat types. At one time they occurred by the thousands, widely scattered over the floodplains of the Missouri and its tributaries. They supported various plant species, each in its proper place according to the depth of the water, the type of substrate, and the salt content of both. Great bulrushes grew in water often deeper than 6 feet, while cattails rooted in intermediate depths and reeds took root in shallow water. Water lilies often sailed on semi-open marsh waters along the Missouri.

Once marshes have accumulated sediment and begun to fill in, the soil becomes waterlogged but rarely bares standing water. Small marshes along stream banks and on pond edges once covered hundreds of miles of undrained or poorly drained floodplains along the Missouri. These marshes were characterized by thick stands of sedges, mixed with some horsetail and smartweed in their moist centers; toward their drier outskirts grew coarse grasses. Marshes may alternate between deep and shallow phases; wetlands in general follow cyclical patterns and often fall into relative classifications.

The coarse grasses occupied vast acreages of the floodplain where the soil was too wet and too poorly drained to support the prairie grasses of the plains, yet too dry to become a marsh. Cordgrass, which may become 5 to 10 feet tall, is an excellent soil stabilizer and is the most common coarse grass on the Missouri River floodplain. Other common coarse grasses are reed canary grass, eastern grama grass, switchgrass, and Virginia wild rye.

Some of the lower floodplain areas are highly saline, principally because of the release of salty water from springs. Such areas support broad belts of salt grass, western wheatgrass, and other salt-tolerant species.

Once young floodplain forests have established themselves, organic matter begins to build up and the soil develops distinct horizons. These more mature floodplains support a richer variety of vegetation. Their dominant species may include red elm, American elm, box elder, green ash, hackberry, honey locust, wild black cherry, and black walnut. Pioneer shrubs (the first shrubs to colonize the site), such as elder, coralberry, bittersweet, and grape, are dispersed into these forests by birds that are attracted by their showy fruits. Forests such as these develop most often in the shelter of high bluffs and hills, which protect floodplain trees from the harsh, dry winds that whip across the prairie. Under natural conditions, unprotected areas along the Missouri River rarely support stable forests.

The mixture of plants once found on the Missouri River floodplain was influenced by numerous factors, including soil texture and salt content, amount of available moisture and frequency of flooding, width and slope of the floodplain, and the presence of protective bluffs. Interspersed thickets of willows and red elm saplings with understories of rough-leafed dogwood, indigo bush, wolfberry, sumac, prairie rose, prickly ash, and elder occurred in many areas along the river. The unordered arrangement of habitat types was further confused by massive tangles of forest grape, virginia creeper, and poison ivy, which often snapped the spines of young willows with their weight.

Highly diverse habitats support highly diverse animal populations. Many Missouri River valley species evolved within one specific habitat type, while others satisfied their needs in various habitat types.

Mid-channel sandbars provide predator-safe resting grounds for migrating waterfowl and soft-shelled turtles. Killdeers, upland sandpipers, and spotted sandpipers feed near the sand-water interface. These species, along with the least tern (recently proposed for listing under the Endangered Species Act), use sandbars for nesting. The combination of sandbars and channels provides feeding grounds for shovelnose sturgeon and paddlefish and serves as nursery areas for immature fish of many species. Bald eagles and ospreys, which nest in large trees along the shores, find easy meals in the dense fish populations in the shallows by the sandbars.

More than twenty-five mammal species occupy floodplain habitat along the Missouri. These include the masked shrew, little brown bat, fox squirrel, raccoon, striped skunk, coyote, eastern cottontail, deer mouse, white-footed mouse, muskrat, prairie vole, silver-haired bat, hoary bat, mink, river otter, red fox, badger, meadow jumping mouse, western harvest mouse, and beaver. White-tailed deer make heavy use of the floodplain. Snowshoe hares depend on the floodplain's young willow thickets for food and shelter in the southern limits of their range. Gray squirrels and eastern fox squirrels use mature floodplain forests almost exclusively because of their need for interlocking canopies and the lack of trees elsewhere in the region.[1]

More than 250 species of birds occur in the Missouri River basin. Sixty percent of these nest in the river corridor. The Missouri River is a major component of the central flyway and provides migratory habitat for ducks, geese, swans, pelicans, and various shorebirds. Several million ducks regularly use the main-stem lakes and open water reaches for resting and the adjoining uplands for feeding. At one time, the river supported large, breeding populations of brightly colored wood ducks. The area now supports a few breeding mallards, gadwalls, blue-winged teals, shovelers, and Canada geese.

Pheasants, quails, prairie chickens, and sharp-tailed grouse are upland species that use the mosaic of floodplain habitats along with cultivated uplands. Wild turkeys occur in wooded breaks along the river, which are also important winter habitat for the prairie grouse.

The Missouri River is a transition zone for eastern and western songbird species. Vireos, nuthatches, goldfinches, orioles, and woodpeckers use the wooded areas. Swamp sparrows, bitterns, herons, killdeers, plovers, and yellow-headed and red-winged blackbirds feed and nest in the wetlands.

The most common reptiles and amphibians along the floodplain include snapping turtles, western painted turtles, plains garter snakes, red-sided garter snakes, king snakes, bull snakes, prairie rattlesnakes, tiger salamanders, plains spadefoot toads, Great Plains toads, chorus frogs, and leopard frogs. These animals find the shelter, food, and moisture near the river that are not available on the windswept prairie uplands.

Navigation on the Missouri

The Missouri River rises in southwestern Montana at the confluence of the Jefferson, Madison, and Gallatin rivers. The river flows north from its source through steep, narrow canyons and short reaches of wider valleys, falling an average of 6 feet per mile, to a deep gorge known as Gate of the Mountains. This stretch of the river is protected from development under the federal wild and scenic rivers program. Captain Meriwether Lewis described the landscape as follows in 1805:

> The hills and river Clifts which we passed today exhibit a most romantic appearance. The bluffs of the river rise to the hight of from 2 to 300 feet and in most places nearly perpendicular; they are formed of remarkable white sandstone which is sufficiently soft to give way readily to the impression of water; two or three thin horizontal stratas of white freestone, on which the rains make no impression, lie embedded in these clifts of soft stone near the upper part of them. The water in the course of time in descending from those hills and plains on either side of the river has trickled down the soft sand clifts and woarn it into a thousand grotesque figures which . . . are made to represent eligant ranges of lofty freestone buildings. As we passed on it seemed as if those scenes of visionary inchantment would never have [an] end, for here it is too that nature presents to the view of the traveler vast ranges of walls of tolerable workmanship, so perfect indeed are those walls that I should have thought nature had attempted here to rival the human art of masonry had I not recollected that she had first begun her work.[2]

It is at this reach of the river that nature's work becomes obscured by man's, for there the river exits the pristine stretch of perfect art and drops into Canyon Ferry, its first reservoir.

Lewis and Clark were the first white men to successfully navigate the Missouri north of the mouth of the Platte River, but they were certainly not the last. In 1819, 13 years after the brave captains had returned from their voyage, the U.S. government sponsored three steamboats on the river: the *Thomas Jefferson*, the *Independence*, and the *Western Engineer*. The *Thomas Jefferson* sank.

The American spirit remained undaunted. In 1842, Congress authorized the Army Corps of Engineers to aid navigation on the Missouri by removing dangerous obstructions such as shoals, rocks, and snags (dead trees) from the river channel. In 1829, the first commercial steamboat line was established, traveling between St. Louis, Missouri, and Leavenworth, Kansas. By 1832, steamboats on the Missouri were traveling as far north as the mouth of Yellowstone River, and by 1860, steamboats were unloading cargo at Fort Benton, Montana, about 2,300 miles above the river's mouth.

The corps surveyed the Missouri River and its navigation hazards in 1867, and in 1878, the chief of engineers initiated a survey for improvement of navigation on the river up to Sioux City, Iowa.

The late nineteenth century was the heyday of the nation's romance with steamboats. For the adventurous spirit, a river trip combined the excitement of travel with enjoyment of the distinct personalities of the rivers. Mark Twain commented on the character of the Missouri's flows in 1883:

> Here was a thing which had not changed; a score of years had not affected the water's mulatto complexion in the least. A score of centuries would succeed no better, perhaps. It comes out of the turbulent, bank-carving Missouri, and every tumbler full of it holds nearly an acre of land in solution. . . . If you will let your glass stand half an hour, you can separate land from water as easy as Genesis, and then you will find them both good: the one to eat and the other to drink. The land is very nourishing; the water is thoroughly wholesome. The one appeases hunger; the other, thirst. But the natives do not take them separately, but together, as nature mixed them. When they find an inch of mud in the bottom of a glass, they stir it up, and then take the draught as they would gruel. It is difficult for a stranger to get used to this batter, but once used to it he will prefer it to water. This really is the case. It is good for steamboating, and good to drink, but it is worthless for all other purposes, except baptizing.[3]

In 1884, Congress established the Missouri River Commission, whose objective was the "improvement of navigation on the river which consists essentially in contracting the width of the stream to comparative uniformity and fixing the location of the channel by protecting all banks exposed to erosive action of the current."

In 1902, the Missouri River Commission was abolished by Congress because railroads were carrying the bulk of the freight that had previously traveled on inland waterways. The responsibility for maintaining the navigability of the Missouri River reverted to the Army Corps of Engineers.

In 1908, the Kansas City district of the corps issued a report recommending that a 6-foot navigation channel be maintained from the mouth of the Missouri River to Kansas City. A formal study of the proposal was authorized by the 1910 Rivers and Harbors Act, and Congress approved construction of the channel in 1912. In 1925, Congress authorized building of a 200-foot-wide channel between Kansas City and the river's mouth, and in 1927, permission was granted to extend the channel to Sioux City, Iowa. From 1912 until 1927, the creation of a navigable channel entailed revetment (facing with stone or concrete to prevent erosion) of caving banks, closing off of sloughs and minor channels, concentration of low flows using low dikes, and protection of the caving banks with inclined groins (rigid structures projecting out into the stream to redirect erosive forces) or spurs consisting of low pile dikes. In 1933, the 6-foot channel to Sioux City was 95 percent complete, yet commercial traffic on the river had declined to about one-third the tonnage carried in 1867. The United States had already spent $68 million on improving nature's work by that time.[4]

Pick-Sloan: Federal Teamwork

Nature repaid the federal government's manipulation of her handiwork with drought in the 1930s and heavy snowmelt in the early 1940s that overflowed the Missouri's banks and flooded the Omaha airport. Colonel Lewis Pick of the Army Corps of Engineers asked for volunteers to man levees along the river in 1943; on April 15 of that year, the river crested at 22 feet — 12 feet above its normal level. When the flood subsided, the corps was asked to provide a solution, one that would address the wide variety of perceived problems and opportunities in the valley. Since some of the solutions proposed by the corps involved areas in which other federal agencies had jurisdiction, the Pick plan was submitted for comment to the Bureau of Reclamation, the Federal Power Commission, and the Department of Agriculture.

The bureau soon responded with a comprehensive Missouri basin program of its own, developed by W. Glenn Sloan. This plan was merged with the Pick plan, resulting in a comprehensive program for the development of the Missouri River, which was authorized by Congress under the Flood Control Act of 1944. The Pick-Sloan program, created in answer to the prairie people's prayers for control of dust bowls and floods, was a mammoth, multipurpose program that entailed the construction of six major main-stem dams as well as extensive riprapping and levee work on the river. The dams, Gavins Point, near Yankton, South Dakota; Fort Randall, near Wagner, South Dakota; Big Bend, at Fort Thompson, South Dakota; Oahe, at Pierre, South Dakota; Garrison, at Riverdale, North Dakota; and Fort Peck, near Glasgow, Montana, are sediment-swallowers that alter the instream ecology of the river. The half-completed program includes more than 130 separate units.

The Pick-Sloan program may have been as much a political maneuver as an attempt to benefit midwestern Americans. According to resource economist David C. Campbell, the Pick-Sloan Program was a victory of politics and bureaucracy over economics and nature. The Corps had lost a huge chunk of its jurisdiction with the creation of the Tennessee Valley Authority. BuRec, which has converted much of California water resources into an intricate plumbing network, was looking to expand eastward. There was serious talk of creating a Missouri Valley Authority modeled on the Tennessee Valley Authority, which would have displaced both the Corps and BuRec. They, along with the Federal Power Commission and the Department of Agriculture, resisted the proposed MVA.[5]

The corps became responsible for construction of multipurpose facilities on the Missouri River and flood control facilities on its tributaries. The bureau was to build irrigation structures on the Missouri and multipurpose dams on the tributaries. The Pick-Sloan plan provided no comprehensive basin planning authority; instead, the two federal construction agencies simply started building projects. By 1985, the U.S. government had expended almost $3 billion on 150 projects. Some of these have not yet been, and may never be, completed. The main-stem Pick-Sloan reservoirs aid navigation on the Missouri River by providing water flows adequate to float barges, though this is only one of the project's purposes. To further this use of the river, the Rivers and Harbors Act of 1945 authorized the Missouri River Bank Stabilization and Navigation Project. This project, to be executed by the Army Corps of Engineers, included measures to form and protect a now 9-foot-deep, 300-foot-wide, 735-mile-long navigation channel from the Missouri's mouth to Sioux City. By the end of 1981, the Bank Stabilization and Navigation Project was complete.

Inundation of an Indian Nation

Several Indian tribes inhabited the Missouri River basin before the onset of European-American culture. Nomadic hunting groups that depended on horses occupied the upland plains. The river valleys housed more sedentary cultures, such as the Gros Ventre, Mandan, and Arikara tribes, which depended on riparian valleys for their livelihood. These tribes farmed the alluvial soils near the rivers, where the water table was high enough to support crops without using irrigation and temperatures were more moderate than on the plains. The Indians also made use of the wild game that frequented the river valleys, as well as the trees, which they used for firewood and buildings, and the lush, herbaceous vegetation, on which they pastured their livestock.

The corps and the Bureau of Reclamation carefully planned the Pick-Sloan program so that the reservoirs would not inundate any white towns along the Missouri. The justification for construction of Garrison Dam was the provision of flood control for white settlements downstream.

The Indians were not so fortunate, however. Three tribes inhabiting the Fort Belknap Indian Reservation, the Arikara, the Mandan, and the Hidatsa, at first objected to construction of this dam because it would inundate the excellent riparian valley on which their people depended for their entire way of life. When the Department of the Interior, which contains both the Bureau of Reclamation and the Bureau of Indian Affairs, came out in favor of building Garrison, however, the Indians realized that their opposition would not stop the dam's construction. They decided to bargain with the federal government and attempt to soften the coming blow to their culture.

The Indians asked for an acreage of land equivalent to the 155,000 acres of fertile bottomlands that were about to go under water. Because they knew that no land on the frequently hostile and windswept plains could be equal in value to the sheltered river valleys, they also asked for at-cost electricity (20,000 kilowatt-hours per year) to power the pumps that would be necessary to irrigate crops on the uplands, permission to graze and water cattle along the margins of the reservoir, and first rights to the wood from the floodplain trees that would die when the reservoir began to fill.

Secretary of the Interior Cap Krug made an initial agreement with the Indians that complied with most of their requests. Colonel Pick, who had been insulted by an Indian during negotiations over compensation for the loss of the reservation lands, complained to his friends in Congress that the Department of the Interior's version of the bill to resolve this matter was too generous. He persuaded the Committee on Interior and Insular Affairs to pass a bill that prohibited Indians from fishing from the reservoir, grazing or watering their livestock along the edges, or harvesting the timber that would die when the reservoir began to fill. The bill gave the Indians no rights to purchase hydropower, and although it did authorize payment to the Indians of about $33 per acre for the land they were about to lose, it specified that none of this money was to be used to hire attorneys. Secretary Krug signed the bill on May 20, 1948. By this time, the corps had been constructing Garrison Dam for 3 years and had sunk $60 million into it.[6]

Garrison Dam was completed in 1955, 70 miles northwest of Bismarck in central North Dakota. Lake Sakakawea, the 200-mile-long reservoir that stretches out behind the dam, divided the Fort Belknap Indian Reservation into five isolated fragments of upland plains and forced the relocation of 1,700 people. The reservoir inundated the only winter range for wildlife and livestock on the reservation. A cash-flow economy was a very small part of the Indians' life-style; they depended on small crops and wild game for the bulk of their subsistence. Seventy percent of their minute cash economy was based on cattle ranching. The inundation of the riparian winter range virtually destroyed the reservation's carrying capacity for wild game and domestic livestock. The reservoir drowned 90 percent of the reservation's timber, an estimated 39 million board feet, which had been used by the Indians for fence posts, firewood, homes, and shelters.[7]

Other dams constructed as part of the Pick-Sloan program also inundated natural resources used by Indians. Oahe Dam, on which construction began in 1948, backs up the river for 250 miles a few miles above Pierre, South Dakota. Subtribes of the Dakota Sioux inhabited the bottomlands that comprised two Indian reservations, Standing Rock and Cheyenne River. When the Oahe's reservoir filled, 351 families were forced to relocate; 160,000 acres of bottomlands were inundated. Eighty to ninety percent of the timberland was lost from both reservations; 75 percent of the corn land, as well as winter range for 5,000 head of cattle, was put under water. The wild fruits gathered each year by 150 Indian families were forfeited, as were an estimated 1,100 deer and several thousand smaller animals used by tribal members.[8]

The Big Bend and Fort Randall dams inundated more than 20,000 acres of land on several Indian reservations. Bernard Shanks, who studied the social impacts of the program, said of the wildlife losses on these reservations:

> Deer were valued by economists as worth $100 each and each
> Indian family used approximately two deer per year. Such
> estimation of worth seems futile when the animals are virtually
> free for the taking but once the habitat is gone, destroyed by
> impoundments, they do not exist. The same is true for cottontails,
> pheasants, water fowl, and wild fruits and berries.[9]

The planning reports for features of the Pick-Sloan program emphasized the need to reverse out-migration from rural areas, to stabilize economic institutions, and to increase development of the Missouri River basin. Settlers whose dreams of a prairie homestead had been shattered by the violent shifts in weather characteristic of the Great Plains were moving on, usually unreplaced. Since the building of the dams on the Missouri, the population of the Great Plains has grown more slowly than that of any major region in the

United States, and most rural areas have lost people during every census period since 1927.[10] It seems as if the white settlers on the Great Plains would have benefited more from lessons in Indian life-styles than from multimillion-dollar water projects.

Another River Harnessed

The initial channelization and subsequent operation and mainte-nance of navigable waterways eliminates many biological commu-nities and sterilizes others. Channelization of the Missouri River destroyed the quality that is most valuable to any ecosystem—diversity.

The Effects of Channelization

Channelization is the straightening and deepening of a river. Under natural conditions, a river's channel and floodplain assume the most efficient configuration along the stream gradient for distributing available energy. Because of the unique characteristics of individual watersheds and the basic differences among geographic regions, each stream channel takes a different shape, and the living communities that evolve along streams are as individual as snowflakes.

When a stream is channelized, its meanders are cut off from the mainstream so that the stream's energy is focused on rapid, forceful movement through deepened channels. The straightening of the channel halts the process of alluvial deposition on in-stream point bars and erosion of outside curves, resulting in the curtailment of succession in the floodplain bottom because pioneer plant commu-nities can no longer become established. The bank-water interface is altered, leading to a decline in the ratio of riparian habitat to the total water volume contained in the stream. This results in a proportional decrease of all the ecological benefits riparian communities provide. Channelization reduces the length of a river and thereby increases the river's gradient as water moves downstream. The current and flow regimes of the river are altered as a result.

Channelization of a river is intended to direct scouring flows at the streambed, but this energy often is unleashed at the banks as well. Numerous structures have been employed by clever corps engineers to prevent frustrated rivers from gnawing away at their banks: man-made levees, dikes, and revetments are common examples.

Man-made levees stabilize the banks and control flooding. They line the shores of a river, artificially raising the natural levees and preventing bank overflow. Once the levees are raised, backwater swamps and marshes are deprived of nutrients and water and often disappear.

Dikes contract the river channel to a desired width and protect the bank on the downstream side from erosion. These structures, placed perpendicular to the river's flow, force the river's high-velocity flows away from the banks and into the channel. Slower flows, however, will bend around the end of the dike in an eddy current. The eddy causes sediment to drop out of suspension behind and between dikes.

Wing dikes are rock or timber structures extending into a river from both shores. These structures forcefully direct water toward the center of the channel. Silt builds up quickly behind these structures and converts the area behind them to dry land, thus accelerating the transformation of a broad, meandering river into a water slide for barges. Some wing dikes on the Missouri have been extended as much as 2,000 feet as the channel silted in behind them.

Revetment structures are placed beside the river's shore, parallel to the flow, either to establish and protect a desired bank line or to guide the flow along a desired alignment. These structures are usually constructed of rock, primarily limestone. Deterioration of revetment structures caused by ice, freeze-thaw action, wave impact, and under-cutting by bed scouring necessitates continuous maintenance of the structures.

Mechnical bank stabilization efforts on the Missouri are expensive. The U.S. government initially provided $424 million to construct the Missouri River Bank Stabilization and Navigation Project. The Army Corps of Engineers estimates that operation and maintenance expenditures for bank stabilization alone will be more than $9 million per year for the expected life of the project, 100 years.[11]

Maintaining the Water Slide

The maintenance of a navigable channel on the Missouri also involves dredging and pool regulation.

Dredging is the periodic excavation of material from the river bottom to keep the river channel at a navigable depth. The removal of this material wreaks havoc on aquatic organisms, which are subjected to increased in-stream turbidity and the direct removal of their substrates. Disposal of dredged materials can be deadly for riparian habitats, as the material is often plopped into swamps or on top of woodlands.

The maintenance of navigable flows entails fluctuations in the water levels of the Missouri's main-stem reservoirs. On the Missouri, the navigation season runs from mid-March to mid-November. During this time, the lower four dams release twice as much water as they do at other times of the year. The minimum nonnavigational flows range from 6,000 to 8,000 cubic feet per second and are provided to meet the domestic and industrial needs of urban centers downstream of Gavins Point Dam. During the navigation season, flows may be increased to a maximum of 31,000 cubic feet per second. The main-stem reservoirs on the Missouri trap virtually all of the sediment that flows into them, preventing the river from creating new islands, sandbars, levees, and bank habitat downstream from the dams. According to a 1976 report by the corps,

> the normal flow river channel lies in a sandy bed that has been degrading slowly since closure of the upstream dam. A special study of the channel downstream of Gavins Point Dam revealed that the channel bed immediately below the dam has degraded about 7.5 feet since closure of the dam, but only about 3 feet at Yankton, South Dakota, and a similar amount of degradation through the reach to Ponca State Park. Of course, with degradation of the riverbed there has been a parallel lowering of the river surface.[12]

Once channelized, the river became a vengeful, burrowing badger bent on destroying the land it was born to create. Between Fort Peck Dam and Lake Sakakawea, and between Garrison Dam and Lake Oahe, island banks and valley land are chewed away at the rate of 1 acre per river mile per year. Between Gavins Point Dam and Ponca State Park, about 3.5 acres per river mile are lost each year. The yearly land loss below Fort Peck Dam averages 130 acres; below Garrison Dam, 75 acres; below Fort Randall, 300 acres; and below Gavins Point Dam, 200 acres. Lost land most frequently hides under the waters of a reservoir, gradually decreasing its storage capacity. Guernsey Reservoir on the North Platte River, a part of the Missouri's tributary system in Wyoming, lost nearly half of its storage capacity because of siltation within 28 years after the dam was constructed.

The Missouri River Bank Stabilization and Navigation Project has, so far, resulted in the destruction of 100,300 acres of aquatic habitat and 65,300 acres of island and sandbar habitat within the formerly 300,000-acre river channel. Additionally, 309,000 acres of riparian woodlands, sandbars, wetlands, and other habitat types have been directly destroyed within the active erosion, or meander, belt.[13] By the year 2003, the natural channel will be reduced in area from 300,000 to 112,000 acres through the processes of erosion, deposition, and accretion.[14] Finally, channelization of the Missouri River resulted in a 60 percent decrease in total water surface area (from 121,739 acres to 40,311 acres) between 1879 and 1954.[15]

This destruction of diversity has taken its toll on the river's wildlife. Two interesting species that were once relatively common along the Missouri River have suffered severely from the loss of habitat.

River Otters   These playful animals are chocolate brown, with a silvery sheen on their undersides. They are slender and almost snake-like in their movements; they have short, round ears and little pug noses. River otters, with their webbed paws and completely closeable nostrils, are built for the water. Their diet consists mainly of fish, frogs, and crayfish and other aquatic invertebrates, although they also hunt birds and small mammals. They commonly den in stream banks.

River otters are often seen playing on slides that they construct on steep banks. The animals clear debris from the bank and hollow out a ditch. In the Deep South, these slides are often constructed in slick clay. In the North, during the winter, river otters construct slides from snow. Otters come together in groups to play on the slides. As one prepares for its turn, it will tuck its forepaws under its body, lift its nose into the air, and plunge headfirst into the water. No purpose has been attributed to this behavior; it is apparently just for fun.

Otter densities on the Missouri before river improvement averaged about one animal for each 19 miles of stream. By 1935, river otters were virtually extinct along the river. The otter is chiefly piscivorous, feeding on fishes; therefore, a direct relationship exists between otter and fish populations. Between 1947 and 1963, commercial fish catches on the Missouri River declined by 80 percent. Paddlefish dwindled; large blue catfish are no longer part of the creel; and the lake sturgeon was irretrievably decimated.[16] This decline in fish numbers and species has also been credited to human tinkering and must play a large role in otter decline.

Minks   The mink is a semiaquatic furbearer that lives along streams and shorelines throughout the United States, except for Arizona, and in Mexico. For such a small, beautiful animal, the mink is a surprisingly fierce predator. Minks hunt primarily on land, feeding on insects, small rodents, amphibians, birds, and muskrats. Minks sometimes kill excessively; one mink may destroy more than twenty ducks in a night.

To human beings, the richness of a mink's fur is probably plenty of compensation for the poultry losses the animals are capable of

The mink is a surprisingly fierce predator for such a small and beautiful animal (Sketch by author)

inflicting. Throughout their range, with the exception of New Mexico, where they are listed as endangered, minks are extensively trapped. About 1,200 mink ranches throughout the United States produce millions of pelts, which are sold at auctions. Each pelt fetches around $30.

Minks desire the quiet neighborhoods provided by backwaters and marshes. A positive correlation also exists between mink populations and the number of miles of permanent stream in an area. Minks have suffered a drastic decline from their original population levels because of the habitat alterations accompanying the taming of the Missouri.[17]

Other wildlife populations that crashed in the mid-1930s when the river was intensively developed have been making a comeback within the last generation. These include muskrats, raccoons, wood ducks, beavers, and wintering Canada geese. Their recoveries are the result of prudent wildlife management and the creation of refuges along the river, but the animals are still limited by lack of suitable habitat.

Changes in the dynamics of erosion and deposition processes have eliminated many of the sandbar and backwater habitats that marked the Missouri as a distinguished river system. The presence and operation of reservoirs initiated a decrease in the diameter growth rate of floodplain trees and changed the population structure of several important tree species by virtually eliminating early successional stages. Cessation of over-bank flooding and the decrease in the meandering rate of the river have caused a decrease in substrate for cottonwood and willow regeneration and an increase in the proportion of forests that succeed to other types.[18]

The process of establishment of stable forest communities on floodplains and river terraces has important ecological and political implications for one of the Missouri's major tributaries, the Platte River.[19]

Waging War on the Platte

The Platte River originates in western Nebraska at the confluence of the North Platte and South Platte rivers. It flows for 310 miles and drains a 29,811-square-mile basin before merging with the Missouri River at the Nebraska-Iowa border. Before the Platte lazily wanders through the arid midwestern prairies, much of her water has already been kidnapped and put into forced labor in cultivated fields. Six main-stem and ten tributary dams on the North Platte and nineteen reservoirs on the South Platte divert more than 80 percent of the rivers' flows.

The Platte, a shallow, meandering plains river like the Missouri, once contained bare mud flats and sandbars in her channel. Seedlings that germinated on these areas were usually drowned by high flows in early summer and midsummer or cleared by the scouring action of ice in the winter.[20]

These high flows also maintained a broad and braided channel. Following extensive development in the mid-1800s of diversion structures for crop irrigation on the North and South Platte rivers, the high flows were retained in upstream reservoirs; as a result, vegetation became established on many of the banks and sandbars, and the channel width decreased.

In 1938, about 24,700 acres of open channel and barren sandbars existed in the river reach between Overton and Chapman, Nebraska. By 1969, approximately 11,100 acres remained—a 55 percent decrease in open channel and sandbar habitat in 31 years. Heavily vegetated communities have replaced these habitats and continued to increase. The Platte River channel from the confluence of the North Platte and South Platte rivers to just above Overton is only 200 to 600 feet wide, a reduction in original recorded acreage of 90 percent. Downstream, from Overton to Grand Island, the channel expands to an average width of 1,200 feet, probably due to the return flow from the power plant at Johnson Lake, which supplements river discharge about 7 miles upstream from Overton.[21]

In the mid- to late 1800s, the banks and islands of the Platte River had little or no vegetation. Then, in 1873, Congress passed the Timber Culture Act, a bit of homesteading legislation that granted an extra quarter section of land to settlers who planted trees on 40 acres of their holdings.

Settlers planted virtually all of the tree species that are now established on the Platte River in these tree claims, including cotton-wood, red cedar, Russian olive, green ash, slippery elm, American elm, red mulberry, box elder, silver maple, hackberry, and Siberian elm. All of these species have airborne seeds, which drifted easily from home plot to river, except for red cedar, Russian olive, and red mulberry. The seeds of these species probably traveled to the Platte in the bellies of birds.[22]

Willow, a native species, needs only 2 or 3 years to become firmly established. Once the Platte's flows were diverted, willows began the succession of these communities from barren sandbars to mature floodplain forests. Between 1938 and 1976, this change in community morphology was accompanied by a decrease in wet meadow habitat, from 81,000 acres to 52,600 acres between Overton and Chapman.[23]

On first consideration, the increasing establishment of mature floodplain forests along any trained and drained river might seem to be a benevolent gift from nature. The golden rule that neophyte biologists should always keep in mind, however, is that diversity is the key to maintaining a healthy and stable environment. Even a magnificent, multistoried river woodland is no bargain if its price tag reads "$ All Other Habitats.00."

Human manipulation of the Platte River has also led to changes in wildlife use of the floodplain. Animals such as raptors and fox squirrels, which depend on mature timber, should continue to increase as woodlands take root along the Platte. While-tailed deer find thermal and hiding cover in the riparian woodlands and will benefit from their proliferation so long as suitable forage remains nearby. Eastern and desert cottontail rabbits use the woods, along with brushy habitats and adjacent small fields of grain and corn, for feeding and reproduction. Many other wildlife species are highly adapted to wetland and barren sandbar habitat, however.

Thousands of mallards and Canada geese, for example, winter along the Platte. In late winter, large populations of white-fronted geese, pintails, and other waterfowl species gather along the Platte and move into nearby rainwater basins as the ice melts in the spring. Most of the mid-continent population of white-fronted geese spends a few weeks in the Platte River wetland areas preparing physiologically for migration and reproduction.[24]

The interior least tern and the piping plover are two shorebirds that use unvegetated sandbars, separated from mainland predators by river flows, for nesting. The interior least tern is proposed for listing under the Endangered Species Act, and the plover was added to the list in 1985.

Cranes also depend on barren sandbars for evening roosts. These delectable shorebirds need broad river channels and high visibility to alert them to the presence of potential predators nearby. Consequently, cranes avoid roosting in areas where vegetation is tall and channel width is narrow. Eighty percent of North America's sandhill cranes stop in late February through early May along the Platte and North Platte rivers on their way to breeding grounds in Canada, Alaska, and the Soviet Union. These migratory stopovers, known as "staging periods," are essential for the buildup of fat supplies to fuel the birds' flight and subsequent reproduction efforts on their northern breeding grounds.

Whooping cranes are an endangered species. Like all cranes, they are as streamlined and graceful as ballerinas, with their long, dark legs and black mustaches. They stand 5 feet tall, have a wingspan of about 8 feet, and weigh an average of 20 pounds. They are named for their call, a lilting *whoop* that resounds as far as 2 miles.

These birds are relics from the Pleistocene period, more than 3 million years ago, and the modern whooper's skeletal structure is exactly the same as that of its ancestors. In prehistoric times these birds ranged from California to Kentucky, wintered in southern marshes from the Atlantic Ocean to western Mexico, and nested in Illinois, Minnesota, North Dakota, Manitoba, Saskatchewan, Alberta, and the Northwest Territories, which comprise their sole breeding grounds today.

The causes of the whooping cranes' decline include human intrusion on their habitat, drainage of wetlands, and low reproductive potential. Each pair of whoopers requires an undisturbed marsh area of more than 1,000 acres in the summer and between 400 to 600 acres in the winter for feeding. The last whooping crane nest in the United States was found in 1889, about 100 years ago; nesting continued in Saskatchewan until 1922. The remanent wild whooper population was discovered in the Northwest Territories, in Wood Buffalo National Park, in 1954. This flock winters in the Aransas National Wildlife Refuge in Texas.

Added to the problem of habitat destruction is the whooping crane's low breeding rate. The cranes lay two eggs per breeding season, and usually only one of these hatches. In 1985, there were approximately 180 whooping cranes left in the world. Of these, only 80 are members of the Wood Buffalo-Aransas flock.

The Fish and Wildlife Service's Whooping Crane Recovery Plan of 1980 states that in order to reclassify the crane from endangered to threatened, the Wood Buffalo-Aransas population will have to increase to 40 nesting pairs. Because of skewed sex and age ratios, distribution, and behavior of the cranes, the total number of birds necessary to establish 40 breeding pairs may be greater than 200.[25]

Whooping cranes use the Platte as a "nontraditional staging area." Unlike the sandhill cranes, whoopers don't stage on the Platte on a year-to-year basis, nor do they stop there long enough to significantly replenish their fat reserves. Still, degradation of the natural Platte River habitat threatens the survival of these birds.

The river bottom of the Platte provides dictary protein for waterfowl and shorebirds in the form of insects, crayfish, frogs, small fish, and other small animals. The destruction by humans of rainwater basins and backwater wetlands near the river results in concentrations of waterfowl and shorebirds on the remaining wetlands. As densities of these birds increase, so do the risks of their being weakened by food shortages and devastated by disease epidemics.

Disease outbreaks among waterfowl and shorebirds are not uncommon in the Missouri River basin. Botulism, caused by avian ingestion of a toxin produced by a bacteria, develops in wetlands when dead animal material is available to provide an anaerobic environment and the nutrients needed for toxin production. These conditions arise when water level fluctuations drown terrestrial invertebrates or strand aquatic invertebrates on shorelines. Sudden changes in the chemical balance of a wetland may also trigger an outbreak of botulism. Nebraska ranks seventh among the western states and Canadian provinces in waterfowl losses due to botulism; cranes are also susceptible to this disease. Duck plague, a highly contagious disease that afflicts only waterfowl, killed about 40,000 mallards and 270 Canada geese in the Lake Andes National Wildlife Refuge in 1983. Avian cholera probably affects all bird species. Cholera, an infectious bacterial disease, killed 20,000 to 25,000 waterfowl in the rainwater basin area near the Platte in an outbreak that began in 1975. In 1980, more than 30,677 birds died of cholera on at least fifty wetlands in this area, including 9,351 mallards, 8,045 pintails, 6,574 white-fronted geese, 2,787 Canada geese, 1,121 American wigeons, and 1,114 redheads.[26] For a small and slow-breeding group of whooping cranes, one bout with an epidemic disease could mean complete elimination.

Pathogens carried in stream systems can be diluted by increasing in-stream flows in the Platte. Increased flows would also maintain bare sandbar habitat and wide channels for cranes and distribute other shorebirds and waterfowl throughout the Platte River basin, thus decreasing opportunities for disease outbreaks. Western water wars are continually being waged over whether to keep the water in the river or spread it about on the land.

Grayrocks

Grayrocks Dam and its reservoir are components of the Missouri Basin Power Project, a joint regional power supply program developed by six consumer-owned electrical utility systems. The dam sits on the Laramie River, which contributes 17 percent of the North Platte's flows. The purpose of Grayrocks Dam is to store 700,000 acre-feet of water to cool an existing 1.5-million-kilowatt coal-fired generating plant near Wheatland, Wyoming. The plant in turn would supply power to privately and municipally owned utility systems in eight states as part of the Missouri Basin Power Project. This project would consume a maximum of 43 percent of the Laramie's flows each year. The funds for Grayrocks were advanced by the Rural Electrification Administration (REA), a branch of the Department of Agriculture, at below-market interest rates.

The state of Nebraska objected to the plan, however, protesting that it held rights to most of the Laramie's flows. The Supreme Court had issued a decree in 1945 allocating the flows of the North Platte River among Colorado, Wyoming, and Nebraska; Nebraska was to receive 75 percent of the river's flows. Nebraska objected to the proposed diversion of Laramie River water to Wyoming on the premise that the decree implied that 75 percent of the Laramie's flows were also Nebraska's property. Nebraska's attorney general filed suit against the REA on these grounds in November 1976, in the District Court for the District of Nebraska.

The lawsuit was joined by several conservation groups, which claimed that the REA had prepared an inadequate environmental impact statement and was therefore in violation of the National Environmental Protection Act of 1969 (NEPA). (Pursuant to this law, federal agencies must prepare environmental impact statements detailing the significant impacts that any federal action is likely to have on the environment. The state of Nebraska claimed that the guarantee of more than $1 million in loans to the Missouri Basin Power Project by the REA in August 1976 constituted a major federal action, subject to the terms of NEPA.) The environmental impact statement prepared by the REA stated that because 80 to 90 percent of the water in the Platte River's flows are provided by the South Platte, the project's impact on Platte River ecology would be insignificant. What the document failed to mention was that much of the water in the South Platte originated in the North Platte and was delivered to its southern sister via diversions from a reservoir.[27] The report also failed to consider the effects of cumulative depletions on the Platte River.

The plaintiff's lawsuit charged that the REA's environmental impact statement had failed to consider alternatives to Grayrocks or assess its downstream impacts on Nebraska's water quality, fisheries, outdoor recreation, and groundwater resources; whooping cranes and other wildlife dependent on habitat in the Platte River; and the proposed Platte River National Wildlife Refuge being contemplated by the Fish and Wildlife Service.

According to the suit, the REA attempted to avoid regulation under the Endangered Species Act as well. Under this act, a federal agency must consult with the Fish and Wildlife Service prior to funding, permitting, or constructing any project that might affect an endangered or threatened species. On November 16, 1977, the Fish and Wildlife Service requested that the REA initiate consultation. The REA replied that a consultation was unnecessary because "the Missouri Basin Power Project will not have a detrimental effect upon the whooping crane or other waterfowl along the North Platte River."

The Fish and Wildlife Service issued a jeopardy opinion for the Grayrocks project in December 1978. One month later, the congressional Endangered Species Committee (commonly known as the "God Committee" because of its authority to decide whether a species may be allowed to become extinct so that a proposed development may proceed), issued an order allowing construction of the dam in spite of the jeopardy opinion. Grayrocks thus became the first federally sponsored project to be exempted from the Endangered Species Act.

In order to construct a dam on the Laramie, the project's proponents were required to obtain a permit from the Army Corps of Engineers for the placement of fill material into waters of the United States, as required by Section 404 of the Clean Water Act. The Fish and Wildlife Service is obligated by the Fish and Wildlife Coordination Act to provide comments to the corps on pending permit applications. In a letter dated December 10, 1976, the Fish and Wildlife Service stated that "it is impossible to consider the permit application and its impact upon the Platte River flows as an isolated situation. . . . The Fish and Wildlife Service and other government agencies must now consider cumulative impacts of the proposed projects on the Laramie and Platte Rivers."[28] The Fish and Wildlife Service recommended that the permit be denied.

Five months later, the Fish and Wildlife Service reversed its position and recommended that the permit be issued, on the condition that an agreement be implemented between the Missouri Basin Power Project and the Wyoming Game and Fish Department to mitigate

losses *at the reservoir site.* On March 23, 1978, the corps issued a
Section 404 permit for the Grayrocks project.

The plaintiffs in the suit against the REA immediately filed suit
against the corps for noncompliance with NEPA and the Endangered
Species Act. The cumulative impacts of depletions on habitat for
whooping cranes and other wildlife had yet to be addressed.

The district court held the corps's permit unlawful. Judge D. J.
Urbom stated that

> the Endangered Species Act places the burden upon the agencies
> who are authorizing, funding or carrying out programs to insure
> that those programs do not jeopardize endangered species or the
> habitat of the species. The burden is not on someone else to
> demonstrate that there will be an adverse impact.[29]

The court suspended the permit, but the parties involved settled out
of court, designed a mitigation plan, and allowed the completion of
the dam.

The mitigation agreement was a landmark in its own right. The
three provisions of the agreement were as follows: a reduction in, and
replacement of a portion of, the water to be consumed by the project;
guaranteed releases from the reservoir to the mouth of the Laramie;
and a $7.5 million whooping crane trust fund, to be provided by the
Missouri Basin Power Project. Three trustees administer this fund:
one each appointed by the Missouri Basin Power Project, the governor
of Nebraska, and the National Wildlife Federation. The duties of the
trustees include the compilation of a habitat monitoring plan to
describe changes in riparian, wetland, and island habitat; the implementation of the plan under the supervision of a technical steering
committee of highly qualified ecologists and water resource special-
ists; and the distribution to the public of regular reports on implementation of the plan. In addition, the trust is used to manipulate and
manage habitat, acquire land, and purchase water rights. The costs of
conservation were considerably lower than the costs of construction
and litigation in this case. The $7.5 million provided by the Missouri
Basin Power Project for this trust fund is less than one-half of 1
percent of the cost of the project. The financial impact of a 1-year
construction delay on the project is approximately $100 million.

The mitigation agreement granted Grayrocks Dam the use of a
maximum of 40,500 acre-feet of water per year. From October through
March, the dam must release 40 cubic feet of water per second; in
April, 50 cubic feet per second; and in May through September, 40
cubic feet per second or 75 percent of the Laramie's flows, whichever

is greater. This agreement contains the germ of in-stream flow alloca-
tions for fish and wildlife, but many conservationists remain skepti-
cal. No legal constraint exists to prevent the diversion of these flows
as they travel from the Laramie to the whooping cranes and other
wildlife of the Platte.

Riverside

The courts so far have said no to a dam on a South Platte tributary,
Wildcat Creek. The earthen dam planned by the Riverside Irrigation
District would deplete an average of 11,000 acre-feet of water per year.
Because construction of the dam would involve placing fill material in
"a water of the United States," Riverside needed a Section 404 permit
from the Army Corps of Engineers before construction could begin.
Riverside applied for permission under a "general permit," a regulatory tool invented by the corps to permit bunches of similar projects
at one time. The corps, however, had to consult with the Fish and
Wildlife Service under the Endangered Species Act before it could
grant permission for the Riverside project.

In 1979, the service issued a jeopardy opinion, claiming that
additional water depletions from the Platte River system would
increase the danger of whooping crane extinction due to narrowing of
the channel and encroachment of woody vegetation. The service
issued a second jeopardy opinion in 1982, this time including alternative mitigation measures that would allow dam construction without
posing a threat to the cranes. Riverside could either provide flows of
1,100 cubic feet per second in the spring and fall, to scour seedling
vegetation and widen the channel, or maintain a strip of the Platte
River channel 500 feet wide and 1.7 miles long (a total of 102 acres)
free of vegetation. This alternative, carried out in perpetuity, would
cost an estimated total of $193,000. Riverside's own estimate showed
that this cost was about two-thirds of 1 percent of the total project
cost, and less than the cost of 1 month's project delay time.

The corps, basing its decision on the opinion offered by the Fish
and Wildlife Service, denied Riverside the shelter of a general permit
and informed the district that it would have to apply for an individual
permit. Instead of doing so, or complying with the alternatives presented in the service's biological opinion, Riverside decided to "tell it
to the judge." By 1985, the district had spent more than 4 years in
litigation, at a cost of hundreds of thousands of dollars each month, in
an attempt to set a precedent that would effectively exempt water
projects involving the otherwise lawful exercise of state-granted
water rights from the requirements of the Endangered Species Act.

The district court ruled that the corps has the authority to deny the granting of a general permit when the project in question is in violation of the Endangered Species Act. Riverside appealed the case and in April 1985, the appellate court upheld the lower court's decision. Clearly, the Endangered Species Act compels federal agencies to use all methods and procedures necessary to preserve endangered species.

The Narrows Unit

In 1958, a group of residents from the South Platte valley, representing areas extending generally from Denver east to the Colorado state line, appeared before the Colorado Water Conservation Board and requested the board to reinitiate studies leading toward the construction of channel storage on the South Platte River. The board agreed to this request and advanced funds to the Bureau of Reclamation for the studies.

The idea of placing a dam and storage reservoir on the South Platte had been included in the 1944 flood control act that had originally authorized the Pick-Sloan program. As time had passed, however, it had been found that some of the lands in the original scheme scheduled to receive irrigation water were not irrigable and that some of the projects on the South Platte were not economically feasible. Congress therefore had requested studies and individual authorizations for each Pick-Sloan unit on which construction had not yet begun as of August 1964.

Studies on the Narrows Unit were completed by 1967, and the project was authorized in August 1970. The rolled-earthfill structure would be built from 8.8 million cubic yards of embankment, utilizing 30,000 cubic yards of riprap material for the upstream slopes. Among the direct impacts of the dam would be the removal of 2,450 acres of fish and wildlife habitat for the dam, reservoir, and other project features and the removal of about 740 acres of borrow areas (areas excavated to provide fill material). The project would inundate 13,000 to 15,000 acres of uplands and 15.5 linear miles of river valley, including 2,700 acres of wooded bottomlands.[30]

The Narrows Unit would also result in the annual net depletion of 93,600 acre-feet of water from the South Platte. Because of the indirect effects of this depletion on whooping crane habitat in the Platte, the Fish and Wildlife Service issued a jeopardy opinion for the project on January 20, 1983.

The Narrows Unit is still authorized and may yet be built. Colorado's governor Richard Lamm still supported the project in the spring of 1985. However, escalating costs and repayment contracts were raising the cost of water from the project as high interest rates and a burgeoning federal deficit afflicted the American economy in the 1980s. As of 1985, the Narrows Unit would have cost more than $430 million—double its authorized cost ceiling.

As irrigation projects came to be viewed with increasing suspicion by resource managers in the mid-1980s, Colorado began to look for a greater share of municipal and industrial water users to justify the Narrows project. This was to be a difficult task.

A data sheet prepared by the Bureau of Reclamation in 1984 showed that more than $117 million of the project's cost had been allocated to municipal and industrial water uses and would have to be repaid, with interest, over a period of 50 years. Therefore, the cost to users of the water would average $300 per acre-foot. Six Colorado towns had requested 19,000 of the total 21,800 acre-feet of Narrows water allocated for municipal and industrial supplies, but in 1985 none of these towns was interested in the water at a cost of more than $30 per acre-foot, much less $300. In addition, two of the companies interested in the water—Western Sugar, which had requested 2,000 acre-feet per year, and Sterling Beef, which had wanted 150 acre-feet per year—were defunct by 1985.

By August 1985, Governor Lamm had changed his water project perspective a bit. Addressing the Colorado Water Workshop in Gunnison, he stated, "Today 27 percent of our water is consumed to irrigate alfalfa. The return to the state is only $156 million a year. Tourism and recreation grosses over $4 billion and it needs water mostly to remain in the streams. Why should we burden taxpayers with the staggering expense of water projects that may actually impinge on lucrative recreational uses?"[31]

Federal water resources development plans on the Platte River tributaries inflict what their sponsors consider "insignificant" impacts on downstream riparian ecosystems. Fish and Wildlife Service opinions and court cases that delay the construction of these often innocuous-looking projects infuriate western water project developers, some of whom have entertained such schemes as amending the Endangered Species Act and the Clean Water Act so that projects involving the exercise of state water rights are exempted from those acts.

The in-stream flow approach indicates an intellectual revolution in the water resource community. Instead of looking at endangered species in the reflection of Tellico Dam in Tennessee, where one "useless" endangered fish temporarily stopped construction dead in its tracks, water resource managers are beginning to see endangered species as members of ecological communities. Ninety-nine out of one hundred times, a species on the brink of extinction was brought there by habitat destruction. Therefore, the demise of that species is an indication that an entire biological community is in danger. In the Platte River basin, the danger is posed by the cumulative impacts of water projects and flow depletion rather than by one individual project with direct and all-too-identifiable impacts, as was Tellico Dam. These projects and depletions pose grave danger not only to the endangered whooping crane but to the piping plover, the interior least tern, and the sandhill crane, as well as waterfowl, reptiles, amphibians, and other creatures that depend on the natural Platte River habitat. Water project developers, as well as conservationists and the public at large, need to take a broader look at man's destruction of the environment.

NOTES

1. Army Corps of Engineers, Office of the Chief of Engineers, *Review Report, Missouri River: South Dakota, Nebraska, North Dakota, Missouri*, (Washington, DC: Government Printing Office, 1976).
2. B. De Voto, *The Journals of Lewis and Clark* (New York: Houghton Mifflin Company, 1953).
3. Samuel L. Clemens, *Life on the Mississippi*. (New York: Dodd, Mead, and Company, 1883), 156.
4. Missouri Basin States Association, *Analysis of the Pick-Sloan Missouri Basin Program: Interim Report on Navigation* (Omaha, NE: Missouri Basin States Association, 1985).
5. D. C. Campbell, "The Pick-Sloan Program: A Case of Bureaucratic Economic Power," *Journal of Economic Issues* 19, no. 2 (1984): 450.
6. M. Reisner, *Cadillac Desert: The American West and Its Disappearing Water* (New York, Viking Penguin, 1986).
7. B. D. Shanks, "The American Indian and Missouri River Water Development," *Water Resources Bulletin* 10, no. 3 (1974): 573–79.
8. Ibid.
9. Ibid, 576.
10. B. D. Shanks, "Missouri River Development Policy and Rural Community Development," *Water Resources Bulletin*, 13, no. 2 (1977): 255–63.
11. Missouri Basin States Association, *Analysis of the Pick-Sloan Missouri Basin Program*.
12. Army Corps of Engineers, Office of the Chief of Engineers, *Review Report, Missouri River*.
13. National Wildlife Federation, unpublished briefing document, 1982.
14. Army Corps of Engineers, *Missouri River Bank Stabilization and Navigation Project: Fish and Wildlife Mitigation Plan* (Kansas City, MO: Army Corps of Engineers, 1980).
15. J. L. Funk and J. W. Robinson, *Changes in the Channel of the Lower Missouri and Effects on Fish and Wildlife*, Aquatic Series, no. 11 (Jefferson City, MO: Missouri Department of Conservation, 1974).

16. Ibid.

17. Ibid.

18. W. C. Johnson et al., *Altered Hydrology of the Missouri River and Its Effects on Floodplain Forest Ecosystems* (Blacksburg, VA: Virginia Polytechnic Institute and State University, Virginia Water Resources Research Center, 1982).

19. R. E. Wilson, "Succession in Strands of *Populus deltroides* along the Missouri River in Southeastern South Dakota," *American Midland Naturalist* 83, no. 2 (1970): 330–42.

20. Fish and Wildlife Service, *The Platte River Ecology Study—Special Research Report* (Jamestown, ND: Fish and Wildlife Service, 1981).

21. G. L. Buterbaugh, *Narrows Unit Biological Opinion—Whooping Crane* (Jamestown, ND: Fish and Wildlife Service, 1983).

22. J. E. Weaver, "Floodplain Vegetation of the Central Missouri Valley and Contacts of Woodland with Prairie," *Ecological Monographs* 30 (1960): 37–64.

23. Buterbaugh, *Narrows Unit Biological Opinion.*

24. Fish and Wildlife Service, *Platte River Ecology Study.*

25. Buterbaugh, *Narrows Unit Biological Opinion.*

26. Fish and Wildlife Service, *Platte River Ecology Study.*

27. D. J. Urbom, "Opinion for the U.S. District Court, District of Nebraska," *Nebraska v. REA* (12 E.R.C. 1156, 1978).

28. C. Brown, "Grayrocks—A New Approach to Mitigation," in *The Mitigation Symposium: A National Symposium on Mitigating Losses of Fish and Wildlife Habitat* (Fort Collins, CO: Forest Service, 1979), 437.

29. Urbom, "Opinion for the District Court."

30. Department of the Interior, Bureau of Reclamation, *Final Environmental Impact Statement, Narrows Unit, Pick-Sloan Missouri Basin Program, Colorado* (Washington, DC: Government Printing Office, 1976).

31. "Reform Our Water Policy," *The Denver Post,* 1985.

Huck Finn's Habitat:
The Upper Mississippi

The upper Mississippi River is a jewel guarded principally by two federal agencies with what have become fundamentally opposing mandates. One is the Army Corps of Engineers, which is responsible for maintaining the navigability of inland waterways, among other functions. The other is the Fish and Wildlife Service, which is responsible for conserving migratory and endangered fish and wildlife species, along with other wildlife-related duties. The most effective means of conserving wildlife employed by the service is acquisition of habitat.

The Fish and Wildlife Service manages about 90 million acres in the national wildlife refuge system. Two large refuges on the upper Mississippi River are managed by the service, but responsibility for the refuge land is shared with the Army Corps of Engineers. This shared management has led to a conflict that rips at the ecological fabric of the Mississippi River like a thornbush grasping at a fine silk gown.

The Upper Mississippi River's Natural History

The gently rolling corn belt country of the upper Mississippi River basin is the result of intricate sculpting by massive glaciers during the Ice Age. Blocks of ice scoured and filled the consolidated and semiconsolidated sedimentary bedrock of the valley, which consists mostly of limestone, sandstone, and shale. Precambrian rocks underlie much of

UPPER MISSISSIPPI RIVER BASIN

the present surface material, forming a basin in which many types of sediment occur.

Strong winds followed the retreat of the glaciers, depositing fertile silt on top of the glacial drift that the sliding ice islands dropped as they melted. These silt deposits gave rise to the hilly prairies through

The river flows within a floodplain 1 to 5 miles wide, bordered by wooded hills and bluffs. (Photo by author)

which the Mississippi cuts its course. The river flows within a floodplain 1 to 5 miles wide, bordered by wooded hills and bluffs. In the northern section, steep bluffs constrict the watercourse. Like many large "granddaddy" rivers, the Mississippi's lower portion is prone to meander slowly and aimlessly through a broad and worn-down floodplain. The streambed material is composed of reworked glacial deposits, modern sands, and gravel. Bedrock lies deep beneath the alluvial streambeds; the river now drifts over as much as 200 feet of sand and gravel.

As on the Missouri, the shifting of the Mississippi's course has led to the evolution of several forest species associations that are adapted to the microclimates along the riverbanks and islands. When sloughs are filled in and the shoreline is altered by deposition and erosion, pioneer associations spring up to stabilize the new land for more mature forest types. The pioneer phase, characterized by sandbar willow, black willow, silver maple, and/or cottonwood, with cockle-bur, wormwood, and grasses commonly intermixed underneath, lasts 2 to 5 years. In areas where dredged material has been deposited, however, succession may be delayed for 30 years or more.[1]

Seedlings of cottonwood and willow need direct sunlight and are eventually shaded out by their parent trees. The closing of a cottonwood-willow canopy on the Mississippi River gives a competitive advantage to silver maple, green ash, black ash, river birch, mulberry, and basswood. Underneath the forest boughs, dense webs of poison ivy, trumpet vine, grape, bur cucumber, and wood nettle take the place of their shade-intolerant predecessors. On low, excessively moist sites, succession often stops at the silver maple or willow stage. In areas of the channel where sediment accumulation has raised the site, thus improving drainage and providing a drier and more stable substrate, sycamore, blackberry, hickory, pin oak, black walnut, black locust, bur oak, and pecan prevail. Here the understory will likely contain persimmon, red-osier dogwood, flowering dogwood, redbud, hackberry, American elm, and tall paw-paw in an intermediate canopy that is usually absent in pioneer communities. The ground cover typically contains poison ivy, bur cucumber, wood nettle, and miscellaneous weeds.

Mud flats and sandbars on the Mississippi are continually being flooded. Their sparse vegetation is usually limited to scouring rush, wild pepper, smartweed, and sandbar willow.

Some Upper Mississippi Wildlife

Many midwestern animal species depend on the availability of riverine and riparian habitats. Excessive disturbance of these ecosystems may result in the decline or loss of these species.

Wood Ducks   These whistling wonders are considered by many to be the most beautiful ducks in the world. The male, were he not so strikingly painted with rainbow iridescence, might be mistaken for a fifties-style slicker with a "ducktail" hairdo. The female is somewhat duller in color.

Wood ducks inhabit much of the eastern United States and are completely dependent on forests adjacent to streams and ponds. Destruction of riparian habitats lowered their populations drastically throughout the second half of the twentieth century until a movement was born to provide the ducks with man-made nest boxes to replace their natural tree-hole homes.

The natural home of a pair of wood ducks is a hollow tree in a lowland forest. These ducks commonly nest about 20 feet above the ground. Their young are precocial—as soon as they dry off after hatching, they are able to swim and walk. About one day after her eggs hatch, the female calls to her downy ducklings from the ground below the nest. The ducklings stumble out of the opening and fall over the side of the nest, tumbling into grass or leaves below.

Freshwater Mussels   Mussels are probably native North American animals; although they now occur worldwide, they probably evolved in the Mississippi River basin. Like oysters, they produce pearls by coating with a shiny excretion the irritating granules that intrude through their water intake siphons.

Mussels have an unusual life cycle. A female can produce millions of eggs, which hatch into free-swimming, shell-less larvae. Some larvae manage to attach to the gills or fins of fish, living there as parasites for the first portion of their lives while their hosts transport them to new locations. When they are more mature, the larvae drop to the bottom of the river or stream and develop into adults.

Mussels are excellent indicators of water quality. They can't move, so if the water becomes intolerably polluted, they shut their shells and stop breathing. Eventually, they have to open up again or suffocate; if the water is still unbearable, they will die. Excessive instream siltation is also lethal to these animals.

Mussels depend on riparian ecosystems to the extent that these ecosystems filter pollutants from incoming runoff and stabilize banks to prevent excessive erosion and stream sedimentation. The link between riparian systems and healthy fisheries is also important to mussels; if the fish are unable to survive, the mussels will die before they are mature and able to reproduce.

Muskrats   Muskrats are large, chiefly aquatic rodents with dense fur and long, naked, scaly tails. They inhabit both riparian and isolated wetlands throughout the United States.

Muskrats are capable of shaping entire tracts of land. They pile up reeds, sticks, and cattails and plaster them with mud to create large, conical dens. These homes look unkempt from the outside, yet they are really quite sophisticated in design. The floors are built above the water level but have underwater exits. The dens are partitioned into individual rooms lined with grass, and the roof contains vents for air circulation.

Muskrats both expand and contract open-water areas in marshes. When a marsh is heavily populated by muskrats, the animals may eat huge amounts of vegetation, allowing water to inundate areas that were previously fairly dry. When a marsh is filling in and drying up, however, muskrat dens are the first places to be colonized by terrestrial plants. Abandoned muskrat dens frequently provide refuge for minks, mice, and raccoons. Ducks and terns often nest on top of them, and small fish hide in the branches that form the floor of the den.

The Upper Mississippi's Human History

The upper Mississippi region, for management purposes, is 800 miles long by 500 miles wide. In the upper region, 4,400 square miles of surface water pass through five states and are managed by more than ten federal agencies and numerous regional and subregional commissions and authorities.

The first humans in the valley were Indians who, about 13,000 years ago, migrated up the valley to hunt. They were succeeded by nomadic tribes, woodland dwellers, and, from the fourteenth through seventeenth centuries, mound builders. The latter group left burial mounds, grassy lumps resembling miniature hills, scattered throughout the upper Mississippi basin states.

The mound builders were replaced by Kickapoo, Sauk, Fox, Ojibwa, and Dakota Indians in the late seventeenth century. During this time, French missionaries and traders laid claim to the Louisiana Territory.

By 1763, the British controlled the upper valley, only to lose their grip to American settlers in the early 1800s. After the War of 1812, white settlers began to pour into the country that is now Illinois. In response, the native Sauk and Fox Indians fled across the Mississippi River. Chief Black Hawk refused to retreat, however, and formed an alliance between the Winnebagos, Pottawatamis, and Kickapoos to battle the settlers. He was betrayed by a band of Winnebagos who accepted a bribe of twenty horses and $100 to turn him over to the white army; as a result, the United States gained what was called the Iowa Territory. He died a prisoner in 1838. The new governor of the territory kept Chief Black Hawk's skeleton on display in his office.[2]

After the tribes had been subdued, settlers moved into the upper basin to farm and build towns. By 1848, the Indians had mostly disappeared, and the upper valley became a boom area for farming, timber harvesting, mining, and trade. This economic growth in the land that cradles the Mississippi increased the river's importance as a highway for commerce.

The Mississippi is a gentle giant of a river, immortalized by stories of steamship travels, and it is a prime target for the Army Corps of Engineers. If the Bureau of Reclamation "beavers" have a reputation for instinctively building dam after dam, the Army engineers seem to have an inherent drive to deepen rivers and "relax" their curves, ironing out every bend and filling every slough until the flow is smooth and pure as homogenized milk.

The first powered vessels traveled upriver on the Mississippi River to the Twin Cities in 1823. They were hampered by low waters, shifting channels, and other hazards. The Army Corps of Engineers was called in to improve the Mississippi River in 1824. At first, the corps merely removed malignant snags, shoals, and sandbars, dynamited and excavated rocks to clear passages, and closed off meander sloughs and backwaters to confine flows to the main channel.

In 1878, Congress authorized the first comprehensive project on the upper Mississippi — a 4-1/3-foot-deep channel. Mark Twain witnessed the grand plans that the congressionally created Mississippi River Commission had devised for the river:

> The military engineers of the Commission have taken upon themselves the job of making the Mississippi over again — a job transcended in size by only the original job of creating it. They are building wing dams here and there, to deflect the current; and dikes to confine it in narrower bounds; and other dikes to make it stay there; and for unnumbered miles along the Mississippi they are filling the timber-front for fifty yards back, with the purpose of shaving down the bank to the low-water mark with the slant of a house-roof, and ballasting it with stones, and in many places they have protected the wasting shores with rows of piles. One who knows the Mississippi will promptly aver — not aloud, but to himself — that ten thousand River Commissions, with the armies of the world at their back, cannot tame that lawless stream, cannot curb it or confine it, cannot say to it, Go here or Go there, and make it obey, cannot save a shore which it has sentenced, cannot bar its path with an obstruction which it will not tear down, dance over, and laugh at.[3]

In 1907, Congress authorized construction of a 6-foot-deep channel. The 1930 Rivers and Harbors Act authorized the maintenance of a 9-foot-deep navigation channel from Alton, Illinois, to Minneapolis, Minnesota; permission later was granted to extend the channel from St. Anthony Falls to the mouth of the Missouri River. Although the act allows dredging only to maintain a 9-foot-deep channel, master plan studies undertaken for the Upper Mississippi River Basin Commission (UMRBC) showed that barges loaded so heavily that their bottoms extend deeper than the statutory depth of 9 feet are common; these barges may become grounded in shallow water. In fact, in an "emergency" situation, the corps may dredge without a permit. Emergencies include grounded barges, but consideration has been given in planning studies to include dredging without a state permit *before* groundings occur.[4]

Above Alton, Illinois, navigation is made possible by dams, which control the flows and water levels of the river, and locks, which are basically elevators to save the barges and tows from having to make suicidal leaps over the dams. These long, narrow water-filled chambers raise and lower tows and barges to the level of the part of the river into which they are passing. Each lock has an upstream set of gates and a downstream set; one of these is opened at a time. For an upstream-bound tow, the downstream gates are opened, allowing the tow to enter the lock. The gates then close, and culverts opening into the chamber walls pass water by gravity into the locking chamber. When the water level in the chamber is equal to that of the river upstream, the upstream gates open and the tow floats out of the lock. The procedure is reversed for vessels traveling downstream.

By 1977, a series of twenty-eight locks and dams between Minneapolis, which is the head of navigation, and Cairo, Illinois, had converted the upper Mississippi into a chain of slack-water pools. The Army Corps of Engineers has put the river into a box, tied it up with riprap ribbons, and presented it to the inland water navigation industry.

Barging In on Ecology

Loss of a range of biological communities, similar to losses suffered by the Missouri River, accompanied the initial straightening and channelization of the Mississippi River. The 9-foot-deep navigation channel from the mouth of the Ohio River at Cairo to Lock No. 27 at Granite City, Illinois, is maintained by dikes and dredging. Over the past 37 years, one-fourth of the open-water surface on the Mississippi has been converted to dry land. Losses of free-river-dependent biological communities are aggravated by the slow but constant degradation of the channel and banks associated with barge operation. Some of these impacts are as run-of-the-mill and unavoidable in the course of navigation as the wearing down of a shoe sole; others are as sporadic, avoidable, and reckless as a hit-and-run auto accident.

Run-of-the-Mill Damage to the River

The passage of the submerged hull of a barge, and the velocity of the propeller jet of its tow, increase the flow velocity of the surrounding water. The amount of acceleration depends on the proximity of the barge to the riverbed; decreased clearance increases the relative velocity. Increases in tow speed also increase flow velocity. When the flow rate of the river is accelerated, the cutting of the banks and riverbed increases.

Diverging waves from the bow, stern, and sides of a barge amplify the natural currents of a river and increase erosion. Wave amplitudes can be significant even when waves originate a large distance from the shore relative to the width of the channel.

The tows are small in relationship to the barges, so the wave action they create is relatively insignificant. The propellers of the tow, however, add turbulence to the disturbed water flows behind the barges. A stationary towboat, maneuvering a barge into a lock or along a bank, creates a turbulent wash from its propellers that spreads downward to and erodes the streambed.

Towboats and loaded barges cause drawdown in a channel that may last for several minutes as the boats pass. Additionally, in narrow sections of channel, where a tow passes close to the bank, waves lose very little energy before reaching the shore and can cause substantial shoreline damage.

The increased flow velocities and the propeller motion resuspend bottom sediments. A plume of resuspended sediment may stretch as far as 2 or 3 miles behind a tow. Suspended sediment in the water column (the vertical cross section of water) is a major component of, and is proportional to, turbidity in the upper Mississippi. Tows currently contribute 2 to 28 percent of the annual volume of suspended sediment entering the backwaters (those areas not in the main channel) of the upper Mississippi. With the installation of the lock and dam system, large amounts of backwater areas were expanded and stabilized. In these areas, the river's flows are forced to slow down. As they do so, sediments fall out of suspension and the backwaters begin to fill in. Data gathered in 1981 on the upper Mississippi River showed that non-main channel water areas are filling in at a rate ranging from 1/2 inch to more than 2 inches per year.[5] A sedimentation rate of 1 inch per year is equivalent to 8 feet per century. At this rate, in 100 years or less, much of the aquatic habitat of the upper Mississippi River will be converted to dry land. Land created by the deposition of fertile alluvial material can potentially support riparian woodlands of value to terrestrial wildlife. Land created in modern times on the upper Mississippi, however, tends to bear nothing but corn crops and farmhouses.

Meanwhile, back at the swamp, the rich complement of wildlife species once abundant along the Mississippi River dwindles. Mississippi flyway waterfowl, worth millions of dollars each year to the five upper basin states (Minnesota, Wisconsin, Illinois, Missouri, and Iowa) have declined in recent years. Part of this decline follows the reduction or elimination of food sources, such as aquatic vegetation and benthic (bottom-dwelling) organisms, due to turbidity in and filling of backwaters. Nesting and resting areas for waterfowl have decreased as well, a result of the construction of new navigation structures, wave wash, and bank erosion. Traffic on the river frightens and flushes staging waterfowl, stressing them into burning valuable calories needed for migration.

Bald eagles are also declining in number because of the degradation and contamination of their environment. Declines in fish populations, which form the prey base for these birds, result from silting and pollution of backwater spawning areas. River traffic interferes with the eagles' foraging attempts.

Aquatic furbearers are also significantly affected by decreases in their forage base. Increases in turbidity can decrease the germination rate of arrowhead, an aquatic plant that is an important item in the beaver's diet, because of decreased light penetration and the accumulation of soft, flocculated sediments unsuitable for rooting.

The survival and productivity of muskrats depends on the availability of emergent marshes for lodge construction and of suitable bank denning areas. If the water in a marsh is not deep enough, both muskrats and beavers may be frozen out in the winter.

Declines in muskrat populations affect minks, which use the "rats," particularly their young, as steak and potatoes. Similarly, river otters are set back by the loss of native fish populations.

Winter navigation exists on the upper Mississippi to the extent that ice conditions permit and towboat operators are willing to operate. Federal authority allows navigation at any time of year. During the winter, wildlife is especially vulnerable to assaults by predators and climate. Winter traffic breaks the ice on the river, disrupting the movements of animals such as deer, coyotes, foxes, bobcats, and small mammals as they seek food and shelter. Human disturbance stresses animals at a time of year when they need to conserve energy. Excess human disturbance in the spring can stifle the animals' reproductive activity.

From 1973 until 1977, the Illinois Natural History Survey Division of the state's Department of Registration and Education conducted a heron and egret census along the Illinois portion of the Mississippi River and in other portions of the state. The survey found decreases in numbers of colonies for several species and severe population declines for others. Great egrets, for example, decreased in number by 80 percent over the course of the survey. Survey data indicated "a serious decline in the green heron population in this century" and included destruction, pollution, and increasing disturbance of habitats among the reasons for this decline.[6]

The Natural History Survey results were confirmed in aerial survey data compiled by the Waterways Experiment Station (WES). WES cited human disturbance as a key factor deterring herons and

egrets from potential breeding areas. Barge operations were specifically cited as a component of this disturbance that is especially
troublesome to nesting birds. Barge fleeting operations, by disturbing
birds engaged in nesting, feeding, and other life-support activities,
could also decrease breeding along the river.

Barge fleeting is the linking together of a number of barges so that
they may all be nudged and prodded along by one towboat. As many as
sixty barges may fleet in an area; these fleets are broken apart when
their paths diverge and are dismantled and reassembled at the locks.
Fleeting areas are generally placed off the normally maintained navigation channel and may therefore necessitate additional dredging.

. . . And Unregulated River Damage

If dredging or filling is involved, or if the Army Corps of Engineers
determines that fleeting might interfere with winter navigation, the
corps will require a permit for fleeting operations. The corps will
probably not require a permit, however, if these factors are not
involved in the operation. According to River County Voices, a local
conservation group, "in many cases, fleeting sites can be chosen and
operated without any responsible agency reviewing 1) the need for
fleeting; 2) the choice of the fleeting area, including the impacts of
fleeting in that area and possible alternate sites and 3) the manner of
fleeting."[7]

While Mississippi River valley settlement was increasing in the
late nineteenth and early twentieth centuries, problems of improper
land use threatened the river's biological communities. Congress
established the Upper Mississippi River National Wildlife and Fish
Refuge in 1924 to conserve these communities. When Congress
authorized a 9-foot-deep navigation channel 6 years later, lands
acquired by the corps to establish a channel were added to the refuge.
The refuge now encompasses 194,000 acres spread over 260 miles
from Wabasha, Minnesota, to Rock Island, Illinois. It contains more
than 1,000 varieties of plants, 113 kinds of fish, 270 species of birds,
and 60 forms of mammals. The refuge is composed of marshes,
woodlands, and sandy grasslands. It harbors bald eagle roosting areas,
provides nesting boxes for wood ducks, and preserves habitat for
songbirds, wading birds, and shorebirds. Waterfowl, upland game,
deer, and furbearers may all be harvested on the refuge.

Congress established a second refuge, the Mark Twain National
Wildlife Refuge, in 1958. It spans the riverbanks from Rock Island,
Illinois, to St. Louis, Missouri. Since 1928, almost 300,000 acres have

been designated as refuge land by the federal government and the states on the upper Mississippi River.

The corps still has administrative responsibility for much of the refuge land. The Fish and Wildlife Service manages the land under a limiting cooperative agreement with the corps. The agreement provides that management for wildlife will not interfere with navigation. The corps considers fleeting a component of navigation, but the Fish and Wildlife Service does not.[8]

The corps, though it is responsible for navigation, is not responsible for the mooring of barges, "except where such activity interferes with navigation, where a mooring structure is created below ordinary high water line, or where a mooring structure is on Federal land controlled by the corps." According to the corps, "any safety problems created by the barges should be resolved by the U.S. Coast Guard."[9]

Barge operators often moor their vessels by cabling them to trees along the shoreline of refuge land, and these trees are often yanked out

This tree was girdled by a cabled barge on the upper Mississippi River. (Photo by Merlin Howe)

by the roots. When this occurs, the only recourse a peace officer has is to issue a $50 to $100 ticket to the barge operator — if witnesses saw the operator tie the barge to the tree, and if someone can prove that the tree was injured. John Husar, a columnist for the *Chicago Tribune,* likened the barge companies to "the 600-pound gorilla that gets to do precisely what it pleases."[10]

Merlin Howe, a police officer with the Illinois Department of Conservation, has been reporting on upper Mississippi River fishing conditions for 35 years, on the longest-running radio shows in the nation. Howe says he has witnessed the slow death of the river — the destruction of trees used for roosting by eagles and herons, along with the wasting of banks and subsequent toppling of more trees. In 1943, a drawdown at Pool No. 30 destroyed thousands of fish. Howe reported this incident to the colonel at the corp's Rock Island arsenal. The colonel, who had issued the drawdown order, shook his finger in Howe's face and said, "I want you to understand one thing . . . we're interested in traffic and traffic only."[11]

The states have at least some hesitation in adopting this view. For them, fish and wildlife, woodlands and water, have more than an obscure moral right to exist. These resources are worth dollars to states such as Wisconsin, which in 1980 grossed $373.5 million from tourism and recreation in the ten counties that border the Mississippi River.

Recognizing the channeled view of the primary federal manager of the murky Mississippi, the governors of Illinois, Wisconsin, Iowa, Missouri, and Minnesota petitioned President Nixon in late 1971 to establish a planning commission for the Mississippi River basin under the Water Resources Planning Act of 1965. On March 22, 1972, Nixon issued Executive Order No. 11652, establishing the Upper Mississippi River Basin Commission (UMRBC) to

> encourage the conservation, development and utilization of water and related land resources on a comprehensive and coordinated basis by the Federal Government, states, localities and private cooperation of all affected Federal agencies, states, local governments, individual corporations, business enterprises and others concerned.

Lock and Dam No. 26

The Army Corps of Engineers appears to have intentions to increase the navigation capacity of the upper Mississippi River. If unimpeded by political opposition, the corps may dredge the waterway to a depth of 12 feet, construct second locks at all the lock and dam sites, and permit new fleeting areas on the main stem and tributaries. These alterations of the river would essentially change it from a dual-purpose, wildlife-and-navigation waterway to a waterway with a single purpose — navigation. The move toward this change began with a battle over Lock and Dam No. 26.

In 1968, the corps's St. Louis district engineer requested the replacement of a "deteriorating" lock and dam, No. 26, at Alton, Illinois. The existing structure, constructed in 1938, contained one 600-foot-long locking chamber and a 300-foot-long auxiliary chamber. The St. Louis district recommended that a new dam with double locks, each 1,200 feet in length, be constructed. This recommendation was approved by the independent, congressionally established Board of Engineers for Rivers and Harbors (BERH), which urged in its report that the new structures be built immediately. The BERH report was reviewed by the secretary of the army, who approved the construction pursuant to Section 6 of the Rivers and Harbors Act of 1909. This act authorized the secretary of the army to order the repair and maintenance of existing navigation facilities.

Between 1968 and 1974, the corps prepared a series of design memorandums and an environmental impact-statement for the double-lock project. Congress appropriated funds for construction in 1974.

In August 1974, the Izaak Walton League, along with eighteen midwestern railroads and two other environmental groups, filed suit against the army in the District Court for the District of Columbia, requesting that construction activity at Lock and Dam No. 26 be enjoined. The district court immediately granted a temporary restraining order that halted bidding on construction contracts. Shortly afterward, the court issued a preliminary injunction stopping all further activity on the project.

The corps was apparently pulling a fast one. The Rivers and Harbors Act of 1909 authorized only repair and maintenance of existing projects. New construction projects, like all major federal water works, must be authorized by Congress before tax dollars may be expended on them.[12]

The corps's legislative bait and switch was not what worried the plaintiffs, however. The railroads were worried that the estimated 18 percent increase in navigation capacity along this stretch of the river would burst their dreams of an eventual $135 million per year in increased revenues. The environmental groups worried that the increased capacity at Lock and Dam No. 26 would merely create a barge bottleneck upstream which would trigger the construction of more double locks. More double locks would mean more traffic, more bank erosion, more backwater sedimentation, more in-stream turbidity, more trees yanked out of the earth, and more general harassment of wildlife, both between the banks and atop them. Conservationists still believe that the plans for a double lock at site number 26 were part of a grander strategy for final corps victory in the resource conflict on the upper Mississippi.

This view was later substantiated in various documents regarding the status of the 1938 structure. A 1974 technical paper by a corps engineer in St. Louis said of the dam, "The core testing and ultrasonic programs indicate that the concrete is of good quality and should remain in serviceable condition for a period extending on the order of 50 years."[13] A report by corps personnel detailing an inspection of the lock and dam in 1974 stated, "The dam, which is pile supported, is surprisingly free of any cracking or signs of deterioration."[14] A report issued by the St. Louis district of the corps dated December 1975 stated that the reason the integrity of the dam was endangered was that "the amount of stone protection downstream of the dam is less than that required to protect the structure from being undercut" and that "the replacement of the stone is considered necessary for safe operation."[15]

After the district court issued the preliminary injunction, the corps decided to seek congressional authorization for the project. In 1975, the corps's St. Louis district engineer issued a formulation evaluation report that evaluated a number of alternatives, including rehabilitation of the existing structure. The report concluded that replacement would be safer and less costly than rehabilitation of the old structure and recommended that a new dam and two new locks, each 1,200 feet long, be constructed.

The BERH reviewed this proposal and issued a report recommending construction of a single 1200-foot-long lock. The BERH's rationale for this idea was that a double lock would have unpredictable environmental impacts, while the impacts of a single lock would be insignificant. The corps, temporarily defeated, accepted the BERH's recommendation. In March 1976, the corps's chief of engineers issued a report describing a single-lock project to the secretary of the army. The secretary terminated his approval of the double-lock project and requested that Congress authorize construction of the one large lock until studies could demonstrate the need for another.

In 1978, the district court dissolved the outstanding preliminary injunction, since the army's withdrawal of the two-lock project had removed the plaintiffs' cause for complaint. In the same year, despite strenuous objections from the railroads and environmental groups, Congress authorized the single-lock project. The corps, shortly after project authorization, began to replace the deteriorating stone below the dam that had threatened the 1938 structure, at a cost of only $1 million.

The act that authorized construction of the new lock and dam at site number 26, known as the Inland Waterway Authorization Act of 1978, contained three major provisions. First, it approved the construction of the single-lock project and the study of a second lock. Second, it imposed a user charge on the heavily subsidized barge industry. A fuel tax, which began at $.04 per gallon in 1981 and will rise to $.20 per gallon by October 1998, is paid into the Inland Waterway Trust Fund, which is administered by Congress. The fund has, however, remained basically untouched since its inception (there was no legislative mandate to spend the money until 1986), and Uncle Sam continues to pay 100 percent of the costs of operating and maintaining inland waterways. Still, establishment of the user fee was a major victory for environmentalists and railroads because it paved the way for future legislation that could introduce free market forces into the corps's dredging and riprapping operations. The third provision of the act was a prohibition of further expansion of the capacity of any lock, dam, or channel in the system, apart from Lock and Dam No. 26, until a study on the effects of system expansion was completed and Congress approved a comprehensive development plan for the upper Mississippi basin.

Such studies and plan formulation were indeed a formidable task, and Congress had given the Upper Mississippi River Basin Commission, now the age of a kindergarten tot, little more than 2 years to accomplish it. By January 1981, the UMRBC was to evaluate the potential impacts of increased navigation on the environment, the railroad industry, and cultural and recreational resources and make recommendations to Congress regarding the optimal plan for future development.

Meanwhile, the Izaak Walton League was initiating further legal action against the corps. The corps, itching to begin construction, had decided not to fully reevaluate the Lock and Dam No. 26 project because in its final planning stages, it did not differ from the single-lock project as originally proposed and authorized by Congress. The plaintiffs held that the corps had failed to comply with the Water Resources Planning Act of 1965 in their preauthorization benefit-cost analysis, that the corps was not in compliance with the National Environmental Protection Act (NEPA) of 1970, and that the corps's postauthorization planning was inadequate.

The district court responded that except for the requirements stipulated by NEPA, the standards established by planning statutes were for the benefit of Congress in deciding whether a project should proceed. Congress had already authorized the new lock at site number 26, so it was not proper etiquette for the court to interfere. As for NEPA, the court found the corps in compliance except for a post-authorization public meeting, required by the corps's own regulations, that the agency had failed to hold. The court would not, however, enjoin the corps to hold such a meeting, because the plaintiffs had had plenty to say about the project over the previous 5 years and the delay would only harm the corps. After a 5-day trial in September 1979, the district court ruled in favor of the corps.

The plaintiffs appealed to the U.S. Court of Appeals for the District of Columbia Circuit. The appellate court affirmed the lower court's finding, in 1981, taking exception only with the latter's leniency on the matter of public hearings. The case was then remanded to the district court so that the corps could be enjoined to hold a public meeting. Seven years of litigation over the future of commerce and ecology on the United States' largest river system had ended in a fizzle over a public meeting.

By 1985, the new lock had been built and Congress had authorized construction of a second lock, 600 feet in length, at site number 26. By 1987, the corps had prepared a draft environmental impact statement, as well as a supplement to the draft when the conservation community complained that the draft was inadequate. In the meantime, the Fish and Wildlife Service was attempting to quantify the environmental impacts that could reasonably be expected to result from an increase in navigation capacity on the upper Mississippi River. "We've gone round and round with the Corps trying to quantify impacts and have found that it's just about impossible," moaned a frustrated Fish and Wildlife Service biologist.

The Fish and Wildlife Service is presently considering a "pay as you go" strategy to quantify and mitigate for damages to the Mississippi's ecology as they occur. The service is also considering using the Inland Waterway Trust Fund to help finance the mitigation. Since 1986, this fund has been earmarked to pay a portion of the cost of new construction on corps projects. Again, conflicts in policy play a role in natural resource management. The Fish and Wildlife Service considers mitigation for impacts on fish and wildlife part of the cost of constructing a waterway project. The corps, which is ready to classify the construction of new locks and dams under "operation and maintenance" rather than construction, will not accept the idea that mitigation constitutes part of the cost of constructing new facilities. The corps insists, in fact, that a brand new authorization and appropriation from Congress will be necessary to fund mitigation for the new locks and dams. Money for wildlife mitigation, especially when the project is already authorized and tentatively funded, is hard to come by.

In 1978, during the first courtroom trial over Lock and Dam No. 26, witnesses from the corps were asked whether they had any plans to reconstruct all the locks on the upper Mississippi. The witnesses replied that no plans existed, but the idea had been considered. One river watcher in Wisconsin stated that he had seen preliminary sketches of flood control dams, which Congress had not authorized the corps to construct, in a corps district office. He postulated that the corps meant it had no *authorized* plans for an increase in locking capacity upstream, but that sketches of second locks up as far as the Twin Cities could well be "lurking someplace in the files, waiting for daylight."

Suiting Up for Another Round

In 1985, the corps requested funding from Congress for major repairs on three locks on the upper Mississippi River navigation system, including the construction of a second lock at site number 26. These repairs are part of a major rehabilitation program (MRP) on the system. The work planned for the locks and dams, many of which are more than 50 years old, would increase the navigation capacity of the system. The MRP may be found to be in violation of several statutes, including the Inland Waterways Authorization Act of 1978 and the National Environmental Protection Act of 1970.[16] The former, which authorized the new lock at site number 26, prohibits any replacement, construction, or rehabilitation that expands the navigation capacity of the system until a management plan for the system has been approved by Congress. The management plan, submitted to Congress in 1981, has not yet been approved, but the corps claims that the MRP is necessary for operation of the system.

NEPA requires the preparation of an environmental impact statement for any federal action that will significantly affect the environment. The Izaak Walton League contends that the MRP will "increase systematic navigation capacity and related environmental impacts" and that an environmental impact statement should be prepared assessing the cumulative impacts.

The corps's current approach is to evaluate project impacts on a site-by-site basis, essentially ignoring the cumulative effects of navigation increases on river ecology. The legal issues may or may not be settled in court, but Paul Hansen, the Izaak Walton League's regional representative, promised that the MRP would trigger the biggest river battle of the 1980s. It may well have done so.

The Fleeting of the Wildlife

The state of Wisconsin is also watching the actions of the corps and the barge companies on the upper Mississippi. In reaction to an apparent lack of response by the Fish and Wildlife Service to habitat destruction, Wisconsin began a program to license barge fleeting areas in December 1982. Approval of fleeting areas, including the areas used prior to the program, requires an environmental assessment by the Wisconsin Department of Natural Resources. Of the more than thirteen applications received by the department's La three were for new fleeting areas. One of these new areas contains a population of a federally listed endangered species, the Higgin's eye pearly mussel. Populations of this mussel have decreased by 53 percent in their original range in the Mississippi River, due largely to river improvements for navigation. Some of the mussels are physically removed from their environment by dredges, and disturbance of their substrate by dredging operations and river traffic smothers remaining mussel beds. Water turbulence caused by river traffic resuspends sediments, which may then accumulate in the bodies of these filter feeders.[17] Filter-feeding animals, which obtain food by filtering it out of the water, are extremely sensitive to chemical changes in their environment; thus, the Higgin's eye pearly mussel serves as an important indicator of the altered nature of the Mississippi River.

The aid that the Mississippi River border states are able to provide to native wildlife is limited. Even attempts at establishing a fleeting area licensing program in Illinois were stemmed by the lobbying of the powerful barge industry.

Another endangered mussel, the orange-footed pearly mussel, is churning the waters on the Ohio River, a major Mississippi tributary. The Consolidated Grain and Barge Company of St. Louis, Missouri, requested a permit from the Army Corps of Engineers, under Section 10 of the Rivers and Harbors Act of 1899, to construct a fleeting area on this river. The corps consulted with the Fish and Wildlife Service, and the service issued an opinion stating that the proposed fleeting area would pose jeopardy to the mussel. Consolidated then applied for an exemption from the Endangered Species Act. The exemption process, created by amendments made to the act in 1978 in the wake of Tellico Dam, allows a plan that poses jeopardy to a species to proceed if no reasonable and prudent alternatives to the plan exist and if the plan is clearly in the public interest. An application for an exemption is essentially a request for federal permission to eliminate a species. Consolidated's exemption application states that grains comprise the majority of commodities to be shipped. According to the Endangered Species Committee,

> there is evidence that in recent years, the strength of the dollar in the international exchange market has severely eroded the demand for agricultural commodities from the United States and, hence, for barging services.[18]

Between the Army Corps of Engineers and the barge industry, the upper Mississippi River, currently a recreational hot spot and a haven for midwestern wildlife, could well become even more heavily industrialized. Barges follow increases in waterway capacity as uprooted refuge trees follow barges; increased commercial river traffic will be welcomed by many riverside cities. La Crosse, Wisconsin, for example, has applied for a license for a new fleeting site and has established a harbor commission to attract any increase in barges that might float their way. Dr. Thomas Klaflen of the University of Wisconsin's Water Resources Center sees the increased navigation capacity as an attractive hazard, with one activity begetting another one. Additionally, creation of a fleeting site constitutes a dedicated use of an area. Barges will fleet there to the exclusion of all other activities.

The upper Mississippi River riparian habitat is most threatened not by a single lock or dam or fleeting area but by a trend toward single-purpose use of the river and floodplain for commercial navigation. The river is already losing the bottom of its food chain, the aquatic invertebrates, because of habitat perturbations caused by barge traffic. Shorebirds and raptors are declining because of the decimation of their food base and the destruction of their habitat. Much of the environmental degradation is occurring in national wildlife refuges, areas set aside to preserve their unique wildlife values. The nation must take care to protect the natural characteristics of the upper Mississippi River; once the river becomes a sterile highway for barges, its value as a wildlife and recreational haven will be gone indefinitely.

NOTES

1. Army Corps of Engineers, *Environmental Assessment: Mississippi River Forestry, Fish and Wildlife Plan, Pools 11–22* (Rock Island, IL: Army Corps of Engineers, 1981).
2. D. Brown, *Bury My Heart at Wounded Knee* (New York: Bantam Books, 1971).
3. S. Clemens, *Life on the River* (New York: Dodd, Mead, and Company, 1883), 191.

4. River County Voices, *Our Rivers: A Citizen's Plan for the Upper Mississippi and Illinois Rivers* (Madison, WI: River County Voices, 1982).

5. Environmental Work Team, *Comprehensive Master Plan for the Management of the Upper Mississippi River System: Environmental Report* (St. Paul, MN: Upper Mississippi River Basin Commission, 1981).

6. J. W. Graber, R. R. Graber, and E. L. Kirk, *Illinois Birds: Ciconiiformes*, Illinois Natural History Survey, Biological Notes, no. 109 (Urbana, IL: State of Illinois Department of Registration and Education, Natural History Survey Division, 1978), 22.

7. River County Voices, *Our Rivers.*

8. J. Husar, "Reality Barges In on a Peaceful Spot," *Chicago Tribune,* 21 April 1985.

9. Army Corps of Engineers, *Mississippi Review* 1, no. 2 (1983): 83.

10. Husar, "Reality Barges In on a Peaceful Spot."

11. M. Howe, personal communication, 1985.

12. *Izaak Walton League et al.* v. *John O. Marsh, Jr., Secretary of the Army et al.* (655 F.R. 2d Series).

13. G. E. Anderson, unpublished briefing document (Chicago, IL: Railroads Traffic Association, n.d.).

14. Army Corps of Engineers, *Lock and Dam No. 26 Periodic Inspection Report No. 1* (St. Louis, MO: Army Corps of Engineers, 1974).

15. Army Corps of Engineers, *Maintenance and Repair: Lock and Dam No. 26, Mississippi River, Phase 1* (St. Louis, MO: Army Corps of Engineers, 1975).

16. P. Hansen, *An Analysis of the Corps of Engineers Major Rehabilitation Program for Upper Mississippi and Illinois Rivers Lock and Dams* (Minneapolis, MN: The Izaak Walton League of America, Upper Mississippi Regional Office, 1986).

17. Fish and Wildlife Service, *Endangered Species Technical Bulletin*, vol. 9, no. 1 (Washington, DC: Government Printing Office, 1984).

18. 50 F.R. 49983, no. 235 (6 December 1985).

8

The Lower Mississippi Valley: Southern Swamps and Soybeans

I n the southern portion of our nation, in the fragile, fertile bottomland hardwood forests and river delta wetlands, wildlife again is
losing ground under federal management.

The Mississippi Rivers and Tributaries Project, a regional river
system control effort authorized in 1928 to control flood flows, grows
every year at taxpayers' expense. This project includes many levee,
floodway (the area necessary for conveyance of the 100-year flood),
channelization, dam, control structure, and pumping plant subprojects. Expenditures for the Mississippi Rivers and Tributaries Project
in 1985 were more than $388 million, about one-fourth of total federal
expenditures on inland waterways.

The fate of America's rivers and riparian habitats lies, to a large
extent, in the hands of people such as Brigadier General Thomas A.
Sands, division engineer of the Army Corps of Engineers' lower Mississippi valley division, who sees the Mississippi River as a "tough
adversary" and states that "appropriate construction, maintenance
and rehabilitation are essential to safeguarding the valley from the
river's menace."[1] This statement demonstrates the army's affinity for
structural alterations of rivers, which is compounded in the lower
Mississippi River valley by the Soil Conservation Service's flood
control programs.

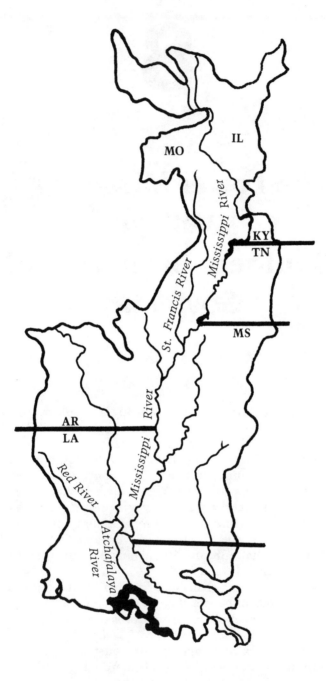

LOWER MISSISSIPPI RIVER BASIN

Oftentimes, after the federal agencies have done their best to control the rivers and drain the floodplains, private landowners, for whom the bulk of the chore has already been accomplished, move in to make use of the floodplain land for economic gain. In the Mississippi basin, upper as well as lower, these landowners frequently clear and level bottomland forests and cultivate soybeans in the fertile alluvial soils deposited by the rivers.

Riparian habitats, such as bottomland hardwood forests and coastal wetlands, are indirectly subject to management by the Army Corps of Engineers under Section 404 of the Clean Water Act of 1977. Any transformation of land use in a wetland or other water of the United States that involves the deposition of dredged or fill material requires a permit in accordance with this law. Although the courts have ruled that the conversion of bottomland hardwood forests to soybean fields requires a permit, much dispute exists over the definition and delineation of wetlands and over the definition of actions that constitute the discharge of dredged or fill material under the law.

Alterations of the Environment and Their Impacts

The Mississippi River valley has been significantly altered to enhance its hospitality to *Homo sapiens.* The restructuring of ecosystems in this region has imposed less advantageous living conditions on other species, however.

Fighting Floods in Fields of Mud

The Mississippi River has caused problems for humanity since its valley was settled. The river builds up its own bed and every few thousand years falls off of it, creating a new delta. Mark Twain noted that the pre-dam Mississippi emptied 406 million tons of sediment each year into the Gulf of Mexico — enough mud to make a mass 1 mile square and 241 feet high.

The river further aggravates valley inhabitants by flooding. In the mid-nineteenth century, floods were battled by private levee districts. The levee inspectors could call out slaves belonging to landowners whose property was threatened by the floods and require the slaves to build levees. The costs of this construction overwhelmed the sparsely settled districts, so Congress passed the Swamp and Overflow Lands Act of 1850. This legislation deeded millions of acres of riparian wetlands to the states, which turned around and sold them to pay for levee construction. Almost 30 million acres of land changed hands, selling for 75 cents per acre if it bore commercially salable timber and 12.5 cents per acre if it did not. The new, private-sector owners of the land proceeded to cut down the riparian woodlands, farm the soil, and demand more levees to protect them from floods. The new levees were insufficient to prevent damages to private property during the floods of 1862, 1866, and 1867.

In 1879, Congress created the Mississippi River Commission to plan new methods of flood protection. The innovative commission recommended newer, bigger levees, many of which were built and proven virtually useless during the floods of 1882, 1884, 1890, 1891, 1897, 1912, 1913, 1922, and 1927.[2]

The Mississippi River and Tributaries Project (MR & T) emerged in the wake of the 1927 floods on the Mississippi River. In response to extensive flood-related damages, Congress passed the Flood Control Act of 1928, which charged the Army Corps of Engineers with the task of creating a comprehensive flood control system for the Mississippi River and portions of its major tributaries. By February 1985, the MR & T was 76 percent complete, with more than $3.5 billion invested in it, and federal funds have not yet stopped flowing.

The MR & T escaped the cost-sharing requirements legislatively applied to other federal water projects in the House version of the Omnibus Water Projects Bill of 1986. Conservationists believe that one reason this project remained exempt was that Congressman Jamie Whitten, a Mississippi democrat, was chairman of the House Appropriations Committee. Congressman Bob Edgar, the sponsor of an amendment that would include the Mississippi River and Tributaries Program under the cost-sharing requirements of the bill, said that "people who take on the chairman of the Appropriations Committee very seldom win" and that "residents of the lower Mississippi are moved to the front of the list. The rest are treated like second-class citizens."[3]

The loophole through which the MR & T escaped was a clause in the legislation that applied cost-sharing requirements only to projects not yet under construction when the bill was passed. Although the MR & T involves several rivers and subprojects not addressed specifically by the 1928 legislation, Congress treats the entire program as one project on which construction began in 1928. Therefore, individual "subprojects" do not have to be authorized before they are constructed. They merely require appropriations from Congress.

Wildlife mitigation is a different ball game. The purchase of titles to and easements on bottomland hardwoods and other riparian lands to compensate for habitat destroyed by the MR & T requires a separate authorization from Congress. When the federal budget gets tight, wildlife funding is often cut.

In 1979, for example, fifty projects of the Army Corps of Engineers were authorized or under construction in the lower Mississippi valley. The Fish and Wildlife Service had requested mitigation for thirty-nine of these projects, including the acquisition of 610,740 acres of wildlife habitat to be managed for the preservation of its natural values. Congress authorized the acquisition of 18 percent of this land, but in 1979, only 36,683 acres, or 6 percent of the total amount requested, had been acquired and were under management. The Fish and Wildlife Service estimated that when these fifty projects were complete, direct and induced losses of bottomland hardwood forest would amount to more than 2 million acres, and channel modifications would have destroyed 6,657 miles of stream habitat.

A large part of the problem with implementing mitigation was public opposition to federal acquisition of land for wildlife conservation; thousands of acres of land had already passed into federal ownership in fee titles and easements simply for project construction. Another part of the problem was the corps's bias toward engineering solutions rather than habitat preservation. Steve Gard, a biologist with the Fish and Wildlife Service, commented that

> next to lack of public support, no other reason for mitigation
> failure stands out so clearly as does opposition to the mitigation
> recommendations of the Fish and Wildlife Service. The Corps has
> consistently opposed the majority of the recommendations or
> proposed their own. In cases where they proposed their own, they
> were usually strictly structural and minor in nature.[4]

The Atchafalaya River, a major distributary (a channel that transports water away from, rather than into, the main channel), normally carries about 30 percent of the Mississippi's flows to the sea. This river provides an example of wildlife's vulnerability to Washington politics. The Atchafalaya subproject began when Congress constructed a 25-kilometer-wide floodway through the center of the basin for controlled floodwater diversion from the Mississippi. The subproject includes maintenance of a floodway, a levee system, and other features.

A management plan for the Atchafalaya floodway was 10 years in the making. The Louisiana Wildlife Federation helped construct a constituency to support a floodway plan that included wildlife enhancement and recreation measures. Dave Treen, Louisiana's governor at that time, adopted the plan and gave it the support that its creators believed would sail it through Congress. Robert Dawson, former assistant secretary of the army for civil works, nearly scuttled the plan's wildlife and recreation provisions in November of 1985 by recommending to the Office of Management and Budget that the provisions not be funded.[5] The Louisiana Wildlife Federation mounted a campaign against Dawson's recommendation, enlisting the help of Treen, Senator J. Bennett Johnston, and the Louisiana congressional delegation. Finally, the management plan was incorporated intact into the omnibus funding legislation passed by the House in 1985.[6]

Not every flood damage reduction plan blueprinted under the MR & T was intended to protect people and houses from floods. Some, such as the proposed Yazoo backwater pumping plant, derived the bulk of their estimated benefits from "agricultural intensification." Often, farmers who clear and cultivate floodplain lands in the lower Mississippi valley are surprised when their fields flood in the spring, reducing their productivity to one or no soybean crops per year. This problem is common in the Yazoo River delta, where approximately 19 percent of the cultivated land lies within the 1-year floodplain (the area likely to be flooded every year).[7]

The Yazoo River delta is a 4.5-million-acre chunk of alluvial floodplain between the Yazoo and Mississippi rivers, extending south to their confluence. The delta was once completely covered with high-quality wetlands and bottomland hardwood forests. Agricultural expansion, aided in part by numerous flood damage reduction programs, has caused the loss of nearly 4 million acres of these forests and wetlands. The Environmental Defense Fund estimates that construction of a pumping plant in the delta will result in the conversion to agriculture of 30,000 more acres.[8] In fact, almost 79 percent of the anticipated benefits from the pumping plant would come from the pumping of water off frequently flooded farms and forests rather than the protection of people, homes, and businesses.[9]

Waterfowl and water quality are two natural resources that would suffer most from construction of the pumping plant and the resulting land conversions. These resources have already been hit hard by flood damage reduction programs in the Yazoo delta.

Waterfowl using the Mississippi flyway depend on bottomland hardwood forests. This is particularly true of wood ducks, which gain feeding areas, cover, nesting cavities, and brood-rearing habitat from these forests. Other waterfowl species, including mallards, pintails, wigeons, black ducks, ring-necked ducks, green-winged and blue-winged teals, gadwalls, hooded mergansers, and many other species, feed on acorns, fruits, nuts, crawfish, insect larvae, and other items found in flooded hardwood stands. As the extent of these stands decreases, waterfowl are forced to supplement their diets with what remains of crops after the fall harvest. Increased efficiency of harvest machinery and decreased flooding of agricultural lands due to flood damage reduction programs diminish the amount of food available to wintering waterfowl.[10]

The corps estimated that the Yazoo Area Pump Project would result in the loss of 1,178 man-days per year of waterfowl recreation.[11] The cumulative impacts of increased clearing, intensified agricultural practices, and altered flood frequency would adversely affect migratory and resident waterfowl. Long-term cumulative impacts could include altered migration patterns, affecting the physical condition, and thus the breeding success, of waterfowl returning to their breeding grounds, and reduced quality of nesting and brood habitat for resident waterfowl.

Water quality is enhanced by bottomland hardwood forests. The effects of nearly half a century of flood damage reduction measures and induced land clearing are evident in the water of the Yazoo basin. In 1970, the Soil Conservation Service estimated that erosion in the Yazoo basin measured more than 28 million tons per year, 15 million tons (55.8 percent) of which were probably passing into the streams. The primary causes of the high erosion rates were channelization and the clearing of bottomland hardwoods for agriculture. Additionally, pesticides applied to cultivated fields adhere to soil particles, and when the particles erode, the pesticides flow along into streams and lakes. The Fish and Wildlife Service found in 1979 that

> flood control works in the basin have led to degradation of water quality, reduction of fishery populations, increased sedimentation and associated pesticide levels, and the overall reduction in the quality of the aquatic ecosystem. The ecosystem has declined such that recent studies have found that only 20 percent of the stream miles in the Yazoo Basin are capable of supporting a fishery of any kind, with even fewer miles supporting a sport fishery.[12]

By approving a little-noticed amendment to the Omnibus Water Projects Bill of 1986, Congress excluded the Yazoo Area Pump Project from the local cost-sharing exemption that allows total federal funding for MR & T projects. For a short while, the project seemed to have evaporated for lack of local support, but as of August 1988 it appeared that it might be resurrected.

Some Southern Riparian Residents

Ivory-Billed Woodpeckers   The striking ivory-billed woodpecker has been reduced to a mere apparition of the bottomland hardwood forests in the lower Mississippi valley. This impressive bird, with its black crest and torso, ivory-colored bill, and sporty white racing stripe down its dark neck, once thrived in great stands of virgin timber throughout the South. Today all that remains of the U.S. population of the bird are unsubstantiated rumors of its existence.

The ivory-billed woodpecker is more than mere legend, however; it is a living creature with habitats and habits unlike any other's. The birds burrow for insects beneath the bark of dead or dying trees. They nest in dead trees, typically 15 to 70 feet above the ground. They breed between January and April, the male and female clasping bills in a courtship ritual. Incubation is a joint venture: the female generally nest-sits during the day and the male, at night. The parents also share in a vigorous defense of their young.

The ivory-billed woodpecker once inhabited large contiguous tracts of bottomland hardwood forest. These forests have been so extremely altered by man that the woodpeckers were considered extinct for about 30 years, until biologists rediscovered the birds in Cuba in 1986. Cuba is now taking pride in this piece of natural history and is taking stringent measures to protect the birds.

American Alligators America nearly lost its alligators to the leather and pet industries. The alligator was persistently hunted for its skin, which was manufactured into ornamental leather goods. Baby alligators were sold to tourists as pets in the Gulf states until Congress placed them under the protection of the Endangered Species Act. By 1987, alligator populations had bounced back sufficiently for the animals to be removed from the list of threatened and endangered species.

American alligators inhabit the backwaters of large rivers, ponds, lakes, abandoned rice fields, and freshwater marshes and swamps. (Sketch by author)

American alligators inhabit the backwaters of large southern rivers, ponds, and lakes as well as abandoned river fields and fresh-water marshes and swamps. They are designed for semiaquatic living; their nostrils and ears are valvelike, closing when the animals are submerged. As an alligator dives under water, its heart rate may drop from about 28 beats per minute to about 5 beats per minute.

Female alligators lay their eggs in late spring. The female builds a nest mound in a shaded area near the water, scooping up mud in her large jaws and mixing it with mouthfuls of marsh vegetation. The mound is usually about 3 feet high and 5 to 7 feet in diameter at the base. The alligator lays between twenty and seventy eggs in a hollow on the mound, covers the eggs with material from the edges of the mound, and crawls about on top of the structure to smooth it out. She then guards the mound faithfully against all intruders until the eggs are ready to hatch, in late summer or early fall. When the eggs are ready to hatch, the young alligators make peeping sounds from inside. The female responds by uncovering the eggs and helping to free her children, 8-inch-long creatures emerging from 3-inch-long eggs. She takes the hatchlings into her mouth and gently carries them to the water.

Alligators shape marsh ecology to a large extent. The mounds they build serve as nesting sites for turtles and colonization areas for plants. Trees and shrubs root on old mounds, and birds nest in these. The mound may initiate the transformation of an open-water marsh into an upland forest.

The converse is also true. The female alligator usually builds her nest mound near a "gator hole"—a hole dug by an alligator into the floor of the swamp or marsh and used for overwintering. If an alligator hollows out the same hole several years in a row, the hole may take on the dimensions of a small pond. These holes may provide the only open-water habitat available to small aquatic animals during droughts, so they often save the lives of amphibians and fish and the predators that depend on them. The alligator also works toward creating open-water habitat by burrowing holes several feet deep in mud flats. Alligators also maintain open-water habitat by tearing aquatic and emergent vegetation out of marshes.

Where Have All the Sweet Gums Gone?

A little-known nineteenth-century naturalist, William Elliott, mourned the habitat losses in southeastern ecosystems:

> Undoubtedly, the most obvious cause of the disappearance of the
> deer and other game, is the destruction of the forests, that of the
> river swamps, especially; which being, in their original state,
> impracticable to horsemen, secured them against pursuit; for, if
> pressed by hounds, they could escape by swimming the rivers.
> These lands being cleared and cultivated, no longer afford them
> refuge. Their feeding and hiding-places being more contracted,
> they can more easily be hemmed in and destroyed.[13]

In fact, biologist R. K. Yancey postulated in 1970 that if the destruction of bottomland hardwood forests in the floodplain of the Mississippi River continued at its current rate, the habitat carrying capacity
for deer (the number of deer that the ecosystem is capable of supporting) would decrease from a pristine original of about 280,000 animals
to a mere 31,000 by 1985. The number of recreational man-days, and
the revenues produced by expenditures for hunting excursions, would
decrease by 75 percent between 1968 and 1985, according to Yancey.[14]

The potential harvest of gray and fox squirrels in 1968 was
2,150,000 by Yancey's estimate. By 1985, this number would have
decreased to 240,000 squirrels, with a resulting loss of approximately
90 percent of recreational man-days. The rate of clearing of hardwood
forests has slowed somewhat since the mid-1970s, but significant
losses of woodlands and wildlife continue.

The conversion of bottomland hardwood forests to tofu fields is
one of the most blatant demonstrations of inside-out land management in the twentieth century. The alluvial valley of the Mississippi
River and twenty-five other major rivers contained, at the time of
European settlement, approximately 10 million hectares of bottomland hardwood forest. In 1978, about 2.1 million hectares, or 21
percent of the original area, remained. By 1995, probably fewer than
1.6 million hectares will be left, and these will be reduced to 810,000
by the year 2000 if the present rate of clearing continues.

The Fish and Wildlife Service recognizes two basic types of
bottomland hardwood forest. The first type, composed of seasonally
flooded basins or flats, is dominated by sweet gum, hackberry, bitter
pecan, elm, ash, and several species of oak. These forests occur on
soils that are moist or saturated or inundated by headwater or backwater flooding during a portion of the year. Headwater flooding follows the occurrence of rainstorms over the drainage basins of a river's
tributaries. This condition, augmented by snowmelt in the upper
tributary basins, creates spring floods. Backwater flooding occurs
when the stage of a river rises enough to cause water to back up on its
tributaries. This phenomenon can cause the tributaries to flow backward and inundate their floodplains for long periods of time. In the

lower Mississippi River basin, the seasonally flooded hardwoods produce mast crops, such as acorns, which are a primary food source for white-tailed deer, squirrels, wild turkeys, and wintering waterfowl.

The second type of bottomland hardwood forest consists of wooded or shrub-covered swamps. These often form in old river channels and are normally wet throughout the growing season. Tupelo and cypress trees dominate most wooded swamps and provide prime real estate for minks and raccoons. Water often stands several feet deep in these communities. Shrub swamps are generally shallower and support buttonbrush, water elm, swamp privet, and willow.

Bottomland hardwood forests in the lower Mississippi valley provide wintering habitat for half the nation's wood ducks, more than 20 percent of our mallards, about 55 percent of our woodcocks, and more than 220 species of nongame birds.

From Evergreens to Soybeans

Destruction of bottomland hardwoods really got rolling after Congress passed the Flood Control Act of 1936, which authorized the activities of federal river wrestlers on the Mississippi River, its tributaries, and their floodplains. From 1937 to 1947, the dates of initiation of major flood control projects in the St. Francis River basin in Arkansas appear to coincide with dates of heavy losses of forested bottomlands. From 1947 to 1957, forest clearing rates dropped. During this period, only minor, local flood protection projects were tackled by the Army Corps of Engineers. In 1954, Congress passed PL-566, the act that established the Watershed Protection and Flood Prevention Program, and the Soil Conservation Service initiated its small watershed program. Under this program, the service provides assistance to local groups in implementing a variety of land treatments, including dams, channel clearings or realignments, floodways, and similar measures to manage the flow of water. These treatments encourage farmers to drain and clear floodplain forests by providing flood control structures and large drainage ditches to which the farmers can connect their own channels. The design and implementation of small watershed projects must be coordinated with the navigation and flood control programs of the corps. Therefore, a double link exists between the corps's waterway improvements and the clearing of bottomland hardwood forests for agricultural use.

The peak of clearing activities occurred from 1957 until 1967. Over this 10-year period, one-third of the counties in Arkansas lost well over 10 percent of their bottomland hardwood forests. In Mississippi, six counties lost more than 10 percent, and five Louisiana counties suffered losses of similar magnitude. Coincidentally, the corps was completing a large number of major improvements on levees, channels, drainage ditches, and floodgates. A report published in 1979 by the Fish and Wildlife Service documented the link between federal flood control work and riparian habitat clearing:

> Visual inspection of the maps display showing the distribution and magnitude of net losses in bottomland hardwoods overlaid with the map of completed Corps of Engineer and PL-566 projects revealed that 32 out of 33 counties with completed projects had corresponding net losses in bottomland hardwood forest. It is also apparent from the data that the counties with very high losses are the same counties with a combination of several completed projects. This seemingly significant relationship could mean that farmers and other clearing operators were responding to their expectations of additional flood control measures by expanding their clearing operation to suitable bottomland hardwood areas.[15]

From 1967 through 1977, streamside counties in Louisiana, Mississippi, Arkansas, and Missouri lost substantial areas of their bottomland forests. The report by the Fish and Wildlife Service stated not only that clearing of bottomland hardwood forests seemed directly related to projects carried out by the Army Corps of Engineers and the Soil Conservation Service but that acreages of lost forest were low (10,000 or fewer acres) in almost all counties with no associated corps or Soil Conservation Service projects.

The wildlife-rich bottomland hardwood forests were losing their appeal to the residents of the lower Mississippi valley. After years of service and production, they had been overcut, and smaller, thicker woods had grown in where more mature stands once existed. The decrease in the average diameters of trees in the alluvial soils decreased the timber's market value, and by the 1960s, little merchantable timber was left. From 1963 to 1972, the output of hardwood veneer logs from the valley declined from 125 million board feet to 60 million board feet. Barely one-third of the trees that were cleared for agricultural purposes were sold to industry; they were more often piled into windrows and burned.

From the late 1950s until the mid-1970s, the world developed a growing hunger for soybean products as technological advances increased the utility of the lucrative legume. The soybean's short growing season (90 to 100 days) and a wide range of suitable soils added to farmers' incentives to clear floodplains and make room for larger soybean crops. Federal agencies subtly encourage this conversion of forests to fields. The corps stabilizes stream banks, so farmers become more confident that the river will not steal their croplands from under their feet after a year or two of production. The Soil Conservation Service offers assistance ranging from advice for the do-it-yourselfers to complete engineering jobs for drainage ditches in agricultural communities. The Department of Agriculture's price support programs minimize the risk of lost investments, and the farmers' federal crop insurance program compensates them for losses caused by natural disasters such as flooding.

From the river's point of view, however, the federal crop insurance program adds insult to injury. Within the array of federal incentives to clear floodplain forests, it is difficult to assess how much of the clearing is attributable to the existence of this program. Payments for flood-caused crop failures have been sufficiently significant to prompt the Federal Crop Insurance Corporation to exclude flood as a cause of loss covered by the general insurance program since 1982. Farmers may purchase flood insurance from the corporation, but they will pay higher premiums than they would under the general program.

Since its inception in 1948 and until 1984, the federal crop insurance program has paid a total of almost $18 million to farmers for flood-caused losses of soybean crops. Most of these losses were caused by Mississippi River flooding, as the following figures indicate. Of the more than $17 million paid to soybean farmers, the top three recipients were states that border the Mississippi River, and two of these are part of the lower basin: Iowa received 20.4 percent of the payments; Missouri, 14 percent; and Mississippi, 13.3 percent. An additional total of 22.7 percent of the payments went to the states of Louisiana, Illinois, Arkansas, and Minnesota, resulting in a total of 70.4 percent of federal insurance payments for flood-caused losses of soybean crops going to states along the Mississippi River.[16]

The Fragile Coastal Zone

Bottomland hardwood forests are not the only highly productive wetland types threatened by development in the lower Mississippi River basin. Louisiana's coastal wetlands are just as valuable, and they are being slowly swallowed by the sea.

Conversion of wetland to cropland is only one of the factors involved in the loss of natural habitats in Louisiana's coastal area. Near the ocean, nature is at her finest — and it is here that she is most vulnerable to the corps's attempts to alter her.

The marshes of southern Louisiana were formed by more than 5,000 years of sediment deposition around the active outlets of the Mississippi River. Existing vegetation trapped the sediments and clays deposited by spring floods. This process resulted in the accretion of nutrient-rich land. Under natural conditions, Louisiana's coastal area is constantly molded and reshaped by the river. Over geologic time, the Mississippi has occupied seven major courses leading to the ocean, building a new deltaic "lobe" or land mass at the end of each course. The river is now in the early stages of building an eighth lobe in the Atchafalaya Bay area. As a lobe is built, the river's channel lengthens and its gradient decreases. The river then begins to search for a shortcut to the Gulf of Mexico. Once a new channel is established, the old channel is abandoned, and the land the river built during formation of the old channel erodes and subsides into the ocean.

The Atchafalaya has been flirtatiously beckoning the Mississippi for more than 100 years, daring the mighty river to jump out of its channel and join the Atchafalaya in a matrimonial march to the sea. The Army Corps of Engineers was the matchmaker in this relationship, although, as happens in most strong attractions, the Mississippi may have tried to change course without outside help. In 1828, Henry Shreve, the corps's superintendent of western river improvements, dredged a cutoff through a large, horseshoe-shaped meander formed by the Mississippi at its confluence with the Atchafalaya. The cutoff caused an increase of the Mississippi's flow into the Atchafalaya, and ever since, the corps has been fighting to keep the river in its original channel.

There is a long list of reasons for keeping the Mississippi in its current channel. At the top of the list are the cities of New Orleans and Baton Rouge. Other reasons include B.F. Goodrich, Reynolds Metals, E. I. du Pont, Shell Oil, Mobil Oil, Union Carbide, Hydrocarbon Industries, Vulcan Materials, Nalco Chemical, Freeport Chemical, Dow Chemical, Allied Chemical, Stauffer Chemical, Hooker Chemical, Rubicon Chemical, American Petrofina, and other corporations that depend to some extent on their locations along the river.[17] These reasons call loud and clear for structural modifications of the Mississippi and the Atchafalaya that will allow some of the Mississippi's flows to depart down the Atchafalaya's channel while retaining most of the flows in their "proper" channel.

Similarly, reasons exist to protect the Atchafalaya River from sudden water fluctuations and the sterilization of habitat that often results from overzealous river control. These reasons include the barred owl, prothonotary warbler, anhinga, blue heron, pileated woodpecker, and other species that depend on healthy aquatic, riparian, and wetland habitats along the river.

The Army Corps of Engineers saw the Mississippi balking in her bridle, struggling to free herself and gallop down the Old River channel (a man-made channel connecting the Mississippi and Atchafalaya rivers), through the Atchafalaya River, and into the Gulf. Such a switch of channels would deprive the cities of Baton Rouge and New Orleans of a sufficient supply of fresh water.

To prevent this from occurring, in 1954 Congress authorized construction of a massive water project to prevent the Mississippi from changing courses. In 1963, construction of the Old River control structure was complete. The project consists of several structures. One of these is the Low-Sill control structure, made of reinforced concrete and consisting of eleven gate bays and inflow and outflow structures. The Low-Sill control structure determines exactly how much Mississippi River water is allowed to pass down the Old River channel. In conjunction with this feature, to provide better flow conditions in the overflow area, 4,500 acres of land adjacent to the inflow and outflow channels were cleared.

Other project features include an overbank control structure, consisting of seventy-three gate bays; a navigation lock that provides continuous navigation between the Atchafalaya River, the Ouachita and Black rivers, the Red River, and the Mississippi; a 16-mile-long levee; and bank stabilization structures. Because of scouring caused by high flows in 1973, $15 million was spent on rehabilitation of the Old River control structure. By 1981, the federal government had spent a total of nearly $2.4 billion to keep the Mississippi on course.[18]

Although the Mississippi Delta's dominant habitat type is bottomland hardwood forest, a wide array of communities exists. Among these are wooded swamps and freshwater marshes, intermediate marshes, and brackish and saline marshes. Wooded swamps are usually located inland from freshwater marsh areas and are dominated by bald cypress, tupelo, Drummond red maple, and buttonbrush. Herbaceous vegetation includes duckweed, alligator weed, and bulltongue. Intermediate marshes become more prevalent as the river approaches the ocean. Wire grass, deerpea, bulltongue, wild millet, bullwhip, and saw grass characterize this marsh type. Saline marshes are most common along the shorelines of the Gulf of Mexico and large bays. Oyster grass, glasswort, black rush, saltwort, and salt grass are the most abundant plant species in these areas.

Louisiana contains more than 40 percent of all coastal wetlands in the conterminous United States, and these wetlands support almost 70 percent of the wintering waterfowl that use the Mississippi flyway.

This figure includes more than 20 percent of the flyway's puddle ducks (or "jump ducks" — nondivers such as mallards, pintails, teals, and gadwalls), 70 percent of the coots, and 50 percent of the lesser snow geese. More than 90 percent of the Mississippi flyway's lesser scaup winter in Louisiana; most of these stay in the coastal zone. More than half of the continent's mottled ducks vacation there. The coastal wetlands of Louisiana provide breeding range for rails, upland game birds, wading birds, and shorebirds. These areas also harbor the largest concentration of bald eagles in the south-central United States.

One acre of these wetlands can produce 1,000 pounds of fish in a year. The nation's commercial fishing industry harvested 24 percent of its fish and shellfish from Louisiana's coastal wetlands in 1979.

The largest fur harvest in North America, and 40 to 60 percent of that in the United States, is taken annually in Louisiana's coastal wetlands. In the 1978–1979 trapping season, more than 3.2 million pelts, worth a total of over $24 million, were taken from these wetlands. In 1979, more than 16,000 alligators, worth about $1.7 million, were harvested.[19]

The marshes also act as storm buffers between the Gulf of Mexico and developed areas of the coastal zone, and they have the capacity to absorb water pollutants.

The Delta, however, is disappearing, and it is taking with it its valuable wildlife habitat. By damming, channelizing, and building levees on the Mississippi River, the Army Corps of Engineers has pushed the river's mouth, where it flows into the Gulf of Mexico, nearly to the edge of the continental shelf. Instead of depositing the fertile soil it has carried from midwestern farmlands into marshes, swamps, and floodplain forests, the river is forced to carry it to the Gulf and dump it off the continental shelf.[20] Robert Jantzen, former director of the Fish and Wildlife Service, testified before Congress as follows in 1981:

> Construction of dams on tributaries of the Mississippi River
> during the past 35 years has caused a significant reduction in the
> amounts of sediments coming down the river that could be used
> for marsh maintenance and building. Navigation projects, levees
> and upstream diversions and flood control reservoirs that have
> been constructed on the Mississippi River since 1927 have
> virtually eliminated overbank flooding, preventing nourishment of
> adjacent marshes with nutrients and riverborne sediments, and
> accelerating land losses.[21]

Losses of native riparian communities in Louisiana's coastal area are effected by several mechanisms. First, since the erosion process continues but eroded lands are not replaced by sediment deposition, open water tends to fill in where land and marshes once existed. This tendency is exacerbated by dredging of wetlands to form canals and harbors. Second, the corps and private landowners commonly deposit spoil materials in wetlands. Spoil banks in the region increased by more than 200 percent, and scrub communities established on old spoil areas increased by 100 percent, from 1956 through 1978. Third, the spoil banks and wetland drainage isolate the remaining wetlands from sources of sediment and nutrients.[22]

Exploration and exploitation of oil and gas reserves also affect coastal wetlands. Barges creep through canals cut into the soft and spongy wetland terrain; exploratory wells are sunk from the barges. In 1979, canals comprised about 1.4 percent of the area of the entire Louisiana coastal zone.[23] These canals impact wetlands by altering hydrology, sedimentation rates, and biological productivity. Once established, the canals do not stabilize. In fact, they widen as a result of wave action, boat traffic, and altered hydrologic patterns. An average canal cut through a wetland will double in width in 7 to 50 years.[24] Currently, 1 acre of Louisiana's coastal wetlands disappears every 14 minutes, adding up to 60 square miles per year. Since oil was discovered in the area in the 1930s, petroleum companies have dredged more than 10,000 miles of canals through Louisiana's coastal wetlands.

The cutting of canals through these delicate wetlands allows salt water to intrude on freshwater or intermediate marshlands. The salt gradually kills freshwater vegetation, and before more salt-tolerant plant species can revegetate the area, the vacant spaces become open-water zones. As the interface between marshes and open-water areas increases, the marsh areas erode more quickly. Wildlife productivity decreases as well, and valuable nursery grounds for fish and shellfish are decimated.[25]

Between 1945 and 1968, saline marshes moved inland an average of 2.1 miles and brackish marshes, 3.8 miles. The corps estimates that unless something is done to control saltwater intrusion in the coastal area, by the year 2035 the saline zone may reach inland 14 to 20 miles under drought conditions.

The Corps and 404 — Indirect Impacts of Water Policy

Dredging a canal through a wetland usually involves either placement of fill material into a wetland or sidecasting (throwing aside) of the dredged material. Placing dredged or fill material into a wetland

generally requires a permit from the Army Corps of Engineers under
Section 404 of the Clean Water Act of 1977. The corps, however, has
created a general permit that covers any wetland dredging activity
that the state of Louisiana finds consistent with the Louisiana
Coastal Zone Management Program.

The general permits are part of a regulatory reform program
devised in 1977 and revised during the Reagan administration to cut
the corps' paperwork load. These permits exempt a wide range of
activities from the scrutiny involved in processing an application for
an individual project permit. When the corps came up with a general
permit for Louisiana's coastal zone, it effectively transferred the
responsibility for regulating wetland ditch diggers to the state. Incidentally, the oil and gas industry generates a large proportion of
Louisiana's income. Louisiana ranks second among the states in
extraction of petroleum, natural gas, and natural gas liquids.

The Army Corps of Engineers does not believe that Section 404
was intended as a wetland protection mechanism. In fact, Robert
Dawson, former assistant secretary of the army for civil works,
illustrated his views on Section 404 in senate hearings on his
confirmation:

> One significant point to recall is that the Congress did not design
> Section 404 to be a wetland protection mechanism and it does not
> function well in that capacity.

Senator John H. Chafee, chairman of the Senate Committee on Environment and Public Works, responded as follows to this and similar
statements by Dawson:

> Well, I don't know who told you that, Mr. Dawson, but you ought
> to read the legislative history of the 1977 Clean Water Act
> amendments. You can start on page 644 of the Senate volume,
> which reads, and I quote to you, ". . . The unregulated destruction
> of these areas is a matter which needs to be corrected and which
> implementation of Section 404 has attempted to achieve."[26]

If Congress did indeed intend the Army Corps of Engineers to
"protect" wetlands under the Clean Water Act of 1977, one may
reasonably wonder why the draining of wetlands and other potentially devastating activities are not regulated by this law. The intent
of the act is to "maintain and restore the physical, chemical, and
biological integrity of waters of the United States," including wetlands. The purpose of Section 404 is unclear; for now, however, it is

virtually the only tool available on a federal level to protect these vital ecosystems.

The corps and the Environmental Protection Agency (EPA), which also has responsibilities under Section 404, share a definition of wetlands that established their sphere of responsibility under the Clean Water Act. Since 1977, that definition has read:

> The term "wetlands" means those areas that are inundated or saturated by surface or ground water at a frequency and duration sufficient to support, and that under normal circumstances do support, a prevalence of vegetation typically adapted for life in saturated soil conditions. Wetlands generally include swamps, marshes, bogs and similar areas.[27]

Although this definition solves the problem of corps jurisdiction on an administrative level, it is a useless tool if the corps's district offices ignore it in the field. Many districts apply the wetland definition more conservatively than do the Fish and Wildlife Service and the EPA, effectively excluding large wetland tracts from the protective wing of the regulatory program. The National Wildlife Federation has documented examples of cases in which this has happened.

In 1983, for example, Jimmy Winemiller purchased 24,600 acres of forested wetlands near the confluence of the Arkansas and White rivers with the Mississippi; some were adjacent to the White River National Wildlife Refuge. The Little Rock district of the corps determined that only 1,900 acres on two tracts totaling 6,460 acres were wetlands subject to Section 404 regulation. If the ratio of this determination were extended to all of Winemiller's holdings, only 7,235 acres of the 24,600 would fall within the jurisdiction of Section 404. The Vicksburg, Mississippi, office of the Fish and Wildlife Service maintains that most, if not all, of Winemiller's holdings are Section 404 wetlands. The Fish and Wildlife Service was excluded from the field excursion, led by Winemiller and a private consultant he hired, during which the corps's wetlands determination was made. The EPA did not become involved. By the spring of 1985, Winemiller had cleared nearly 3,000 acres of land without applying for a Section 404 permit and was continuing to clear more.

In another instance, the Chicago Mill and Lumber Corporation planned to clear as much as possible of its holdings of bottomland hardwood forest in order to put the land into agricultural production. The corporation requested the EPA to determine how much of its land was wetland and would require a permit under Section 404. The

Dallas office of the EPA asked the Vicksburg office of the Fish and Wildlife Service to assist in the determination process.

The Fish and Wildlife Service determined that 105,000 out of 110,000 acres of Chicago Mill and Lumber's holdings were forested wetlands subject to Section 404 jurisdiction. The service was quite thorough in making this determination. It used the methodology that it had jointly developed with the EPA and the corps; it employed forty-four transects to cover the full range of topographic variability; and it recorded observations on vegetation, soils, and hydrology for each transect. The service's findings were scientifically documented and completely replicable.

The EPA used the Fish and Wildlife Service's determination in its July 1, 1981, wetland determination for the company's land. In May 1983, however, the EPA discussed these findings with Chicago Mill and Lumber and with the corps. The EPA subsequently dropped its determination that almost all of the land was wetland and asked the corps to make the final call.

The corps determined that about 10 percent of the land was wetland, but as of 1985, it had not officially released a final determination. By the spring of 1985, 15,000 acres of these bottomland hardwoods had been cleared without an application for a Section 404 permit, and the clearing was continuing.[28]

Opposing viewpoints stemming from the different mandates of the three agencies often prevent efficient enforcement of Section 404. A panel composed of representatives from the Forest Service, the Fish and Wildlife Service, the Environmental Protection Agency, the National Marine Fisheries Service, and the Army Corps of Engineers convened in 1984 to study the loss of bottomland hardwood forest in the lower Mississippi valley and to identify the relationship of these losses to the Section 404 program. The panel agreed that approximately 9 million acres of bottomland forest existed in the river valley and that the current rate of forest-to-field conversion was about 100,000 acres per year. Agreement among the agencies then disintegrated. The Fish and Wildlife Service believed that 86 percent (or 7,740,000 acres) of the remaining forest is wetland subject to Section 404 regulation. The EPA called 68 percent (6,120,000 acres) of the forest Section 404 wetland, and the corps claimed it had responsibility for only 60 percent (5,400,000 acres) of the remaining forested lands under Section 404. The differences in these estimates resulted from the various field techniques used by the agencies to determine wetland areas.

An even greater discrepancy exists in agency opinions concerning how much of the clearing of the wetlands should be regulated under

Section 404. The Fish and Wildlife Service and the EPA maintain that all clearing of forests results in deposition of dredged material, composed of root wads and debris and therefore requires a Section 404 permit. According to the Fish and Wildlife Service, 86,000 acres per year should be evaluated by the corps, with subsequent issuance or denial of a Section 404 permit. According to the EPA, however, this figure should be 68,000 acres. The corps, on the other hand, feels that only a small portion of the clearing operations in the Mississippi alluvial valley constitutes a dredge and fill operation subject to Section 404 regulation. In short, the Fish and Wildlife Service believes that 86 percent of the annual conversion of forest to cropland should be scrutinized and regulated by the corps, but the corps ignores 95 percent of the clearing that goes on each year.[29]

Natural riparian habitats in the southern region of the United States are vanishing; we are rapidly losing many unique and irreplaceable combinations of plants and animals. The agency primarily responsible for maintaining these habitats is a manifestation of our society, a tool of our federal government. The people of the United States, by becoming aware, can halt and even reverse the unnecessary destruction of those communities.

NOTES

1. House Committee on Appropriations, Subcommittee on Energy and Water Development, *1985 Hearings on Energy and Water Development Appropriations for 1986*, 99th Cong., 1st sess., 1985, 1539.
2. J. McPhee, "The Control of Nature," *The New Yorker*, 29 February 1987, 39–100.
3. D. Shirbman, "House Votes Record Water Project Bill That Seeks New Tax on Cargo at Port," *The Wall Street Journal*, no. 14 (1985).
4. S. W. Gard, "Unmet Mitigation in the Lower Mississippi and Tributaries," in *The Mitigation Symposium: A National Workshop on Mitigating Losses of Fish and Wildlife Habitat* (Fort Collins, CO: Forest Service, 1979), 423.
5. R. K. Dawson, letter to James C. Miller III, director of the Office of Management and Budget, Washington, DC, 1 November 1985.
6. R. P. Lanctot, executive vice president of the Louisiana Wildlife Federation, personal communication, 1986.
7. J. T. B. Tripp, "Statement of the Environmental Defense Fund, Inc., on the Yazoo Area Pump Project," draft of testimony before the Senate Appropriations Committee, 1982.
8. Ibid.
9. S. W. Forsythe, *Draft Environmental Impact Statement, Yazoo Area Pump Project* (Vicksburg, MS: Army Corps of Engineers, 1985).
10. Fish and Wildlife Service, *The Yazoo Basin: An Environmental Overview* (Vicksburg, MS: Fish and Wildlife Service, Division of Ecological Services, 1979).
11. Army Corps of Engineers, *The Yazoo Area Pump Project Reevaluation Report: Vol 2 — Technical Report* (Vicksburg, MS: Army Corps of Engineers, 1982).

12. Fish and Wildlife Service, *The Yazoo Basin.*
13. P. Laurie, "The Vision of William Elliott," *South Carolina Wildlife* 32, no. 5 (1985): 41–45.
14. R. K. Yancey, "Our Vanishing Delta Hardwoods," *Louisiana Conservationist* (March–April 1970).
15. P. O. MacDonald, W. E. Frayer, and J. K. Clauser, *Documentation, Chronology and Future Projections of Bottomland Hardwood Loss in the Lower Mississippi Alluvial Plain* (Fish and Wildlife Service, Division of Ecological Services, 1979).
16. W. Grotman, of the federal crop insurance program, personal communication, 1985.
17. McPhee, "The Control of Nature."
18. Army Corps of Engineers, *Water Resources Development in Louisiana, 1981* (New Orleans, LA: Army Corps of Engineers, 1981).
19. House Committee on Merchant Marine and Fisheries, Subcommittee on Fisheries and Wildlife and the Environment, statement by R. A. Jantzen, director of the Fish and Wildlife Service, concerning wetland losses, 97th Cong., 1st sess., 1981.
20. S. Begley, "Setting the Mississippi Free," *Newsweek,* 20 September 1982.
21. House Committee on Merchant Marine and Fisheries, statement by R. A. Jantzen.
22. Ibid.
23. Bahr and Wascom, "Wetland Trends and Factors Influencing Wetland Use in the Area Affected by the Lower Mississippi River," unpublished report, n.d.
24. Ibid.
25. Army Corps of Engineers, *Louisiana Coastal Area, Louisiana Freshwater Diversion to Barataria and Breton Sound Basins Feasibility Study Draft Main Report, Draft Environmental Impact Statement* (New Orleans, LA: Army Corps of Engineers).
26. Senate Committee on Environment and Public Works, Subcommittee on Environmental Pollution, *Oversight Hearings on Administration of Section 404 of the Clean Water Act,* 97th Cong., 1st sess., 1985.
27. Clean Water Act of 1977 (33 CFR 323.2c and 40 CFR 230.3t).
28. Senate Committee on Environment and Public Works, Subcommittee on Environmental Pollution, *Oversight Hearings on Administration of Section 404 of the Clean Water Act,* statement by R. P. Davidson, J. Jackson, and C. E. Hunt of the National Wildlife Federation, 97th Cong., 1st sess., 1985.
29. J. E. Alcock et al., *Blue Ribbon Panel for Bottomland Hardwoods* (Washington, DC: Army Corps of Engineers, Office of the Assistant, 1984).

Southeastern Shipping Lanes

Throughout the United States, and particularly in the Southeast, rivers and riparian habitats have been transfigured to provide highways for barges. The operation and maintenance of these inland waterways have severe environmental repercussions for river-related ecosystems. Periodic dredging to maintain channel depth can alter the hydrologic connection between the river and the floodplain. Disposal of dredged materials often results in the burial of floodplain wetlands. The regulation of river flows to maintain navigable water depths can alter the timing and intensity of floodplain soil inundation so severely that native plant communities, such as cypress swamps, no longer regenerate. Development induced by the creation of navigable waterways frequently displaces some of the nation's last remaining riverine wildlands.

Many economists would argue that if a perfect market system existed, society as a whole would obtain optimum utility from existing resources simply by letting the market balance relative costs and benefits. Our market system in the United States is not perfect and self-regulating, however. Even if we were able to place appropriate price tags on all the goods, services, and amenities that can, in one form or another, be exchanged or transformed via market deliberations, we would find the scales still tipped because some goods are subsidized by the government. When the benefits of inland navigation projects are weighed against the value of existing ecosystems, the ecosystems lose out on both grounds. Their benefits are much more difficult to estimate monetarily, and the waterway projects are heavily subsidized.

Federal Funding of Wasteful Waterways

The Army Corps of Engineers operates and maintains more than 25,000 miles of inland waterways at the expense of the taxpayers. Despite new cost-sharing requirements established in 1986 for the construction of federal water projects, the private-sector beneficiaries of the inland waterway network do not share in the expense of operating and maintaining the waterways.

Compared with other modes of freight transportation, inland waterways are heavily subsidized. According to the Congressional Budget Office, in 1982 domestic inland waterway transportation received subsidies of 3.3 mills per ton-mile (a mill is one-thousandth of a cent; a ton-mile is 1 ton carried for 1 mile), compared with 1.4 mills received by the railroads, 1.3 mills received by trucking companies, and nothing received by pipeline operators. The Congressional Budget Office calculated that in 1982, federal subsidies covered more than 28 percent of all shipping costs for waterways, as compared with 4.2 percent for railroads and less than 1 percent for the trucking industry.[1] In 1983, more than 11 percent of the annual federal expenditures for operation and maintenance of inland waterways went to a series of waterways that collectively carried less than 1 percent of the nation's river-borne traffic.[2]

The Inland Waterways Trust Fund, established by the Inland Waterways Authorization Act of 1978 (see Chapter 7), was a first step toward preventing free-for-all use of federal funds for navigation projects of dubious long-term value. If the user fees that created the trust fund were used to partially fund the construction, operation, and maintenance of the waterways, as the Highway Trust Fund finances national roads, some of the politically motivated and environmentally unsound water projects might never pass the planning stage, and others would not be maintained unless their rates of return were up to snuff.

The omnibus water projects bills passed in 1986 by the Senate and the House both contained provisions for using the Inland Waterways Trust Fund to finance portions of new project construction. From 1978, when Congress created it, until 1986, no expenditures had been made from the trust fund, which in 1985 grossed $39 million in new receipts for a total of $197 million. As of 1987, all costs for operation and maintenance of inland waterways were still being paid by the Treasury. These costs average more than $350 million per year.

Some southern waterways carry so little commercial barge traffic that if the cost of maintaining them as navigation channels were borne by the private sector, they would close down. Examples of these are the Apalachicola-Chattahoochee-Flint, Red River, Alabama-Coosa, White River, and Tennessee-Tombigbee waterways.[3]

The Apalachicola-Chattahoochee-Flint Waterway

The Apalachicola-Chattahoochee-Flint (A-C-F) waterway is shaped like a wishbone. The Chattahoochee and Flint rivers converge at Jim Woodruff Dam, also the shared boundary of Alabama, Georgia, and Florida, to form the Apalachicola River. This river empties into Apalachicola Bay in the Gulf of Mexico, where 80 percent of Florida's oyster catch is produced, along with shrimp, blue crab, and other seafood. The tri-river system is maintained for navigation by the Army Corps of Engineers. In 1983, only 690,000 tons of traffic, less than one-tenth of one percent of the nation's total inland waterway traffic, moved on this waterway, and $5.67 million was spent to maintain it. This averages out to more than 70 mills per ton-mile. The national average cost for waterway operation and maintenance is about 1 mill per ton-mile.

From 1828 to 1831, the corps removed obstructions to navigation from the Apalachicola. Throughout the nineteenth century, the transition to deeper draft vessels and the desire for a more dependable channel to keep the region competitive with other areas of the nation's industrial and agricultural society put pressure on the corps for more intensive management.

In 1874, Congress authorized construction of the present-day A-C-F waterway. The project was modified periodically over the next few years to provide for a 1.6-foot-deep, 100-foot-wide channel on the Apalachicola; a 4-foot-deep, 100-foot-wide channel on the Chattahoochee; and a channel 3 feet deep at extreme low water and 100 feet wide on the Flint from the river's mouth to Albany, Georgia.

From the 1870s to the 1930s, the corps maintained the Apalachicola River mostly by snagging (removing dead trees) and limited dredging. The first training works, including dikes, groins, and sills, were constructed in Moccasin Slough in 1878, followed by additional work in 1900. In 1902, Congress added the Chipola cutoff and the lower Chipola River channel, which joins the Apalachicola in northwesten Florida, to the project. In the early twentieth century, the corps performed intensive snagging and dredging operations on the rivers.

In 1934, the level of maintenance dredging on the A-C-F shot up from about 35,811 cubic yards per year to 251,125. The Rivers and Harbors Act of 1944 authorized the 9-foot-deep by 100-foot-wide channel that now exists on the A-C-F system. Alteration of the waterway was gradually accelerating.

The corps initiated construction of Jim Woodruff Dam in 1947 and completed its work a decade later. The 9-foot-deep navigation channel on the Apalachicola was completed in the same year; the corps had dredged a total of 2,700,000 cubic yards of material from the river to construct it. Since 1958, the corps has annually removed an average of more than 1 million cubic yards of riverbed from the Apalachicola.[4]

Because rivers often change their minds about which turns to take, they migrate into bedrock and degrade their silty beds. These mindless meanderings may expose bedrock at a depth potentially hazardous to barges. In 1984, the corps blasted 112,817 cubic yards of rock out of the Apalachicola River to improve navigability.[5]

Barges have trouble maneuvering through the tight turns caused by wandering rivers. To assist navigation, the corps "eases" the bends by excavating banks to widen tight river sections. Two such easings have been accomplished on the A-C-F: the Lower Elbow on the Apalachicola River in 1957 and Suck Bend on the Chattahoochee in 1976.[6]

Although low traffic volume currently makes the Apalachicola an economically inefficient waterway, the corps believes that alteration of the natural river will lead to a dramatic increase in commerce. According to Brigadier General Forrest T. Gay III, division engineer for the corps's South Atlantic division in 1985, due to environmental concerns Florida withheld from the corps a state permit for the blasting of rock outcroppings from 1977 until 1982. During the same period, river traffic dropped from 1.1 million tons in 1977 to 875,000 tons in 1982. The navigation industry lobbied the state of Florida, and in June 1982, the state issued the necessary permit. The brigadier general stated that as a result, he expected "a dramatic upsurge in the use of this river system. I have already noted increased interest by shippers who had earlier written off this waterway as a viable artery of interstate commerce."[7] The year after the permitted rock blasting began, traffic on the Apalachicola decreased by 180,000 tons.

The Apalachicola's floodplain contains a variety of natural habitats. The predominant species on the narrow upper floodplain include water tupelo, Ogeechee tupelo, bald cypress, Carolina ash, swamp tupelo, sweet gum, and Overcup oak. The lower floodplain is characterized by coastal-plain pine flatlands, coastal dunes, and freshwater and brackish marshes. In dry to damp soils, associations of sweet gum, sugarberry, water oak, and loblolly pine are common. In the upper and middle regions of the basin, associations of water hickory, sweet gum, Overcup oak, green ash, and sugarberry prevail. Along waterways and abandoned waterways in the lower reaches of the river basin, the water tupelo, Ogeechee tupelo, and bald cypress association thrives. Pioneer associations are dominated by a thin strip of black willow in areas inundated by high flows more than 25 percent of the year. Marsh areas occur along the lower river. These ecosystems have been greatly diminished by the digging, damming, diking, and dynamiting operations of the corps.

The flooding that maintains the presence of riparian pioneer communities and marshes is also a major force for mobilizing organic matter and nutrients into Apalachicola Bay. Jim Woodruff Dam now traps almost all particulate matter from the waters of Chattahoochee and Flint rivers before they pass into the Apalachicola. As a result, the Apalachicola and Chipola rivers and their riparian ecosystems bear all the responsibility for supplying the bay with nutrients.[8]

Since the corps has been manipulating the A-C-F, ecological conditions have changed greatly. The massive amounts of dredged material pumped up from the river bottoms must land somewhere in the floodplain, and they often land in the valuable riparian and wetland communities bordering the rivers. According to a 1979 report by the Florida Game and Fresh Water Fish Commission,

> depositing dredged material on the forested floodplain caused the loss of most plants within the deposition area. The levee mixed hardwood plant community is the most valuable wildlife habitat in the floodplain and is receiving the greatest adverse impacts from disposal activities.[9]

The report described spoil deposits placed in sloughs or creeks that blocked or altered natural drainage patterns. Spoil deposited to a depth of 2 to 6 inches around the base of a tree decreases the vigor of the tree's growth. Deposition of 3 or more inches of silt or sand may seal the soil and smother the tree roots. The depth of deposition on the areas investigated was sufficient to kill virtually all of the trees within the spoil disposal area.

Attempts at establishing vegetation on spoil areas are common, but the creation of completely new habitats, such as on spoil deposits, has dangerous consequences. Exotic species of plants and animals are potential invaders of unnatural environments and can introduce parasites and diseases to which the native ecosystems have not developed an immunity. For example, several active mounds of fire ants were observed on an old spoil site. Exotic species often compete with or threaten native species as well.[10]

Such revegetated spoil areas may eventually provide plant diversity similar to that of the original habitat, but plant density is extremely low. Wildlife habitat on these sites is therefore inferior to natural habitat. Gray squirrels, otters, raccoons, opossums, beavers, wild turkeys, and deer are among the mammal species that suffer from this degradation.

Corps alterations on the A-C-F system have impacted in-stream as well as riparian habitats. Before Jim Woodruff Dam was built, the A-C-F supported a viable striped bass fishery. This is no longer so. The presence of dams on the Chattahoochee and Flint rivers, and dredging and spoil disposal along the upper Apalachicola have eliminated the striped bass spawning grounds from the system.[11]

Sandbars and spoil disposal areas are now common throughout the Apalachicola River; in the upper river, gently sloping natural bank habitat has been gradually eliminated over the past 30 years by dredging operations. Biologists project that because of such habitat alterations, the fish species composition will continue to shift from game species to rough and forage species.[12] (Rough species are species of low economic value that can survive in poor habitat.) The loss of natural habitat is also associated with the loss of the river's sturgeon fishery, which puttered out in 1970, when only five fish were taken.

The navigation industry, despite signals of environmental disturbance and a lack of traffic volume, wants to greatly increase the navigability of the A-C-F. In engineering studies undertaken in 1950, the corps decided that a flow of 9,300 cubic feet per second would be sufficient to provide the authorized project dimensions. In 1985, however, the corps was negotiating with the Fish and Wildlife Service and various state agencies to increase these flows to 13,000 cubic feet per second. Such a program would require huge fluctuations in upstream reservoirs, and according to a briefing package on the new navigation plan, "quantitatively, the extent of adverse environmental impacts on the upstream reservoirs would be much more extensive than the beneficial impacts on the Apalachicola River."[13]

The most dangerous proposal for the tri-river system is a 25-year permit that would allow the corps to dredge and perform related operation and maintenance activities. The corps applied for this permit from the Florida Department of Environmental Regulation in 1986. The department issued a 3-year permit instead, giving the corps a temporary "carte blanche" for dredging and snagging and possibly for other operations. The corps may reapply for a 25-year permit in the future. Environmentalists are upset over the issuance of any permit because several ecological studies on the A-C-F, including an analysis of the water flows necessary to maintain the productivity of the bay, have not been completed.

Dr. Robert J. Livingston, who has studied the ecology of Apalachicola Bay for more than 13 years, stands in steadfast opposition to a long-term permit. He holds Congress responsible for the advancement of an expensive operation and maintenance program that has destroyed two anadromous fisheries and threatens one of America's most productive estuaries. He also fears for the well-being of 73,000 acres of riparian wetland, recently purchased by the state of Florida and added to the Apalachicola River and Bay Estuarine Sanctuary. The aspect of A-C-F mismanagement that most infuriates this activist-biologist is that the taxpayers are forced to fund it.[14]

Audrie Eloson, secretary of the Chipola Bay Protective Group, also opposes the permit. Like Dr. Livingston, she feels that the ecology and economics of the bay and waterway should be thoroughly assessed before a permit is even considered. Her fears for the living rivers go beyond the impacts of operation and maintenance activities and extend to movements of the barges on the waterway, such as an overloaded oil barge that crashed and spilled on the Chattahoochee in March 1986. The corps closed down two dams to contain the spill. Other barges containing toxic chemicals frequent the A-C-F, loaded with potential doom for river communities. "What we really want," Eloson wistfully concluded, "is to get the corps off of the river."[15]

The Red River

The Red River, a Mississippi tributary, is another waterway that would shut down if subjected to a market test. This half-completed waterway moved 7.5 million tons of commerce in 1983 at an operation and maintenance cost exceeding 10 mills per ton-mile, more than ten times the average national expense. In the spring of 1984, construction on the system's first lock and dam was complete. In 1985, the river carried only 3.3 million tons of traffic, less than before the locks were opened for shipping. Most of the barges using the river carry rock to supply the river riprapping activities of the Army Corps of Engineers.[16]

Congress authorized the Red River Waterway Project in 1968, calling for a 9-foot-deep, 200-foot-wide channel extending from the mouth of the Red to Shreveport, Louisiana, and then through Twelvemile and Cypress bayous to a turning basin in Lake O' the Pines, Texas. This ambitious project was later scaled down to exclude the reach from Shreveport to Lake O' the Pines. A lack of funding creates a constant specter of potential doom for future stages of the project.

The stretch from the river's mouth to Shreveport involves the construction of five locks and dams. Work on the first lock and dam commenced in 1977 with a ground-breaking ceremony attended by the governor of Louisiana, virtually all of the Louisiana congressional delegation, and a few corps employees.

The banks of the Red River between its mouth and Shreveport are highly erodible. The river's alluvial floodplain developed from periodic overflows that occurred prior to the corps's installation of flood control improvements. When the river flooded, coarse, sandy sediments were deposited on the existing banks. This process led to the development of banks that slope downward from the river. Further from its channel, the river deposited finer soil particles; these formed swampy, semipermeable lowlands.

The Red River did many a dance through its floodplain before the corps "improved" it. The 80-mile-long Red River raft, a conglomeration of debris that formed a natural dam, stopped navigation on the river for 160 miles in the early 1800s.[17] The raft converted about a million acres of farmland into swamp. James Michener described an 1805 trip down the river as follows:

> The river itself, and the lands bordering it, was fascinating, a true
> frontier wilderness with just enough settlement scattered
> haphazardly to maintain interest. . . . [The boat approached the
> Red River raft and] when it seemed the boat would crash, it veered
> off to the left to enter a bewildering sequence of twists, turns,
> openings, and sudden vistas of most enchanting beauty. The boat
> was picking its way through a jungle fairy land stretching miles in
> every direction.[18]

The natural drainage patterns and claylike soils in low areas along the Red River made them more difficult to drain and till, and less productive than the higher, sandy loam of the natural levees.[19] Thanks to the corps, channelization of the river has made the flow faster, which has tended to dry up the river basin, prompting farmers to cut their woods and plant soybeans. To maintain and improve the river's navigability, more cropland-creating techniques will be applied.

Construction of the stretch to Shreveport, including channelization, bank revetment, and meander cutoffs, would result in the alteration or loss of more than 2,300 acres of bottomland hardwood forest and more than 15,000 acres of cottonwood, willow, and sycamore associations. An additional 6,680 acres of woodland would fall victim to induced clearing, the conversion of forests to fields on floodplain lands that federal projects have stabilized.

Cottonwood, willow, and sycamore woodlands are the dominant natural floodplain association in the Red River Valley, although by the mid-1970s agriculture had already replaced most woodlands. Early successional communities of sandbar and black willow generally precede and intermix with this river-front association. The plant density in the willow communities is relatively low. These areas are used by shorebirds (sandpipers and plovers, for example), waterfowl, aquatic furbearers, American woodcocks, and many species of reptiles and amphibians. The American alligator uses this habitat type extensively for lounging. The more mature river-front forests often include young box elder, hackberry, and other hardwood trees. The ground cover and understory are composed of poison ivy, pepper-vine, dewberry, grape, trumpet creeper, and Virginia creeper. This woodland type is used by white-tailed deer, raccoons, swamp rabbits, woodcocks, and numerous species of reptiles, amphibians, invertebrates, and birds. Beavers and wood ducks thrive in these forests, especially during high-water periods. Extension of the Red River Waterway Project would destroy as much as 20,742 acres of cottonwood, willow, and sycamore woodlands.[20]

The Fish and Wildlife Service found that construction of the stretch of waterway between the mouth of the Red River and Shreveport would change the region's aquatic habitats from riverine to lacustrine, or lakelike, and change the terrestrial habitats from forest types to open-land types. Terrestrial species such as gray squirrels, red foxes, wild turkeys, American woodcocks, and white-tailed deer would be replaced by eastern cottontails, mourning doves, and bobwhites, species that prefer open lands to forests. The baseline potential of 25,530 man-days of sport hunting for terrestrial species in the project area would drop to 16,813 by the year 2040 if the project is completed.[21] More important, habitat diversity, which is the key to ecological stability, would decline. Because the riparian lands along the Red River have already suffered massive agriculture conversion, those that remain are even more precious.

The project may never be completed as planned, however. When the Red River Waterway Project was first authorized in 1968, Congress anticipated spending $1.6 billion to make the Red navigable. The combination of the dubious value of a modern waterway in a river valley already serviced by railroads, the possibility of environmental problems, and a likely increase in the project's price tag led David Stockman, President Reagan's budget director, to put on ice the $93 million in project funds scheduled for the Red River waterway in 1981.

The project was rescued by two Louisiana democrats. Senator J. Bennett Johnston, who chaired the Energy and Water Subcommittee when the project was authorized, and Senator Russell Long talked to their colleagues, visited President Reagan, and managed to replace $50 million of the frozen funds.[22]

The second lock on the system, the John H. Overton Lock and Dam, was opened to navigation in November 1987, allowing commercial traffic to pass right up the Red to Alexandria, Louisiana, where that city is planning to construct a port to harbor it. The corps expects construction on the third structure, a lock and dam opposite Colfax, Louisiana, to commence in the spring of 1988. Whether this structure, or intended waterworks upstream, will ever be completed is in doubt, primarily due to tight Treasury strings. The corps anticipates heavy use of the waterway, whether it stretches to Shreveport or just to Alexandria, by farmers barging their soybeans to market.[23]

The Alabama-Coosa Waterway

The Coosa River is formed by the confluence of the Oostanaula and Etowah rivers near Rome, Georgia. It flows west for 110 miles and joins the Tallapoosa River to form the Alabama River about 18 miles north of Montgomery.

The Rivers and Harbors Act of 1946 authorized development of the Alabama and Coosa rivers for navigation. A restudy of the project released in 1977 concluded that the benefit-cost ratio, at the low interest rate of only 3-1/4 percent, was, at best, .46 to 1.[24] In 1983, the Alabama-Coosa waterway carried 2.61 million tons of commerce and cost taxpayers $3.62 million to maintain, resulting in an average expenditure of 20.69 mills per ton-mile, nearly twenty times the average national expenditure.

The corps would like to provide a 9-foot-deep, 150-foot-wide navigation channel from Montgomery to Gadsden, a distance of 192 miles. The Alabama River section of the project was completed in 1972. In 1983, the corps compiled a draft general design memorandum describing a plan to increase the availability of a 9-foot-deep navigation channel on the Alabama. Nearly three-quarters of the projected navigation benefits used to justify this project were attributed to future shipments of limestone and clay by the Ideal Cement Company, which had never used the waterway before. By 1985, Ideal's Alabama River plant had closed its doors. The corps is currently reevaluating its plans for expansion of this waterway.

The Fish and Wildlife Service anticipates that as much as 3,000 acres of valuable wildlife habitat would be destroyed by the development that would be induced by an intensified navigation program on these rivers. Associated with the loss of habitat are predictions for declines in animal populations, including a 48 percent decline in eastern cottontail populations, a 36 percent decline in the number of wild turkeys in the project area, and a 36 percent decline in

Mechanical dredging from the Alabama River. (Courtesy of Tom Thornhill)

populations of nongame wildlife such as indigo buntings, green herons, and redtailed hawks.

The service also predicted that

> industrial discharges, accidental spillage of potentially toxic materials, increases in municipal wastewater discharges, and urban runoff could cumulatively degrade water quality conditions to a point where fish populations could be severely suppressed, thereby reducing sport fishing opportunities.[25]

Three species of sturgeon, listed respectively as endangered, threatened, and species of special concern in Alabama, already may have disappeared from the Coosa River because dams have eliminated their free-flowing habitat.

The corps and the Fish and Wildlife Service are looking for sites on which to dispose of material dredged from the Alabama River in the course of maintaining the current channel. The corps has been depositing the dredged material in the river, in piles 30 to 40 feet high. These spoil piles often wash into the river, degrading aquatic ecology and necessitating more dredging.

Alternatives to within-bank disposal exist, but they have drawbacks. One alternative is the disposal of the dredged material in bottomland hardwood forests, essentially a sacrifice of important and already diminished wildlife habitat. Another alternative is the pumping of spoil material from the dredging site 4 or 5 miles upriver to cropland, pasture, and abandoned mine sites on private land. The corps would have to acquire the land in fee title or easement, and it has not found willing sellers. Until innocuous disposal sites are found, severe degradation of the Alabama River's natural resources will continue.[26]

The White River

The White River is a tributary of the Mississippi. Alteration of the White for navigation began in 1870, in conjunction with work on the Mississippi. Congress authorized construction of the existing channel, from Batesville, Arkansas, to the river's mouth, in 1892. Maintenance of the river for navigation was suspended from 1951 to 1961 because of a lack of traffic. The Rivers and Harbors Act of 1960 reactivated and enlarged the project.

In 1983, this waterway carried only half a million tons of commerce and cost $1.6 million to operate and maintain, for an average cost per ton-mile of 23.1 mills, about twenty times the national average. Yet the corps wants the waterway expanded, deepened, and widened. More than half of the anticipated benefits of intensified

Hydraulic pumping of dredged spoils on the Alabama River. (Courtesy of Tom Thornhill)

navigability on the White are attributed to the movements of petroleum products that do not currently travel on the waterway.

Since 1940, 58 percent of the riparian zone along the river, including 1.1 million acres of bottomland hardwood forest, has been cleared. Dredged spoil disposal areas have claimed at least 216 additional acres of wetlands.[27] Intensified management under the corps's plan would likely result in a significant loss of aquatic resources, including declines in commercial and recreational fisheries.[28]

The Tennessee-Tombigbee Waterway

The Tennessee-Tombigbee Waterway is a 234-mile-long canal (longer than the Panama Canal!) that connects the Tennessee and Tombigbee rivers in Alabama and Mississippi. The corps predicted that this aquatic highway, which cost nearly $2 billion to construct, would carry 27 million tons of commerce in 1985, its first year of operation. Instead, the Tenn-Tom carried only 1.7 tons, barely 6 percent of the corps's prediction.[29] The corps had predicted that soft coal from Kentucky would account for 70 percent of the total Tenn-Tom tonnage, but by 1980, the world soft coal market had crumbled. In 1985, the corps was estimating that coal would comprise only 54 percent of the traffic on the waterway. Coal traffic had picked up slightly by 1987, to 1.2 million tons, but the waterway is now being touted as primarily recreational.

In a report on the anticipated environmental impacts of this project, the Fish and Wildlife Service stated that

> the river corridor provides the most productive, least disturbed wildlife habitat . . . the large, unbroken expanses of bottomland hardwoods intermixed with oxbow lakes, streams, [and] abandoned and current agricultural lands provide ample food and cover for a variety of game and non-game species.[30]

The service predicted that 64 percent of the 105,000 acres of project area would suffer habitat losses; nearly 45,000 acres of bottomland hardwood forest would lose virtually all of their value as habitat for terrestrial species, and 22,500 acres would be degraded by spoil disposal and construction of recreational facilities. Deer, turkey, squirrel, and furbearer populations would all drop below half of their preproject levels, according to the service's estimates.

So long as the operation and maintenance of our inland waterways is financed entirely by the Treasury, the specter of long, deep, wide, and infrequently traveled waterways in corridors that once provided food and shelter to thriving fish and wildlife populations looms large before us. It is quite likely that simply removing or reducing operation and maintenance subsidies on the inland waterways would bring American society closer to a true balancing of the costs and benefits it incurs by keeping them in operation. If shippers had to pay the full costs of moving their goods, they would be encouraged to seek the most efficient mode of transportation. The total cost of shipping goods by waterway (including the average federal construction and operation and maintenance subsidy of 25 percent of the total cost) is not currently factored into shippers' decisions. An inland waterway system financed partially or entirely by users would promote more efficient use and maintenance of the system, conserve environmental resources of value to the general public, and eliminate unnecessary drains on the Treasury.

NOTES

1. Congressional Budget Office, *Charging for Federal Services* (Washington, DC: Government Printing Office, 1982).
2. C. E. Hunt, "Reducing Environmental and Economic Costs of Inland Waterway Operation and Maintenance." (Paper presented at the Annual Meeting of the Transportation Research Board, Chicago, IL, 23 July 1986).
3. Department of Transportation, Office of the Secretary of Transportation, *Inland Waterway User Taxes and Charges* (Washington, DC: Government Printing Office, 1982).
4. Florida Department of Environmental Regulation, *Apalachicola River Dredged Material Disposal Plan* (Tallahassee, FL: Florida Department of Environmental Regulation, 1984).
5. Ibid.
6. Ibid.
7. House Committee on Appropriations, Subcommittee on Energy and Water Development, *Hearings on Energy and Water Development Appropriations for 1985,* 98th Cong., 2d sess., 1984, 909.
8. R. J. Livingston, *The Ecology of the Apalachicola Bay System: An Estuarine Profile,* Fish and Wildlife Service publication OBS-82/05 (Washington, DC: Government Printing Office, 1984).
9. N. F. Eicholz, D. B. Bailey, and A. V. McGehee, *An Investigation of Dredged Material Disposal Sites on the Lower Apalachicola River* (Tallahassee, FL: Florida Game and Fresh Water Fish Commission, 1979).
10. Ibid.
11. Livingston, *Ecology of the Apalachicola Bay System.*
12. Ibid.
13. Army Corps of Engineers, *Briefing Package on the A-C-F Waterway Navigation Maintenance Plan* (Mobile, AL: Army Corps of Engineers, 1985).
14. R. J. Livingston, personal communication, 1986.
15. A. Eloson, personal communication, 1986.
16. Army Corps of Engineers, Tulsa District personnel, personal communication, 1987.
17. J. McPhee, "The Control of Nature," *The New Yorker,* 29 February 1987.

18. J. Michener, *Texas* (New York: Random House, 1985), 596.
19. Army Corps of Engineers, *Red River Waterway, Louisiana, Texas, Arkansas, Oklahoma; Mississippi River to Shreveport, Louisiana: Design Memorandum No. 2* (New Orleans, LA: Army Corps of Engineers, 1976).
20. Army Corps of Engineers, *Red River Waterway, Louisiana, Texas, Arkansas, Oklahoma; Mississippi River to Shreveport, Louisiana: General Reevaluation Report and EIS Draft Supplement No. 2* (New Orleans, LA: Army Corps of Engineers, 1982).
21. T. Hardaway and P. Yakupzak, *Red River Waterway Project, Mississippi River to Shreveport, Louisiana, Reach and Planning Aid Report* (Lafayette, LA: Fish and Wildlife Service, Division of Ecological Services, 1981).
22. H. Kurtz, "Congress' Budget Cutters Protect the Home Folks," *The Washington Post*, 15 January 1982.
23. Army Corps of Engineers, Vicksburg, Mississippi, personnel, personal communication, 1985.
24. Army Corps of Engineers, *Restudy on the Coosa River Navigation Project, Alabama-Georgia* (Mobile, AL: Army Corps of Engineers, 1977).
25. Fish and Wildlife Service, *Coosa River Navigation Project: Alabama; Fish and Wildlife Coordination Act Report* (Decatur, AL: Fish and Wildlife Service, Division of Ecological Services, 1982).
26. T. Thornhill, biologist for the Fish and Wildlife Service, personal communication, 1986.
27. Army Corps of Engineers, *Feasibility Report, White River Navigation to Batesville, Arkansas* (Memphis, TN: Army Corps of Engineers, 1979).
28. A. H. Hulsey, director of the Arkansas Game and Fish Commission, letter to Colonel Robert W. Lockridge, Jr., district engineer for the Memphis district of the Army Corps of Engineers, 4 April 1979.
29. W. E. Schmidt, "Tombigbee Use Falls Short of Forecasts," *The New York Times*, 16 February 1986.
30. Fish and Wildlife Service, *Fish and Wildlife Coordination Act Report, Tennessee-Tombigbee Waterway, Arkansas and Mississippi* (Decatur, IL: Fish and Wildlife Service, Division of Ecological Services, 1981).

10

The Growth of Small Hydroelectric Projects in the Rivers of the Northeast

Nature is composed of cycles of all sizes, from the wheels of our solar system to the turning of the seasons, so it is appropriate to end the discussion of federal impacts on riparian ecosystems where it started: with hydropower generation. This use of riverine resources is altering streams in the Northeast at a rapid, but rarely recognized, rate. Unlike the grandiose, federally financed dams of the Pacific Northwest, the northeastern dams are mostly small and privately constructed. The federal government's role lies in the licensing of the dams, a task accomplished by the Federal Energy Regulatory Commission, or FERC.

FERC, formerly named the Federal Power Commission, was born in 1920 when the Federal Water Power Act became law. Congress created the Federal Power Commission to oversee the development of national water resources and to market power produced by water projects. Before 1920, responsibility for licensing and marketing hydroelectric power had fallen almost randomly on the shoulders of the Department of War, the Department of the Interior, and the Department of Agriculture, a situation leading to inefficiency and confusion. The Federal Water Power Act indicated a congressional intent to promote a uniform plan for developing public water resources and to eliminate the divided jurisdiction over power development.

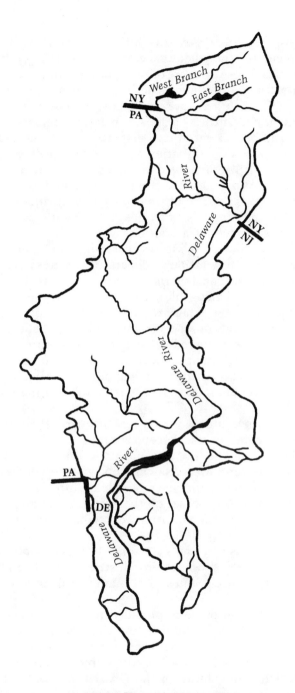

DELAWARE RIVER BASIN

Since 1920, the Federal Power Commission and its replacement, FERC, have regulated the wholesale energy sales of privately owned utility companies. These sales are of two types: requirement sales and coordination sales. Requirement sales occur when a private utility that has the ability to generate and transmit power (known as a "vertically integrated" utility) agrees to meet the demand of a publicly owned distribution enterprise that has little or no generation capacity of its own. A coordination sale involves two or more vertically integrated utilities involved in one agreement. Different regulatory standards are applied to requirement and coordination sales of various types. FERC is also responsible for approving rules and regulations under which power pools, or groups of energy-producers, operate and for approving intrapool transactions.

FERC has the authority to issue licenses for periods not exceeding 50 years to citizens, corporations, cooperatives, states, and municipalities authorizing the construction, operation, and maintenance of water power projects on navigable waterways, on streams over which Congress has jurisdiction, where the project affects interstate commerce, or on public lands or reservations of the United States. FERC can also issue licenses to nonfederal interests to use surplus water or water power from government-owned dams. FERC can issue preliminary permits for a 3-year period so that applicants will have priority for licenses after they complete surveys and studies of their proposed developments.

Water power drove much of this nation's early industry before electricity was in common use. Legend speaks of a brilliant Irishman named Matthew Lyon who, in 1783, moved to Fair Haven, Vermont, and built the first water-powered sawmill and gristmill. This epitome of American entrepreneurship then proceeded to hire the first teacher, erect the first meeting house, set up the first printing press, publish the first newspaper, and sponsor iron works and a paper mill in his community.[1]

Lowell, Massachusetts, and Paterson, New Jersey, followed suit and used falling water to power their industries. Lowell and Paterson became two of the United States' first manufacturing towns in the early 1800s.

Small hydroelectric projects provided most of the energy that made New England prosperous during the nineteenth and early twentieth centuries. Thomas Edison built the world's first electric generating station in Manhattan in 1882. Less than a month later, the world's first hydroelectric plant, built on the Fox River, generated enough power to light 250 light bulbs in Appleton, Wisconsin. In 1896, Westinghouse constructed the first major hydroelectric plant.[2]

Electrically powered industry followed the pioneer gristmills in New England towns, and soon the cool but fertile New England states were chock-full of woodworking, shoe, textile, furniture, and machine tool factories. As hydroelectric technology increased in sophistication, sturdy stone dams replaced the early wooden works. One stone dam, built in 1848 at Lawrence, Massachusetts, stands as strong as when it was first built. Dams of this ilk powered New England for about a century and a half, and by 1900, 57 percent of the energy used in the United States was generated by hydroelectric dams. Then came the fossil fuel glut of the mid-1900s.

The availability of cheap coal and oil during the first half of this century transformed the United States briefly into a hard-driven energy empire. The old hydroelectric dams were dismantled, their turbines removed and their penstocks, the pipes that carried water to the turbines, cemented shut. New England became the greatest fossil-fuel-burning region in the United States.

In 1920, coal accounted for 78 percent of American energy consumption and oil accounted for 14 percent. As the nation became increasingly industrialized, our dependence on oil, and on foreign oil imports, increased also. Following World War II, the airline industry blossomed, bringing oil use to a level equal to that of coal: 39 and 38 percent, respectively, of our energy consumption. In 1950, the United States extracted 1.97 billion barrels of domestic oil reserves and consumed 2.37 billion, leaving a 12.5 percent deficit, which was filled by foreign imports. In 1973, the year that marked the beginning of the 6-month Arabian oil embargo, the deficit in national production had climbed to 35 percent.[3]

Energy prices climbed in response to production quotas set by the Organization of Petroleum Exporting Countries (OPEC), and the New England states were hit hard. Residents began to look for less expensive and more reliable energy sources.

What they found was an old energy source — hydropower. Restoration of the old stone dams became a regional hobby. The stone dam at Lawrence was fitted with hydraulic turbines, which have since replaced the old waterwheels in many such structures. Hagley Museum in Delaware refurbished a turn-of-the-century hydropower plant on Brandywine Creek, which now supports almost all of the 500-kilowatt demand from a 180-acre building complex. Mill Dam on the Goose River in Maine was reactivated. This 6-foot-tall dam has a penstock that increases its head to 21 feet.

By December 31, 1975, 106 conventional hydropower plants were operating in New England under Federal Power Commission licenses and generating almost 1,200 megawatts.[4] In October 1976, Congress

passed the Water Resources Development Act, which authorized a
3-year national hydropower study. The Army Corps of Engineers
conducted this study for the Institute of Water Resources. The corps's
report, published in July 1977, indicated that more than 2,800 existing
dams built by the corps in New England had no hydropower facilities.
The New England River Basins Commission and several states also
surveyed potential hydropower sites, both undeveloped and at existing dams, in the mid-1970s. Surveys and preliminary screening by the
states indicated ten potential sites in Vermont, twenty-four in Massachusetts, and thirty-one in Maine.[5] Many of these sites became the
targets of preliminary applications as soon as the studies identified
them. By 1977, the federal government had made low-interest loans
worth a total of $10 million to private and public utilities to reacti-
vate existing dam sites. In spite of this small bit of fiscal encourage-
ment, small hydropower projects continued to be relatively unattrac-
tive to private developers because the high construction cost per
kilowatt of capacity of such projects increased the relative cost of the
energy they produced above that of the larger fossil fuel developments
sponsored by major utilities.[6]

The push for development of hydroelectric power gained substantial momentum during the Carter administration. Carter merged
several energy functions, including those of the Federal Power Commission, into the newly created Department of Energy. A 3-year
program of regulatory reform accompanied this reorganization. The
program included establishment of a simplified procedure for licensing projects designed to generate less than 1.5 kilowatts, an exemption
from the licensing requirements for small-conduit hydroelectric facilities, and a program of exemptions for projects designed to generate
less than 5 megawatts.[7]

The most significant impetus for hydropower development
sprang from the passage of the Public Utilities Regulatory Policies
Act (PURPA) in 1978. This act mandated local utilities to purchase
power generated by small projects at the "avoided cost" rate, the rate
of expense the utility would incur if it generated the energy itself.
This created a guaranteed market for electricity generated by small
hydropower plants.

In the wake of PURPA, license applications for small hydropower
projects soared. Between 1976 and 1979, FERC had received only 100
applications for permits, licenses, and exemptions. Between 1980 and
1983, however, the agency received 4,500 applications.[8] Congress
added to the encouraging effects of PURPA when it passed the Crude
Oil Windfall Profits Tax Act of 1981, which provided an 11 percent
investment tax credit for the construction of hydroelectric facilities

with capacities of less than 25 megawatts. This subsidy is in addition to the standard 10 percent investment tax credit. The total investment tax credit would be $4.2 million on completion of a $20 million plant.

America has traditionally viewed electricity generated by small hydropower projects as an innocuous form of energy because of what it doesn't do, such as create acid rain, color the sky brown, and irradiate people. But little dams have the same impacts on the environment as big dams, just on a smaller scale. To compensate for their compact impact, there are more of them, often concentrated in single river basins. The cumulative impacts produced by numerous small dams may degrade natural resource networks.

Since the site studies done in the 1970s indicated a wealth of old hydropower facilities that could be rehabilitated and a number of existing nongenerating dams where powerhouses and turbines could be installed, PURPA did not greatly worry the conservation community. PURPA states that the small power production facilities qualified for mandatory interconnection to utilities are those that produce electric energy solely by use of "biomass, waste, renewable resources, or any combination thereof." Neither the statute nor the regulations that FERC published to implement the statute defines "renewable resources," but the conference report that accompanied the legislation in 1978 stated that "the conferees intend that water be included within the meaning of the term renewable resources with respect to hydroelectric facilities *at existing dams*" (emphasis added).[9] Thus, conservationists did not anticipate the act's fertilizing effects on new construction.

FERC, however, interprets the report's language differently. In regulations promulgated by FERC in 1980, the agency stated that

> the Commission has reviewed the conference report and has determined that the conferees did not intend to restrict the term renewable resources to water use only at existing dams. Therefore, the Commission intends that the term renewable resources applies to water used at existing and new hydroelectric facilities of less than 80 megawatts.[10]

As the number of preliminary applications quickly surpassed the number of sites with existing dams qualified for hydroelectric development, the number of applications to build totally new facilities on free-flowing rivers increased. During the first 3 months of 1982, FERC received more than 300 applications for small hydropower projects. Almost half of these involved construction of new dams, and at least twenty involved rivers that the National Park Service had included in its 1982 nationwide rivers inventory.

The National Park Service's inventory identified approximately 61,700 miles of rivers in 1,524 segments that possessed sufficient natural or cultural attributes to qualify for inclusion in the national wild and scenic rivers system. In the Northeast, only two rivers, the Allagash in Maine and a section of the Delaware in New Jersey, are designated members of this system. Since the Wild and Scenic Rivers Act is the only federal law that specifically protects rivers, all other New England rivers were vulnerable to FERC hydropower licensing until 1986. One hundred and forty-four other New England river segments were identified by the Heritage Conservation and Recreation Service as candidates for national designation due to high scenic or recreational value.[11] These 144 segments were fair game for FERC licenses, along with river segments such as the East and West branches of the Penobscot in Maine and the Shepaug and Housatonic in Connecticut, whose status as national wild and scenic rivers has expired; all the rivers included only in state wild and scenic river segments; and all the rivers under study by the Forest Service for inclusion in the national wilderness system.

In October of 1986, Congress passed the Electric Consumer Protection Act. Among other provisions, this law demands that FERC give environmental concerns "equitable treatment" with the development purposes of the Federal Water Power Act.

The 1986 law also created two requirements for new small dams and diversions. The first was that licenses or exemptions for projects must include conditions to protect, mitigate damage to, and enhance fish and wildlife. FERC must determine that the project will not have a substantial adverse effect on the environment, including recreational value and water quality, and it must take into account the effects of the project alone and in combination with all other facilities on the same watercourse or relevant related waterway.

The second requirement is that FERC must determine that the project is not located on any segment of a waterway that is included in or designated by law for potential inclusion in a state or national wild and scenic river system or that the state has determined, under state law, to possess unique natural, recreational, cultural, or scenic attributes.

Impacts of Small Hydroelectric Dams

Since the undeveloped streams in New England are relatively narrow and because of the diminutive nature of small hydropower projects, the majority of the new dams are operated in a run-of-the-river mode. Many of these are diversion projects, projects that divert water from the natural stream channel into a pressurized pipe, or penstock, that runs downstream and descends vertically until it reaches the turbines. The head, or vertical elevation drop, in the penstock creates the pressure needed to turn the turbines and generate power before the water returns to the stream channel.

Permanent flow reductions often occur when the hydropower projects divert water from the main streambed. Even if the project's permit mandates that minimum in-stream flows be maintained, the environmental impacts on the stream segment between the intake and the return flow may be severe.

In-stream impacts of stream dewatering include shrinkage of the channel and decreased flow velocity of the water. The former may lead to the encroachment of riparian vegetation on aquatic habitats, such as fish spawning sites. The latter may cause the disappearance of aquatic species adapted for life in swiftly flowing streams.

For natural riparian communities, stream dewatering can mean the removal of drinking water for terrestrial wildlife, altered flow patterns and volumes that affect aquatic mammal populations, lowered floodplain water tables that cannot support the more drought-intolerant riparian species, and changed flood patterns that are incapable of supplying wetlands with recharge water and nutrients.

The extent of the impact of small hydropower projects on New England riparian ecosystems has not been comprehensively assessed. The damage amounts to the sum of impacts from individual projects. Some of these projects are clustered in river basins, leading to what are probably very significant impacts on the basins. FERC, though directed to adapt the plans for proposed projects to comprehensive plans for improving or developing a waterway,[12] is just beginning to consider the licensing of clusters of projects in a single river basin a major federal action subject to NEPA requirements. In 1985, FERC was initiating cumulative impact studies on several "clustered" basins, but only in western states. One of these basins was *not* the West Branch of the Penobscot in Maine.

Maine Rivers and the Plight of the Penobscot

The state of Maine is blessed with a complex geologic history that left as its legacy a uniquely sculpted landscape. Most of the state's bedrock formations were originally deposited on the bottom of the ocean during the early Paleozoic era, formed by the extrusion of

molten rock material from deep within the earth. During the Paleozoic, the Appalachian mountains burst forth from within the earth's
crust, creating intense pressures and temperatures that caused fold-
ing, faulting, uplifting, and volcanic activity. These restructuring
processes left durable igneous and metamorphic rock formations in
the mountainous Maine uplands and along parts of the Atlantic coast.
Following the Appalachian geologic revolution, an accumulation of
glacial snow and ice scoured the bedrock and sheared the tops off the
ridges and mountains. The ice began to melt about 10,000 years ago,
leaving a watery landscape of lakes, ponds, streams, rivers, and
wetlands.

A veneer of boulders, sand, gravel, and clay also remained in a
layer over the uplands, a memoir of the monstrous snowballs that had
scraped and gouged the state. As the meltwater streamed back from
the glaciers like the tail of a comet, it eroded a pathway to the Atlantic
through the bedrock. Occasionally, the meltwater would encounter
cliffs or jumps in the landscape over which it would leap in frantic
enthusiasm, creating waterfalls in its wake. As the force of the water
eroded the bedrock, many of the falls deteriorated into white-water
rapids. Some of the falls with sturdier bedrock beneath them remained, though they migrated upstream as erosion slowly scraped
away at them, leaving deep, tree-lined gorges downstream.

In the central and southern portions of the state, the glaciers left
behind interesting landscape formations, such as linear ridges,
braided streams with complexes of river islands, rivers with sinuous
meander complexes, and glacial outwash plains.

The legacy of these geologic occurrences is priceless. The state of
Maine is graced by tall waterfalls and steep gorges. These, when
harboring a river, create a shaded and highly humid atmosphere that
supports several rare plant species. Bedrock materials outcrop along
the banks of streams and rivers in the northern portion of the state,
serving as fossil museums that contain the "fingerprints" of marine
vascular plants and invertebrates from the early Paleozoic epoch.[13]

Present-day Maine contains a wide variety of northern streamside
habitat types. Along the West Branch of the Penobscot, in the hilly,
northern region of the state, the rich alluvial soils common to midwestern rivers are conspicuously lacking. The river instead lays down
a porous mixture of coarse sand and gravel with little capacity to hold
on to organic matter and nutrients. The West Branch of the Penobscot
passes through spruce-fir country, where red spruce and balsam fir
dominate the landscape to the river's edge. In the lowlands, cedar joins
the spruce-fir association. These magnificent conifer castles are broken by other forest types. Some ridges, for example, support hardwoods such as red maple, sugar maple, yellow birch, and white birch.

Red maple dominates around old river meanders that have become oxbow lakes and swamps. In regions where fire has disrupted climax communities, bigtooth aspen dominates until it is replaced by spruce and fir species that germinate and grow in the shade. At one time, white pine was also abundant in this portion of the state, but heavy harvesting removed most of the marketable timber, leaving only occasional saplings and tall snags that tower over the rest of the canopy.

The Maine forests surrounding the Penobscot's West Branch provide living quarters for a variety of wildlife species. In the lowlands, woodcocks and ruffed and spruce grouse are common. Night herons, blue herons, brown herons, black ducks, and mallards all use the river corridor almost exclusively in satisfying their needs. Weasels, ermines, martins, fishers, and skunks are common inhabitants of the riverside forests. Raptors such as great horned owls, barred owls, screech owls, kestrels, red-tailed hawks, ospreys, golden eagles, and bald eagles roost in the woodlands. More cosmopolitan species such as white-tailed deer, red squirrels, gray squirrels, and black bears frequent the forested floodplain, along with less common northern species such as moose and an occasional Canada lynx.

Development of Maine's rivers, as in other New England states, began early in the history of the United States. During the sixteenth and seventeenth centuries, the British were harvesting trees from the floodplain of the Kennebec (an Abnaki Indian term for "snaky monster") and Penobscot rivers to build ships' masts. The Americans followed suit and harvested timber from Maine's streamside communities for shipbuilding after the Revolutionary War.

In the early 1800s, the first waterwheels appeared along Maine's rivers. These were used at first to mill grain and saw lumber, but their uses quickly expanded into textile, tanning, and other industries. By the 1830s, dams had ruined runs of Atlantic salmon on the Androscoggin, the Penobscot, and the Kennebec and its tributaries. A spurt of growth in the paper industry, on top of the increasing use of hydropower for commercial, industrial, and household uses, sent the construction of dams skyrocketing. By the end of the nineteenth century, about 100 hydropower and water storage dams provided 20 percent of the electricity produced in Maine.[14]

In the 1900s, Maine's rivers faced a different problem. Factories and towns used the pristine streams as sewers; logging operations dumped bark and sawdust into them. By 1941, fumes from the polluted Androscoggin were strong enough to peel paint off houses in Lewiston and Auburn. In 1960, no salmon at all were caught on the lower Penobscot, though they had been common a century before. The waters of Maine were sullied. Something had to be done.

The state cleaned up the rivers in the 1970s with remarkable success. The Penobscot salmon fishery recovered. The rivers once more ran clean, and recreational demand increased rapidly throughout the decade. Private developers began to build marinas, restaurants, parks, and public boat launches along the river.

The 1973 oil embargo was painfully felt in Maine, which had depended heavily on oil during the second half of the twentieth century. A number of Maine's rivers became subject to hydropower development proposals during the 1970s, bringing power developers into a confrontation with river recreationists. In 1981, hydropower developers announced their intention to reconstruct a breached dam on the Penobscot River. The proposal triggered vociferous opposition from the river recreationists.[15]

Joseph Brennan, Maine's governor, was forced to react. He issued the Maine Energy Policy, encouraging the development of hydroelectric power to combat the energy crisis. During the same year, Brennan ordered Maine fishery agencies to develop a fishery management plan and the Maine Department of Conservation to identify river stretches with outstanding natural and recreational values and to propose a strategy for protecting these values. In 1982, the Maine Department of Conservation turned out the Maine Rivers Study.

Production of this study involved a wide variety of groups, including the National Park Service, the Fish and Wildlife Service, the Appalachian Mountain Club, the Maine Audubon Society, and various other state and private organizations. The study identified 4,204 miles of rivers and river segments that possessed significant natural and recreational resource values, out of a total of 31,806 miles of permanently flowing rivers and streams in the state. Study participants classified the outstanding rivers into four groups. Rivers and riparian corridors in category A possessed a composite natural and recreational resource value with significance that extended beyond the borders of the state. Rivers and corridors in the B category had characteristics of outstanding statewide significance. Rivers on the C list were significant statewide, but not outstanding; D list rivers had only a regional significance. A total of 1,663.5 miles made it to the A list; among these were the East and West branches of the Penobscot and the Penobscot's main stem.

Pursuant to the inventory, in July 1982, Governor Brennan designated 1,100 miles of sixteen rivers as eligible for special protection. These segments received legislative protection in 1983, when Maine's legislature authorized the Maine Rivers Act. This act prohibited dam construction on 1,100 river miles unless the legislature specifically authorized the structure. The West Branch of the Penobscot was not on the list of protected rivers.

The West Branch of the Penobscot is only one of Maine's magnificent rivers, but it is a blue-ribbon example of the natural values that are under seige in the state of Maine. The West Branch has been recognized for its outstanding natural values by many organizations. The entire Penobscot, including both the East and West branches, was one of the original twenty-seven rivers in the United States designated for study under the federal Wild and Scenic Rivers Act of 1968. The study of the Penobscot, concluded in 1976, found that a unique landlocked salmon fishery, an outstanding array of wildlife, excellent water quality, and outstanding scenery were among the qualities that made the river eligible for inclusion in the wild and scenic rivers program. The river was never included.

The National Park Service's nationwide rivers inventory, published in 1982, stated that a 21-mile stretch of the West Branch possessed "outstandingly remarkable" scenic values. A study of the national natural landmarks conducted by independent researchers under contract by the National Park Service found that the 16.5-mile stretch of the Penobscot between Ripogenus Dam and Debsconeag Falls qualified for designation as a national natural landmark because it contained the widest variety of diverse geologic, geomorphic, hydrologic, and scenic features to be found anywhere in the state of Maine.

All this glory is attributed to the 110-mile-long West Branch, where dams and reservoirs have already swallowed about 50 miles of the river. Of the nineteen dams that existed on the West Branch in 1985, eighteen belonged to the Great Northern Nekoosa Corporation of Stamford, Connecticut. Great Northern had a license application, already conditionally approved by the state of Maine, pending before FERC in 1985.

The project that Great Northern proposed to build was in Piscataquis County. The existing river in the project area is narrow and fast-moving, a joy for white-water rafters. If dammed, this river reach would be transformed into a flat, wide lake. The proposed dam would have stood 148 feet high, stretched to a length of 2,300 feet, and measured 440 feet wide at the widest section. The reservoir would have backed up the river 4.5 miles, inundating 857 acres of riparian forest. Below the dam, the river's flow would have narrowed to that of a small stream. Above the dam, under the surface of the reservoir, a curious scuba diver would have found the remains of three series of rapids, lying like a sunken schooner. Because the dam would have been constructed 1,000 feet downstream from the base of the Big Ambrjackmockamus Falls, it was known as "Big A."

Like termites in a graceful old New Hampshire home, low-head hydropower projects in New England slowly eat away at riparian habitat and other river resources. On the Penobscot's little West Branch, almost half of the natural stream has already been given away by the federal government without so much as an environmental impact statement. As Chris Brown, former conservation director of the American Rivers Conservation Council, stated, "We repeatedly hear from developers that it is just one short stretch of free-flowing river that they want: 2 miles here, 3 miles there, 4.5 miles now on the Penobscot. But such takings are often actually incremental steps in the progressive destruction of a free-flowing river."[16]

In January of 1986, the State of Maine denied Great Northern the water quality certification necessary for construction of Big A. As March winds and spring rains found proponents of the dam devising strategies around this monumental setback, Great Northern suddenly withdrew its FERC application. For the time being, the Penobscot's right arm is safe.

The Upper Delaware's Fight for Flows

The state of New York's Department of Environmental Conservation has been doggedly trying to guard the flows necessary to sustain the fisheries on the Delaware River.

The Delaware River basin spans five physiographic provinces, ranging in topography from mountains to hills to gentle coastal plains, and it drains about 12,750 square miles of land. Of these miles, 3,423 comprise the upper basin. Congress included a 73-mile portion of the Delaware River that passes through the upper basin as a recreational and scenic portion of the wild and scenic rivers system in 1978. The lower Delaware River basin, below Port Jervis, New York, is heavily populated and industrialized.

The valley floor in the upper Delaware valley is dotted with towns, farms, and forests. Woodlands along the river do not significantly differ in floristic composition from those on basin uplands, but they provide essential wildlife habitat.

Trees common on the floodplain include oak, hemlock, beech, birch, and fir. Mountain laurel sweetly scents the summer air near the river. White-tailed deer, black bears, foxes, rabbits, snowshoe hares, raccoons, opossums, woodchucks, muskrats, minks, and beavers use the upper Delaware's riparian habitat. The upper Delaware provides important wintering ground for bald eagles and ospreys; the survival of these birds depends on riparian trees for roosting and hunting perches and on the aquatic environment for forage fish.

The entire upper Delaware River basin system sustains magnificent fishery resources. On the Delaware's East Branch, brown and

The upper Delaware provides important wintering grounds for bald eagles and osprey. The survival of these birds depends on both riparian trees for roosting and hunting perches and the aquatic environment for forage fish. (Sketch by author)

brook trout are plentiful. Fishermen also pursue these two species, along with rainbow trout, on the West Branch. A warm-water fishery composed of black bass, muskellunge, and sunfish exists from Callicoon to Port Jervis. Walleye populate the entire main stem of the Delaware, and an anadromous American shad run also exists on the river.

The fisheries resources are a long-standing concern of the New York Department of Environmental Conservation. The threat to the fish began in the 1930s when New York City began construction of three reservoirs in the Delaware River basin: Pepacton Reservoir on the East Branch of the Delaware, Cannonsville Reservoir on the West Branch, and Neversink Reservoir on the Neversink River. Agreements between the state of New York and New York City established minimum flow releases from the reservoirs, but the required flows were inadequate to preserve fishing and boating opportunities on the river over a long time period. New York City decided which reservoirs to use to meet the flow requirements with little or no consideration of environmental impacts. Erratic releases from Cannonsville Reservoir in the late 1960s, for example, eliminated the existing warm-water

fishery and periodically made the West Branch of the Delaware un-
fishable and unboatable.[17]

In response to declining environmental conditions, the New York
Department of Environmental Conservation established a team to
determine adequate reservoir release levels for the streams below the
New York City reservoirs. The team issued its findings in 1974. In
1975, the department and the state attorney general's office began
negotiations with New York City so that the flows identified by the
study could be implemented on an experimental basis. The negotiations dead-ended because the city feared that establishing higher
conservation flows would lead to difficulties in appropriating water
for municipal uses during low flow years.

To break the impasse, New York's state legislature passed the
Reservoir Release Law in 1976, giving the New York Department of
Environmental Conservation authority to regulate releases from storage reservoirs in the southeastern portion of the state. The law also
stated, however, that there shall be no impairment of an adequate
water supply for any municipality using the reservoir water for
drinking and other purposes and for power production.

The concurrence of the congressionally established Delaware
River Basin Commission was needed for the New York Department of
Environmental Conservation to establish a permanent conservation
release program. The commission was initially reluctant to adopt a
permanent program based on the department's findings. Instead, the
involved parties embarked on a 3-year experimental release program.
When this program concluded, the data collected indicated that modifications were needed in the flows initially recommended by the
department if it was to accomplish its fisheries conservation goals.
The state and city of New York entered into a new reservoir release
agreement in 1981, but this agreement specified releases based on the
original experimental program, not on the new findings indicating the
need for program modifications.[18] The present reservoir release program would therefore be inadequate to prevent devastating dewater-
ings and flow fluctuations, which could decimate the Delaware River
fisheries.

A Conservation Role for FERC?

Recent plans by New York City to develop hydroelectric facilities
ironically provide an opportunity to correct the shortcomings of the
reservoir release program. New York City must apply for a FERC
license before it may construct hydroelectric facilities. The city has

proposed new hydropower projects for the West Branch Delaware Aqueduct and other outlet works at the three city reservoirs. The state of New York and the National Park Service, which is authorized to manage the Delaware River's recreational and scenic stretch, have requested that FERC refuse to issue exemptions or licenses for these hydropower projects until a cumulative impact assessment is completed regarding the effects of such projects on the upper Delaware River basin.

Although the state of New York seems to be primarily interested in using the FERC licensing process to improve recreational resources on the Delaware River, the National Park Service wants documentation of the entire flow regime in order to obtain a holistic picture of the ecology of the Delaware River corridor and the stream flows necessary to maintain it. The National Park Service is one of a few groups currently examining the ecology of the Delaware River and its riparian communities. The Nature Conservancy recently completed a study on rare plants in the area, and the National Park Service is working with the Forest Service on a long-range study of the carrying capacities of the river's riparian communities and the limits of acceptable change. The National Park Service is also involved in a study of the river's macroinvertebrates (those benthic species large enough to be seen with the naked eye). The service would like to see any cumulative impacts study mandated by FERC fill in missing data gaps in FERC's complex picture of the river's ecology.[19]

FERC has yet to complete an assessment of the cumulative impacts of the projects it has licensed on the ecology of a river basin. The Federal Water Power Act of 1920, however, directs FERC to license only such projects as are "best adapted to a comprehensive plan for improving or developing a waterway or waterways."[20] The legislative history of this provision indicates that Congress intended FERC to develop actual river basin plans against which to judge hydropower licenses.[21]

It was not until December 1984 that FERC attempted to fulfill this responsibility. In that month, FERC's Office of Hydropower Licensing issued a directive to FERC staff describing a cluster impact assessment procedure (CIAP) to be used to "identify basins where there is a potential for adverse environmental impacts from clustered hydropower projects; determine the geographic extent of these adverse impacts (cluster size); determine the interaction of target resources and proposed and existing hydropower projects; perform an impact assessment of the clustered projects; and finally, prepare the appropriate National Environmental Policy Act (NEPA) documents."

The CIAP consists of several phases: a geographic sort to identify the boundaries of the study; a resource sort to identify the proposed hydropower developments that may adversely affect target resources; a multiple-project assessment that weighs impacts using a computer-assisted matrix analysis; and the preparation of NEPA documents.

FERC published proposed rules for implementation of the CIAP in January 1985 and received critical comments from a number of concerned agencies and organizations. Among the most significant comments were that the proposed CIAP failed to consider the ecological integrity of a river basin because it would consider only pending applications and not existing projects, exempted projects, or projects for which only preliminary applications had been filed. The CIAP falls short of comprehensive resource management because it defines clusters in terms of geographic proximity rather than by the cumulative impacts of multiple dams existing in one basin but not situated close enough together to be considered part of a cluster. The danger posed by such an approach lies in double jeopardies being posed to a resource, such as a salmon stock or a deer herd, when different parts of its life history are adversely affected by dams many miles apart. A third major shortfall of the CIAP is FERC's refusal to gather baseline data on the biological and related resources of the basin.[22] FERC completed the first CIAP studies on the Snohomish River basin in Washington, the Salmon River basin in Idaho, and the Owens River basin in California in 1986. A thorough critique of their findings may tighten the loopholes in the assessment process, but tight funding may continue to limit the agency's ability to comprehensively address cumulative impacts.

FERC complains of the time and funding restraints limiting its ability to collect baseline data and assess river basin impacts in a more comprehensive manner than that outlined in the CIAP. The agency may find it necessary to engage the assistance of state and federal resource management agencies in developing plans that address impacts to terrestrial and aquatic resources. An impact assessment that ignores even one harmonic strand of basin ecology will do little to conserve the symphony of the river.

In initiating studies of cumulative impacts, FERC is on the road to balancing the actual energy demand in the United States with environmental concerns. The CIAP should be modified in order to present a more accurate picture of the ecology of a river basin and the extent of the hydropower impacts likely to alter that ecology. Priority in licensing new projects should be given to those that are most environmentally benign. The last decade has taken a toll on free-flowing rivers and the riparian ecosystems that surround them. FERC has a substantial potential to conserve the remaining natural river resources and the mandate to do so.

Society can no longer afford to view hydropower as a cheap and benign energy source. America is in an energy glut, so the nation has an opportunity to develop and implement studies on the impacts of hydropower generation. Such studies, if they are to effectively help conserve riverine and riparian resources, must view river basins as webs woven of water, land, and life, with each strand indispensible.

NOTES

1. Lilenthal, "Lost Megawatts Flow Over the Nation's Myriad Spillways," *Smithsonian* 8, no. 6 (1977): 83–89.
2. T. Palmer, *Endangered Rivers and the Conservation Movement.* (Berkeley and Los Angeles, CA: University of California Press, 1986).
3. T. Szulc, *The Energy Crisis* (New York: Franklin Watts, 1974).
4. New England Federal Regional Council, *A Report on New England Hydroelectric Development Potential* (New England Federal Regional Council, 1976).
5. J. D. Lawrence, "Hydropower Studies in New England," in *Hydropower: A National Energy Resource* (Washington, DC: Government Printing Office, 1979).
6. R. A. Jones, "Small Hydro Projects Create Flood of Worries," *Los Angeles Times*, 6 April 1982.
7. Senate Committee on Energy and Natural Resources, Subcommittee on Energy Regulation and Subcommittee on Water and Power, *Hearings on Licensing of Hydroelectric Projects*, testimony by Georgiana H. Sheldon, vice chairman of the Federal Energy Regulatory Commission, 97th Cong., 2d sess., 1982.
8. C. N. Brown, "Statement of Christopher N. Brown, Conservation Director, American Rivers Conservation Council, before the Land Use Regulation Commission: May 5, 1985" (unpublished testimony prepared by the American Rivers Conservation Council, Washington, DC).
9. House Committee on Energy and Commerce, Subcommittee on Energy Conservation and Power, *Hearings on Licensing of Hydroelectric Projects*, statement on H. R. 6800 by Edward R. Osann, coordinator of the Coalition for Water Project Review, 97th Cong., 2d sess., 1982, 11.
10. 45 F. R. 17966 (20 March 1980).
11. New England River Basin Commission, *Water, Watts and Wilds: Hydropower and Competing Uses in New England. Final Report of the New England River Basin Commission's Hydropower Expansion Study* (New England River Basin Commission, 1981).
12. Federal Water Power Act of 1920 (16 U.S.C.A., sec. 803a).
13. State of Maine, Department of Conservation, *Maine Rivers Study: Final Report* (Augusta, ME: Maine Department of Conservation, 1982).
14. M. Sullivan and R. A. Griffen, "The Maine Rivers Policy," in *Proceedings of the Symposium on Small Hydropower and Fisheries* (Bethesda, MD: American Fisheries Society, 1985), 315–20.
15. Ibid.
16. Brown, "Statement before the Land Use Regulation Commission."
17. J. D. Sheppard, *New York Reservoir Release Monitoring and Evaluation Program — Delaware River — Summary Report* (Albany, NY: New York Department of Environmental Conservation, 1983).

18. J. D. Sheppard, *Synopsis of the Natural Resource Concerns with the Delaware Reservoir Releases Program* (Albany, NY: New York Department of Environmental Conservation, 1985).
19. J. T. Hutzky, personal communication, 1985.
20. Federal Water Power Act of 1920 (16 U.S.C.A., sec. 803a).
21. T. L. Thatcher, counsel for the National Wildlife Federation, letter to Kenneth F. Plumb, secretary of FERC, 26 February 1985.
22. T. L. Thatcher, counsel for the National Wildlife Federation, personal communication, 1985.

11

Creating a New Era

The way that America views rivers and streams is changing. Through the science of ecology, we have learned the importance of wetlands and riparian corridors. Through experience, we have learned how structural approaches geared toward controlling these ecosystems can destroy them. As modern life becomes increasingly stressful and sterile, people turn to natural beauty for relaxation and comfort. Rivers are well suited to this purpose because they are aesthetically interesting, biologically rich, and acoustically soothing. A small bit of land or easement acquisition can place a large piece of river corridor in the hands of the public for recreational pleasure. More utilitarian purposes, such as the construction of homes, are ill suited for floodplains anyway.

The changes in the perspective of American society toward rivers is reflected in recent federal legislation and the fates of some unsound water projects. In the past few years, legislation has toughened non-federal cost sharing for projects constructed by the Army Corps of Engineers, called for consideration of fish and wildlife in projects licensed by FERC, demanded mitigation for impacts to natural resources inflicted by power plant construction in the Columbia River basin, and forbidden most federal subsidies to construction on the floodplain of the lower Colorado River. Unsound water projects, such as Cliff Dam on the Colorado, the Narrows Project on the South Platte, and the Big A hydropower project on the West Branch of the Penobscot, have been shelved for the time being. A steadily growing constituency of environmentally minded Americans is demanding careful evaluation of individual and cumulative environmental impacts, as well as economics, in the use of our natural resources. The analysis and planning necessary to maintain the renewability of our natural resources in times of burgeoning population, intense economic competition, and conflicting and overlapping political jurisdictions require the cooperation of people and governments at all levels. The conservation of riparian communities must be accomplished in three conceptual phases: a halt to destruction of riparian ecosystems, a reversal of national policy to one of conservation, and a restoration of the most valuable resources.

Saving the Remaining Riparian Habitat

In order to conserve the riparian ecosystems that still adorn the nation's streams, all levels of government must provide resources and cooperation.

The Federal Level

The federal government often has more resources and more authority to halt riparian destruction than do state or local governments. The federal government also has more to gain (reduction of the national deficit by eliminating wasteful expenditures) and less to lose (no direct stake in property taxes; financial health dependent on the economy of the nation as a whole rather than just one state) than do state or local governments. Intervention by the federal government in matters of land management may be resented by the lower levels of government, however. The current political trend in the United States seems to be toward minimizing federal regulation and ownership of land.

Regulation   Much of the federal government's regulatory authority over riparian zones is exercised in accordance with the Federal Emergency Management Agency's (FEMA's) flood insurance program and Section 404 of the Clean Water Act of 1977 (this program does not regulate floodplains unless they contain wetlands). Both programs frequently restrict development in riparian zones. Congress designed both of these programs to protect the public interest: the former to reduce national flood losses and the latter to maintain and restore the physical, chemical, and biological integrity of the nation's waters. Regulation of riparian zones can serve well as a method of rendering economic development more compatible with an area's natural ecology, but it seems to be a poor method of keeping development out of floodplains altogether. Thus, despite large tax-dollar expenditures on regulatory programs, development continues to creep onto flood-prone lands, bisecting and isolating wildlife habitats and placing human dwellings in the danger zone. With few exceptions, today's prevention of a development project in a riparian strip by a federal regulatory program provides no guarantee that the area will remain free from this type of encroachment in the future.

Acquisition   Federal acquisition of riparian zones is often more economically feasible than continued subsidized development. For example, it would make more economic sense for the federal government to buy all the land in Arizona's Wellton-Mohawk Irrigation District than to continue irrigating its salty soils. It would make more economic sense for FEMA to buy the 2 percent of the land in the United States that repeatedly floods than to continue disbursing disaster payments to those areas.

The federal government has several programs that enable it to purchase riparian corridors. One major source of funding is the Land and Water Conservation Fund, which provides matching grants to the states to achieve their goals for outdoor recreation and provides money for federal agencies to acquire land. The program garners its funds from a tax on oil and gas extraction. Between 1965 and 1987, the program provided the federal government with $3.6 billion and the states with $3.1 billion. Congress increased the amount to be added to the fund to $900 million per year in 1977. In 1978, total distributions peaked at $804 million, and distribution to the states peaked a year later, at $370 million. The Reagan administration precipitated a decline in distribution of the funds.[1] The report of the President's Commission on Americans Outdoors, released in 1987, recommended that this program, currently subject to annual congressional appropriations, be given the status of an endowment, much like the National Endowment for the Arts. The report also recommended an increase of $1 billion per year in the amount to be added to the fund through taxes on real estate transfers and the issuance of conservation bonds.[2]

The Duck Stamp Act of 1934 provides the federal government with funds earmarked for the purchase of waterfowl habitat, which includes riparian wetlands. These funds are acquired through the sales of duck stamps to hunters and nonhunting conservationists.

FEMA also operates a land acquisition program. If a property already insured by FEMA is severely damaged by floods (damage exceeding 50 percent of the property value in 1 year or exceeding 25 percent of the value in 3 out of 5 years), and if the community containing that property agrees to manage the property as open space, FEMA may acquire the land. FEMA began to purchase property under this program in 1980. By 1987, the agency had acquired 1,000 properties in sixty communities, for a total expenditure of $37 million.

Three conditions increase the probability for success of a FEMA land purchase. First, it is optimal for the agencies to acquire about fifteen contiguous properties. This reduces fragmentation of habitats and allows for the creation of a more substantial open-space area. Second, the time lapse between the flood and acquisition of the property should be minimized to keep costs low. Third, cost sharing cuts the costs to the federal government and gives the community a stake in maintaining the property.[3]

Funds for federal land acquisition have nearly trickled dry in the past few years. The problems with federal land acquisition as a method of protecting riparian habitat include opposition from local landowners and lack of funding. The benefits of such acquisition include complete control of the property for management purposes by the purchasing agency and a guarantee that the land will remain open virtually in perpetuity.

Elimination of Harmful Subsidies   If federal acquisition of flood-plain land is at present politically unpalatable, perhaps a beginning can be made by simply eliminating federal subsidies for floodplain development and other economically unsound river-related activities.

The preceding chapters have identified numerous federal programs that subsidize the destruction of riparian habitats. Hydro-electric power furnished by government-built dams has provided subsidized electricity to homes and industry in the Pacific Northwest for much of the twentieth century, but the environmental costs have been high. The impacts on wildlife in northwestern river basins remain largely unmitigated. Even though fisheries may improve and wildlife habitat may be protected as a result of the Northwest Power Planning Act of 1980, it is not possible to replace the riparian corridors that were lost as a result of this development.

On the lower Colorado River, subsidized irrigation encourages farmers to grow crops that may later receive deficiency payments from the federal government. If floodplain fields are washed away, as frequently occurs in the soybean fields along the Mississippi River, farmers are eligible for federal crop insurance payments.

In the metropolitan areas of our nation, much of the land once used for farming is being converted to urban uses, primarily housing and commercial ventures. Many people speculate that the availability of federal flood insurance encourages, rather than discourages, development on floodplains. Despite structural attempts to reduce flood damage, floods currently cause approximately $5 billion worth of damage each year in the United States. Eighty to ninety percent of all disasters in this country are caused by flooding. Federal taxpayers foot a $3 to $4 *billion* bill every year for flood damages.[4] Recent data indicate that it would be more cost-effective for the federal government to buy floodplain land than to pay for damages to buildings reconstructed in floodplains year after year after year.

The Army Corps of Engineers builds, maintains, and operates inland waterways for barge traffic at little cost to the barge industry. The construction of navigation channels has destructive effects on the environment; the maintenance of these channels adds to these impacts, and commercial traffic on the waterways contributes to ecological degradation so great that it drives species to extinction. Federal law contains no direct provision for commercial barge operators to share in the expenses of maintaining waterways for navigation. The straightening, deepening, dredging, blasting, locking, damming, riprapping, leveeing, and other operations on the 25,000 miles of inland waterways in the United States cost more than $600 million per year.

Small hydropower project development mushroomed after Congress passed PURPA and the Windfall Profits Tax Act of 1980. The environmental impacts of these prolific projects have not yet been adequately assessed.

The federal government misallocates both fiscal and natural resources by subsidizing unwise floodplain development, unneeded irrigation projects, economically inefficient waterway construction and maintenance, and cumulatively destructive small hydroelectric dams. Many of these activities destroy valuable habitat as well, so the elimination of wasteful subsidies would conserve money and wildlife.

Two examples of ecosystem protection by elimination of federal subsidies are the Coastal Barriers Resources Act of 1982 and the Colorado River Floodway Protection Act.

Coastal barriers are migratory islands that are constantly reformed and reshaped by waves, tides, changes in the source and supply of sediments, and sea level fluctuations. Like riparian habitats, coastal barriers contain a great diversity of plant and animal life. The Coastal Barriers Resources Act designated a network of 186 coastal barriers along the coasts of the Atlantic Ocean and the Gulf of Mexico. Within this network, called the Coastal Barriers Resources System, most federal expenditures are no longer available to promote growth and development. The act states that

> no new expenditures or new financial assistance may be made available under authority of any Federal law for any purpose within the Coastal Barriers Resources System, including, but not limited to — 1) the construction or purchase of any structure,

appurtenance, facility, or related infrastructure; 2) the
construction or purchase of any road, airport, boat landing facility,
or other facility on, or bridge or causeway to, any System unit, and
3) the carrying out of any project to prevent the erosion of, or to
otherwise stabilize, any inlet or shoreline, except in cases where
an emergency threatens life, land, and property immediately
adjacent to that unit.[5]

The act contains several exceptions to the subsidy prohibition, including the allowance of proenvironment projects for the study and
management, enhancement, and acquisition of fish and wildlife
habitat.

The Colorado River Floodway Protection Act, like the Mississippi
River and Tributaries Project authorized in 1928, was a congressional
response to disastrous flooding. Unlike its Mississippi River counter-
part, however, the Colorado River law takes a progressive, nonstructural approach to flooding problems by eliminating federal subsidies
to floodplain development. The act states that "certain federal programs which subsidize or permit development within the Floodway
threaten human life, health, property, and natural resources and there
is a need for coordinated Federal, State, and local action to limit
Floodway development."[6] The act established a task force consisting
of representatives from counties, water districts, cities, states, and
federal agencies to advise the secretary of the interior and Congress in
floodway management. The Department of the Interior is to map out a
floodway capable of containing a 100-year flood or a stream flow of up
to 40,000 cubic feet per second. Within the floodway, no new financial
assistance or expenditure would be available for purposes incompatible with floodway establishment.

The State Level

In many respects, the protection and restoration of riparian habitats
can best be accomplished at the state level. Lawmakers and policymakers are more accessible at this level, and constituencies for
individual rivers are more easily built. State and local governments
have police and land use regulation authorities that can be broadly
applied to riparian conservation goals. Further, state resource managers are familiar with the land, water, and wildlife resources under
their jurisdiction.

Twenty-eight states currently have some form of statewide river
conservation program. These range from "mini" wild and scenic
rivers programs to comprehensive statewide plans based on resource
assessments and management tool inventories.[7] State programs often

suffer, however, from a lack of funding and the absence of a broad base of support.

The State and Local Rivers Conservation Bill (S. 317) currently pending in the Senate could be used as an incentive for states to implement river conservation programs and as a vehicle for a federal consistency clause (not currently part of the bill). The bill contains authorizations for federal matching grants to the states for the assessment of rivers and the establishment of state river programs approved by the secretary of the interior.

Although Congress is not likely to fund a new conservation-oriented grant program while the nation is burdened with a national debt exceeding a trillion dollars, a guarantee of protection for rivers with high scenic, recreational, and wildlife values might be sufficient to trigger more state river programs. Such a bill could also carry provisions similar to those of the Coastal Barriers Resources Act and the Colorado River Floodway Protection Act to prevent the granting of subsidies for development within the floodplains of state-designated rivers.

The Local Level

Many states grant local governments sweeping powers to determine land uses through local zoning ordinances. Some local floodplain ordinances are more restrictive than federal or state permit and insurance programs.

Local governments often encourage the use of natural resources to capture the maximum economic return, however. In the case of riverine ecosystems, this may mean sacrificing wildlife, recreational, water quality, and flood mitigation values in return for tax revenues from floodplain development.

In addition, many local governments are afraid landowners will sue them on the grounds of confiscation of private property without just compensation, a violation of a constitutional right granted by the Fifth Amendment, if floodplain zoning restricts development. Ordinances that are well designed to protect the public health and welfare by protecting water quality and minimizing flood hazard have withstood many courtroom tests, however. These ordinances may serve other purposes, such as provision of open space and recreational opportunities, so long as their primary purpose is not to provide the public with benefits that were unavailable before their adoption.

Through local zoning and land acquisition, many communities are developing "greenway" systems. Greenways are linear corridors designed to provide recreational opportunities and open space. They generally link up larger parcels of open land, such as parks. *The Report of the President's Commission on Americans Outdoors* recommended that Americans "light a prairie fire" by creating greenways that reach out from their individual communities and interlink with one another, eventually becoming a network of parks and trails that would connect the entire continent.[8] By establishing greenways along streams and rivers, local governments could provide their communities with flood protection and higher water quality as well as opportunities for biking, hiking, jogging, and bird-watching.

Reversing the Trend

Human alteration of riparian and aquatic ecosystems often destroys the ability of these ecosystems to maintain themselves and sends them on a downward spiral toward the loss of ecological stability and a condition of biological sterility. Actions that contribute to this trend include stream dewatering and use of structural measures, such as damming and channelization, that disrupt the normal mechanics of rivers and streams. In order to preserve riparian ecosystems, waterways must have guaranteed in-stream flows. Nonstructural methods of stream management, rather than expensive and destructive riprapping, dikes, and other structural measures, can be used to reduce flood damage and improve stream bank stability.

Preservation of In-Stream Flows

Riparian ecosystems depend on water for their survival; therefore, their maintenance and restoration depends on the presence of certain quantities of water, which must be supplied in temporal pulses that approximate the natural pulses of streams and underground aquifers. Although rivers have traditionally been associated with water, no guarantees exist that even our most biologically rich river systems will continue to contain the copious waters that now dance through them, do-si-doing around rocky riffles and plunging majestically off high cliffs. Such a guarantee of in-stream water flows is the first step toward reversing the trend of riparian ecosystem destruction.

In-Stream Flows and Water Rights   Many of the ecological problems created by water project development are the result of stream dewatering. High salinity levels in the Colorado River and vegetation encroachment on the island and sandbar habitats of the Platte are examples of major ecosystem disturbances precipitated by diversions of water. Stream dewatering is largely a western problem. In the arid

West, most states have traditionally required a diversion from a river before they will recognize a water right. Thus, in order to maintain the ecological integrity of western rivers and riparian habitats, states must grant in-stream flow rights, and federal, state, and private parties must use any available means to provide the necessary flows.

In the West, states have traditionally used the law of prior appropriation to establish water rights. This "law" is based on several assumptions. First, the law assumes that waters are owned in trust for the public, so state governments have the right to regulate water appropriation. This assumption emphasizes usufructuary water rights (rights to the use of water), since the water is held in trust until it is diverted and put to a "beneficial" use. Second, the law assumes that water use is optimized when public uses, such as preservation of in-stream flows for fish or canoes, are minimized, and private uses, such as provision of water for industry and agriculture, are maximized. Third, water rights are assigned on a priority scale based on the date of filing or first use.[9]

State water law, often structured on this skeleton of antiquated assumptions, is being squeezed by the changing times, however. Federal courts have extended the assignment of water right priority based on seniority to apply to dates of land withdrawal by the federal government. In the case of *Arizona* v. *California*, the Supreme Court held that:

> the principle underlying the reservation of water rights for Indian reservations was equally applicable to other Federal establishments such as National Recreation Areas and National Forests. We agree with the conclusions of the Master that the United States intended to reserve water sufficient for the future requirements of the Lake Mead National Recreation Area, the Havasu National Wildlife Refuge, the Imperial National Wildlife Refuge, and the Gila National Forest.[10]

In the case of *United States* v. *Alpine Land and Reservoir Company*, the District Court for the District of Nevada ruled that the Toiyabe National Forest was reserved and withdrawn from public domain and dedicated and set apart as a national forest for the protection of watersheds and the maintenance of favorable stream flows in and below the watersheds; the production of timber; the production of forage for domestic animals; the protection and propagation of wildlife, including fish; and the provision of recreation for the general public.[11]

In November 1985, in the case of *Sierra Club* v. *Block*, the District Court for the District of Colorado recognized federal reserved water rights for twenty four wilderness areas in Colorado. This court case added to previous water law history by ruling that federal officials are not required by law to file for reserved water rights. This decision was upheld on appeal in 1987.

A federal reserved water right is purely a product of the judge's bench, not a product of the legislature. Federal agencies may also obtain water rights through the traditional state appropriation system, depending on the attitude of the state toward in-stream flows and federal ownership of water rights. In 1985, the Bureau of Land Management obtained from Nevada's state engineer a right to in-stream flows on a series of fishing lakes. The granting of this right set a precedent that may improve the atmosphere for environmentally beneficial water uses in the West.

Federal ownership of water rights for maintenance of in-stream flows is still the exception rather than the rule. Federal water rights are a volatile issue, but a few western states have recently changed their laws to permit appropriations of water rights by the state and by private parties for in-stream uses. Most of the states that now allow in-stream water rights do so to preserve fisheries.

In 1955, the Oregon legislature enacted a policy statement that provided for the administrative establishment of in-stream flow standards. Washington followed suit in 1981, adopting two statutes for flow preservation. In 1983, Montana created a stream flow reservation program and Colorado enacted legislation allowing the state's Water Conservation Board to acquire water rights for in-stream uses. Colorado has since obtained water rights for more than 700 stream reaches. By 1983, sixteen states had programs directed specifically toward in-stream uses of water.[12]

As more states recognize the preservation of in-stream flows as a beneficial use of water, the opportunities for acquiring in-stream flow rights will increase.

In general, the states have been responsible for allocating water among competing uses. The role of the federal government in appropriating in-stream flows remains undefined, but water uses that depend on in-stream flows are becoming increasingly threatened by diversions; thus, both state and federal roles in water appropriation are destined to change.

In-stream flow protection is a three-step process. First, resource managers must decide on the timing and quantity of the flows necessary to maintain the resources in question. Once these factors are determined, a method for protecting the flows must be chosen and implemented. Finally, managers must monitor the stream and resources to ensure that the protective methods are enforced and that the chosen quantity and timing are adequate to perpetuate the resource.

Quantity and Timing Three parameters must be investigated in order to establish an in-stream flow regime to maintain riparian habitats. First, the minimum quantity necessary to water the vegetation must be determined. Second, researchers must estimate the maximum flow that the ecological system can tolerate without being subjected to prolonged inundation or severe scouring. Third, the resource managers must consider the natural variations in flows.[13]

In-stream studies of variability should include consideration of seasonal fluctuations such as spring floods, which are needed to prepare a seedbed for riparian community regeneration and to scour encroaching vegetation out of the river channel. Long-term fluctuations, such as decades of low flow in the history of the stream, should also be considered, and this information should be incorporated into the flow management strategy.

Several methods may be used to determine the in-stream flow regime necessary to maintain riparian habitat. These methods range from a quick-fix establishment of minimum flow standards as a fixed percentage of a stream's average annual flow, to simple transect methods that incorporate site-specific aspects of stream morphology but rest on assumptions of consistent morphology throughout the stream, to highly labor-intensive multiple-transect methods.[14]

The Fish and Wildlife Service's Cooperative Instream Flow Group has developed a multiple-transect method known as the "instream flow incremental methodology" (IFIM). In establishing stream flow requirements for stream-dependent organisms, the service collects data on seasonal and long-term flow variations, geologic and hydrologic characteristics of the stream, and the habitat preferences of fish and aquatic wildlife. The data are fed into a computer model that produces quantitative information on many different aspects of the stream-related ecosystem. This results in an information base that is flexible, precise, and highly credible, but the process is extremely consumptive of time and labor. When adequate in-stream flows must be identified for a large number of streams, shortages of time, money, and labor may limit the practicality of the incremental methodology.

Jones and Stokes Associates, Inc., an environmental consulting firm, has extended some of the Fish and Wildlife Service's work on in-stream flow evaluation to riparian habitat. In one project, researchers sampled vegetation along twenty-two IFIM fisheries habitat characterization transects on the north fork of the Kings River in the western Sierra Nevada. They recorded the rooting locations of all plants on the

the floodplain within a 3-meter-wide belt centered on an IFIM transect. Using data from the IFIM stream cross section survey, the researchers predicted water surface elevations for discharges of various magnitudes. (Discharge levels of given magnitudes inundate the floodplain to predictable elevations.) The inundation elevation data were then related to the elevations of the plant species on the floodplain.[15] This type of study can be used to assess the potential effects of planned water projects on riparian ecology. Such a study provides site-specific information which is important because the response of riparian vegetation to in-stream flows is also influenced by the permeability of the substrate and by the presence of springs, seeps, and aquifers that contribute additional moisture to riparian communities, among other factors.

Timing is as important as quantity in maintaining natural river-dependent ecosystems. Historical records may provide information needed to understand the relationship between seasonal flow variations and the life cycles of natural biota. The regeneration of cotton-woods on the Colorado River, for example, depends on high spring flows that correspond with the release of seeds from mature trees. The continued survival of the endangered Colorado squawfish may partially depend on high spring flows to destroy the eggs of competing, introduced fish species. Timing in-stream flow releases to maintain biological communities is politically problematic, since timing is an essential aspect of water project functions such as irrigation, flood-water storage, and peak hydroelectric operations.

Legal Protection of In-Stream Flows   Three basic mechanisms currently exist for the appropriation of in-stream water rights. The most politically viable of these is the direct setting aside of rights. This may be accomplished through the acquisition of existing water rights, the reservation of unappropriated flows by the state, or the establishment of minimum flows in streams by state agencies. Reservation of these flows via the latter two mechanisms depends on the availability of substantial amounts of unappropriated water.[16]

A second technique for maintaining instream flows is indirect protection, as when flows are identified for conservation of endangered species and preservation of water quality. This technique, often considered a threat to the state water appropriation tradition, has been attacked by western water developers. These developers lobbied Congress to include the following statement in the Clean Water Act:

> It is the policy of Congress that the authority of each state to
> allocate quantities of water within its jurisdiction shall not be
> superseded, abrogated or otherwise impaired by this chapter. It is

further the policy of Congress that nothing in this chapter shall be construed to supersede or abrogate rights to quantities of water which have been established by any state.[17]

Western water conservancy districts and others interested in water development drafted similar language for an amendment to the Endangered Species Act in 1985. The draft amendment was intended to thwart any demands by the Fish and Wildlife Service that planned water projects, particularly those on the Colorado and Platte rivers, release sufficient flows to maintain populations of endangered species. Congress did not appear receptive to such an amendment, so it was not offered during the act's 1985 reauthorization.

The danger in depending on indirect protection of in-stream water rights to maintain riparian habitats is that the quantity and timing of flows sufficient to ensure a target water quality or species breeding level may not be sufficient to maintain riparian vegetation.

A third method of appropriating in-stream flows is through rights displacement. This method rests on the public trust doctrine. The public trust doctrine has traditionally been used for three purposes relating to navigable waters: commerce, navigation, and fishing.[18] In some states, such as Massachusetts, Wisconsin, and California, the courts have placed strict limits on the ability of state and local governments to dispose of public trust resources to private interests.[19] When the federal government or the states use rights displacement to gain in-stream water rights, the acquisition of private rights by the government creates controversy at best, and at worst, hostility.

Monitoring and Enforcement Once an in-stream water right is gained, procedures, responsibility, and authority must be designated to ensure that the right is respected and that it serves its purpose.

During times of low flows, unless a stream is patrolled or metered, in-stream flows may be illegally diverted by irrigators, holders of junior water rights, or other parties with unmet needs for water. Enforcement of in-stream water rights is costly, but without enforcement, all prior labor is for naught.

Monitoring of the resource for which the water right has been appropriated is also necessary for effective use of in-stream flows. If maintenance of healthy riparian habitat is the goal of setting in-stream flow quantities and timing, baseline data must be collected, and the floodplain must be watched for seasonal and long-term shifts in species composition of flora and fauna, vegetation growth rates, densities of plants and animals, and other parameters. If the improvement in the health of the riparian community is unsatisfactory, some adjustment in the flow regime may be necessary. Like enforcement, the monitoring process is quite consumptive of time and resources, but it may be extremely rewarding in the resulting accumulation of scientific knowledge.

Use of Nonstructural Measures

Structural measures modify the amount, quality, location, or timing of the water resource itself through construction projects such as dams, harbors, or channels. *Nonstructural* measures modify the use of a water resource; such measures may include changes in public policy, alterations in management practices, regulatory changes, or modifications in pricing policies that provide complete or partial alternatives to structural measures. *Holistic* measures use human labor and the natural energy of the river to restore a degraded river channel to its natural condition.

Much of the degradation of America's riparian habitat is linked to structural alterations of rivers and streams. On the lower Mississippi River and its tributaries, for example, federal agencies are channelizing streams to reduce flood damage, thus initiating a chain reaction that results in massive destruction of highly valuable bottomland hardwood habitat.

Alternatives to traditional irrigation practices in arid lands provide opportunities to produce crops without severely damaging riverine and riparian ecology. In the desert Southwest, a reduction in the agricultural consumption of river flows would result in the availability of more water for aquatic wildlife, riparian habitats, and recreational uses.

Higher water yields can be obtained from watersheds without resorting to environmentally damaging phreatophyte control. If resource managers increase the ability of small headwater streams to store water in aquifers during high-flow seasons, the streams will naturally release more water during dry seasons. In many watersheds, this job can be accomplished by beavers.

Nonstructural and holistic restoration measures do not allow the intense exploitation of river resources that structural measures do, but they help to preserve wildlife habitat and aesthetic values. Unlike structural measures, which create serious ecological problems that must be monitored and "bandaged" at government expense for the life of the project, the benefits provided by a healthy river system in its natural state are indefinitely self-perpetuating.

Flood Damage Reduction   On small streams, the conventional flood damage reduction measure involves dredging to increase channel capacity. The resulting streamlined, trapezoidal sluiceway passes water quickly downstream so that the farmers upstream are not troubled by it. The corps and the Soil Conservation Service use heavy machinery to remove obstruction to stream flow and to dredge artificial channels. These measures often create or increase downstream flooding, as water passes more rapidly through the dredged channels. A natural channel would retain, purify, and gradually release this water by allowing some percolation into porous soils and through riparian vegetation. Instead, the unimpeded water rushes downstream in one huge, erosive torrent, carrying sediments away from the land to lodge in a reservoir somewhere downstream. Additionally, traditional channelization requires expensive and continuous maintenance work.

Riparian habitat could be protected if the federal water development agencies did not channelize small streams to reduce flood damage. The benefits of large-scale stream alterations are restricted to a few landowners, but the adverse effects touch a broad range of Americans through land losses, downstream flooding, aesthetic degradation, and declining wildlife populations.

Gentle methods may be used to increase the capacity of small streams to accommodate high flows. Native Americans in the Southwest once planted riparian trees as a buffer against short-duration flood flows. These ingenious indigenes also wove semipermeable barriers of seep willow, burrobush, and mesquite and tied them between the trunks of riparian trees to slow floodwaters. Often, indigenous farmers would build such living fences several meters into an eroded stream, forcing the water to deposit sediment and rebuild the river's banks. These fences "tamed" floodwaters without causing channel entrenchment or downstream erosion. The woven fences collected alluvial sediments, which the farmers spread on fields. When this alluvium was mixed with decomposed vegetative debris, it served as a rich soil supplement. The riparian strips also served as windbreaks, decreasing the exposure of crops to the hot, dry winds of the desert that stress plants by increasing water loss by evapotranspiration. The indigenous farmers harvested fuel wood from the riparian trees, and insectivorous birds nesting in the trees helped to control crop parasites.[20] Many of the first Spanish immigrants to the southwestern United States adopted these practices.

A modern-day stream doctor, George Palmiter, has developed and successfully demonstrated holistic management methods to increase the floodwater capacity of small streams while reducing erosion and improving water quality. The major difference between Palmiter's tender stream restoration methods and traditional methods used by federal agencies to channelize and straighten streams is that the former harness human energy and the energy of the river to clear the channel, while the latter rely on expensive and destructive heavy machinery.[21]

To increase the depth of a channel, Palmiter and his work crews manually remove large debris jams so that the water can erode the sediments deposited underneath them. Trenching and removal of vegetation from sandbars that block the flow of water may be necessary before the natural power of the river can quickly dig a deeper channel.

To divert water pressure away from stream banks so that bank erosion will decrease and new land will accrete, Palmiter cuts the tops off trees and cables them lengthwise along gouged areas at the water line. The stream forms eddies around and through the branches, slowing the current so that sediments settle out and begin to build land. This method can also be used to straighten streams; the treetops are cabled to the inside curves of meanders, directing the stream's erosive force to the insides of point bars.

Revegetation of stream banks is an essential part of the Palmiter prescription for stream restoration. Riparian trees bind soil with their roots, thus preventing bank erosion; they shade the stream to maintain cool summer temperatures for cold-water fisheries; and they contribute nutrients to the aquatic ecosystem. This vegetation also preserves the depth of streams, adding to the flood damage reduction benefits of the Palmiter method. Large tree roots that knot and braid below the water line on the riverbank create small whirlpools that churn bottom sediments, keeping them from settling out of suspension, and dig into the stream bottom. Shade provided by riparian trees inhibits the growth of weeds in the channel. Since weeds tend to trap sediments, the presence of riparian trees indirectly prevents the growth of obstructive sandbars in the channel.

Palmiter's methods for increasing the flood capacity of a stream cost one-tenth to one-third as much as methods involving drastic alterations of channel morphology and the use of heavy equipment.[22] Barlow compared Palmiter's channel improvement methods with the conventional methods employed by federal agencies and reported that

> many channel improvement projects cost upwards of $80,000 per mile, paid for by assessments on local landowners and state and Federal taxpayers. Legal and engineering interests, which receive up to 20 percent of these monies, have not been zealously working to change to methods that reduce expenses. . . . Unfortunately, because the political and legal structure that sets a project in motion and guides it to completion is strongly influenced by engineers, alternatives like Palmiter's are being ignored.[23]

On any stream, the best method for preventing flood damage is to keep damageable property off the floodplain. Even structural flood control methods, such as channelization and construction of flow retention dams, merely reduce the frequency of floods; they do not prevent floods.

A report prepared for the Water Resources Council makes the point that new structural alterations of floodplains are not prudent investments for the federal government:

> In the United States, flood-free land is virtually an unlimited commodity. From a national perspective, the creation of additional flood-free land, per se, can have no economic value. . . .Over the last twenty years, a relatively small percentage of authorized flood control projects has been economically justified on the basis of protecting existing development alone. The justification has depended on changing land use and the location in the floodplain of new development which could just as well be located elsewhere.[24]

Different methods exist for preventing development on floodplains. To preclude development indefinitely, conservationists can purchase the floodplain land in fee title or obtain conservation easements on it. State and local governments can prevent construction in flood-prone areas through zoning statutes, permit systems, or voluntary agreements. The federal government can prevent construction in floodplains by purchasing land and placing it into the national park, wilderness, or wild and scenic rivers systems. The government can also charge flood insurance rates that reflect actuarial probabilities of loss.

Precluding construction of housing and commercial property on flood-prone land does not imply precluding all human activity from that land. Communities can create greenways in floodplains near urban centers and provide within them facilities such as fishing lakes and golf courses, which are not seriously impaired by flooding. Many outdoor recreational activities are enhanced by a lack of visual obstruction.

Irrigation Overproduction of many farm crops during this decade has resulted in prices for many farm products so low that farmers often are unable to pay debts on equipment and fertilizer. While the federal government makes deficiency payments and pays farmers to keep land out of production, irrigation districts continue to produce blueprints for water projects that would increase the amount of land irrigated with river water. Not only would an increase in irrigated acreage further depress the farm economy, it would also decrease the productivity of more land through erosion and salinity, decrease the quality of surface and underground water through runoff and percolation of salts and fertilizers, and further threaten wildlife through clearing and dewatering of habitat.

These problems are aggravated in hot and arid lands that, though fertile, are not equipped to produce water-consumptive crops, such as alfalfa, year after year. These lands would remain productive for more years if farmers would switch to crops better adapted to the climate. In the Southwest, for example, Indians have grown and lived on dryland crops for more than three centuries. In fields tended by Papago, Pima, and Yuma Indians, where temperatures routinely reach 121 degrees, tepary beans, Papago corn, and yellow-meated watermelons grow like crabgrass. Other delicious and nutritious foods grown by desert Indians include native sunflowers, Navajo wild potatoes, Hopi lima beans, chiles, and squash. These lands also support indigo, medicinal herbs, and other valuable crops.[25] As the culinary curiosity of American people expands, a market for wholesome native foods could easily be developed.

Even the crops that arid-land farmers now produce can be grown and irrigated more efficiently. Existing varities of cotton, if planted with closer spacing, mature more rapidly than conventionally spaced cotton, so the growing season can be shortened by a month or more. Drip irrigation, the slow application of water to the soil around the root zone of a plant, reduces water losses from evaporation and deep percolation because a small amount of water is applied to a small portion of the soil surface. This irrigation method has many benefits, including better water control, low seedling mortality, greater uniformity of crops, fuel savings, flexibility in the use of fertilizers, little weed growth, erosion control, and increased yields.[26] Drip irrigation is expensive, but recent innovations are decreasing the relative costs of using this method for irrigating row crops. Innovations in irrigation systems promote the conservation of water, energy, and fertilizers.[27]

Increasing Flows Without Cutting Trees   Water developers in arid river basins such as the Colorado's often view riparian trees as competitors for the precious crystal fluid and would therefore prefer to destroy them, but for the benefit of the river, man, and wildlife, the trees should remain where they are. Phreatophyte control, the destruction of riparian vegetation, is unnecessary for providing increased stream flows.

Wise watershed management of headwater streams can provide high water yields without phreatophyte control. Since the land surrounding most small headwater streams is undeveloped, potential flooding is not a problem, and since these streams are generally too small even for recreational craft, channel depth does not influence their usefulness to man. The floodplains of headwater streams can, therefore, be used for water storage.

Introducing beavers into headwater streams can indirectly increase summer flows, so long as riparian vegetation is present to provide the animals with building materials for dams and food. Installing small water-spreading dams can produce the same effect. Small dams on headwater streams, whether created by man or beaver, increase summer flows, possibly because they increase the zone of saturation contained within the valley bottom.[28] Beaver dams also reduce the ability of small streams to transport sediment by reducing the gradient and velocity of the streams. Deposition of sediment increases the elevation of the water table and the water table's ability to store water for much of the growing season.[29] According to Stabler,

> during overbank flows, riparian vegetation encourages better streambottom aquifer recharge. Although removal of riparian vegetation may result in small increases in summer streamflow over the short term the elimination of woody riparian vegetation and debris over the long term may result in eventual loss of summer streamflow, especially along stream reaches susceptible to gullying.[30]

Restoring Riparian Systems

If we were able to freeze the destruction of riparian ecosystems within the next hour, we would still need to replace some of the wildlife-rich habitat that has been so recklessly destroyed. Restoration techniques can be used to bring back essential riparian and wetland habitats on river systems such as the Colorado and Mississippi. These techniques can also be used to restore rivers in urban settings so that human inhabitants can enjoy cleaner water and more wildlife. Restoration projects can range from the planting of trees on denuded banks by a group of weekend volunteers to the design and installation of complex wetland ecosystems on spoil deposit sites or urban watersheds.

Before restoration can get under way, baseline data on the ecology of the basin must be gathered. Then the areas targeted for restoration work should be thoroughly surveyed to determine possible problems that would frustrate restoration efforts. For example, layers of caliche or bedrock below the topsoil layer that would prevent tree roots from reaching groundwater must be avoided or broken up with an auger. High soil salinity can thwart efforts to grow certain tree species on floodplains; salt-tolerant species should be planted in such areas. Some wetland restoration sites are flooded more frequently and to greater depths than others; such site variations should be considered in the planning stage.

However simple or complex the restoration effort, monitoring the work after it is completed is an essential part of the program. The relatively small effort required to survey the site once a week for several months after planting and once a month after that can rescue the entire project from the mandibles of insects and prevent other potential disasters, as well as instill a sense of maternal pride in the project crew.

Collection of Baseline Data

The collection of baseline data is essential if a restoration effort is to be monitored. The purpose of baseline data collection is to assess the state of the river basin's ecology and the trends and functions involved in producing or maintaining that state so that the appropriate restoration techniques may be applied and their impacts later assessed.

In order to successfully restore and monitor a large area of riparian habitat, managers must collect information regarding the ecology of the entire basin within which they are working. Such a collection ideally includes daily wildlife use patterns and daily patterns of change in the river system, such as diurnal (throughout the day) fluctuations of dissolved oxygen and other chemical constituents of the water. A comprehensive data base must include information on seasonal fluctuations in both the aquatic and riparian ecosystems, such as vegetative growth and die-off, microbial activity in water and soil, nutrient uptake and release, fish and wildlife breeding patterns, and temperature and light effects. Annual variations, such as floral and faunal succession, are also important to a complete data set.

Restoration project planners may ascertain current land uses and changes in land use in the basin by reading studies and examining chronological maps and photo series. Communications with basin residents and local officials can provide useful information, as can the evaluation of land use plans, zoning regulations, and building permits.

Finally, it is important to know something about the hydrology of an area for which restoration work is planned. Studying maps of the topography of the basin, locating all current water outlets and drainage tiles, estimating seasonal flows and long-term flow variations, and examining hydrographs and floodplain maps all contribute to a knowledge of the location, quantity, and timing of flows so important to the health of both the riparian and aquatic environments.

Revegetation of Riparian Forests

Planting trees in a floodplain can be a simple and inexpensive process if the substrate is soft and the saplings are available near the restoration site. Trees such as cottonwoods and willows can be started from cut poles. Often, the reward is directly proportional to the effort. Cottonwood poles have a higher survival rate when they are allowed to develop root systems before planting, but many will grow if they are simply nicked at the bottom and treated with vitamin B_1 to prevent shock. Regardless of the preplanting treatment, the holes in which the trees are planted must tap groundwater unless an irrigation system is installed at the project site. Irrigation systems greatly increase project costs and must be consistently monitored for leaks and breakage. If used, they should be employed intermittently so that developing root systems will grow down toward the aquifer instead of laterally. Fencing of the young trees will be necessary if the project site is grazed by livestock or contains a large population of beavers.

Restoration of riparian forest communities with complex seral stages, such as those along the Missouri and Mississippi rivers, requires long periods of time. The most skilled biologist is incapable of creating a climax forest in one step; instead, the project crew must initiate succession by encouraging the colonization of a floodplain or spoil deposit by early successional species and protecting the floodplain until the substrate is stable and succession is evident.

Restoration of Desert Riparian Vegetation

Anderson and Ohmart have been experimenting with restoration of desert riparian habitat for more than a decade under a contract with the Bureau of Reclamation. Their objective, in addition to revegetating banks, is to develop techniques to optimize wildlife habitat while minimizing evaporative water losses from vegetation. The investigators estimated that if less dense stands of high-quality native species replaced salt cedar, wildlife habitat would improve and evapotranspiration would decrease. They initially spent 84 months collecting data on the relationships between wildlife use of riparian areas and plant species composition. When they had interpreted their baseline data, they began revegetation of a spoil disposal site and a site that had been cleared of salt cedar. Bird use of the revegetated sites increased at all times of the year as the native vegetation became established. Populations of small mammals also increased in the cleared site, apparently because the horizontal diversity of the vegetation increased. Anderson and Ohmart found that the per-acre costs of revegetating their study sites were almost $4,000, including irrigation works, administrative overhead, travel, and other expenses. Depending on the condition of the site to be revegetated, the costs can be much lower. Using volunteer labor, the Bureau of Land Management has revegetated sites in southeastern Arizona, complete with livestock fencing, for as little as $100 per acre. The success rate of these projects has been 80 to 90 percent.[31] Clearly, well-planned and effective riparian revegetation is expensive, but Anderson and Ohmart concluded,

> action agencies should explore all alternatives prior to destroying a reach of valuable riparian habitat. Should it be necessary to destroy it, they should be prepared to meet the high cost of replacing it in kind and general proximity.[32]

In 1985, Ohmart wrote to the regional directors of several federal and state agencies with resource management responsibilities along the lower Colorado River and requested the agencies to pool their resources and expand their revegetation efforts along the lower Colorado River. The response has not been encouraging, but such an interagency effort has the potential to maximize the efficiency of revegetation work in the Colorado River basin and in all river basins.

The Corps's New Efforts

The Department of the Army signed a memorandum of agreement with the National Oceanic and Atmospheric Administration (NOAA) in October 1985 committing the agencies to a pilot study of the practicability of restoring wetlands and other fisheries habitat.[33] The memorandum of agreement is the first step in establishing a nationwide habitat restoration and creation program to contribute to the balancing of habitat conservation with water resources development. The agencies within NOAA and the army responsible for the habitat restoration are the National Marine Fisheries Service (NMFS) and the Army Corps of Engineers, respectively. The NMFS, part of the Department of Commerce, has the primary federal responsibility for the conservation, management, and development of the nation's living marine resources. The Army Corps of Engineers has the general authority, under Section 150 of the Water Resources Development Act of 1976, to create wetlands using dredged material associated with construction and maintenance of civil works projects. Under the memorandum, selected NMFS regions will furnish participating corps divisions and districts with proposed areas for habitat creation and restoration and will identify the resources expected to benefit.

The corps will then use its technical and engineering expertise to create and restore habitat.

This move to create and restore habitat has as its precedent the wetlands creation work of the corps's Vicksburg, Mississippi, Waterways Experiment Station under the Dredged Material Research Program. Under this program, the corps has established upland and wetland habitat at seven sites, including Miller Sands Island.

Miller Sands Island, which sits in the Lewis and Clark National Wildlife Refuge on the Columbia River, was built from dredged material in 1932 and used as a disposal site in 1974 and 1981. In 1974, the corps pumped more than a million cubic yards of sandy dredged material onto the island to form a protective cove. An upland habitat site was then prepared by disking and tilling the original spoil material. The corps planted tufted hairgrass, Lyngbye's sedge, slough sedge, broadleaf arrowhead, common three-square, soft rush, yellow flag, and water plantain in the marsh area and European beach grass, Oregon bent grass, reed canary grass, red fescue, and tall fescue on the uplands. The marsh area already contained some willow, and the upland bore Sitka spruce, black cottonwood, and red alder. The corps applied fertilizer to the sandy and infertile meadow habitat. By 1980, the Miller Sands experimental site had a lower vegetative density than do natural sites with comparable habitats, but it was slowly filling in with plant life. By 1982, wildlife use of the area equaled or surpassed that of comparable natural habitats.[34]

As of 1987, the corps was not actively attempting to reestablish bottomland hardwood forests, but such work may be initiated in the future. Although succession into mature hardwood forest could take a century after a restoration site is identified and protected, federal development of bottomland hardwood forests would eventually compensate for some of the valuable wildlife habitat that has been needlessly destroyed. Hardwood habitat restoration could also provide a self-perpetuating commercial timber source if the hardwoods were harvested on a sustained-yield basis.

Urban River Restoration

Restoring riparian forests and wetlands in urban areas can result in improved water quality, enhanced wildlife values, decreased flood damages, and better aesthetics. Wetlands Research, Inc., is in the process of reestablishing a former wetland bordering a 3-mile stretch of the Des Plaines River just north of Chicago, Illinois. The Des Plaines River, once a vital organ in a rich prairie ecosystem, has been channelized and polluted for the past century. The river supports carp and algae and little else. Dr. Donald Hey and associates are widening the river channel, regrading the adjoining land into a gradually sloping floodplain capable of harboring wetlands, and reintroducing native prairie and wetland flora and fauna. The narrow, "pea-soup" river will eventually be transformed into a braided, clean-flowing stream, with the help of an irrigation system that will pump water into the uplands and allow it to gradually pass back into the river. The benefits expected by the Wetlands Research staff include improved water quality, flood control, and wildlife habitat.

The Des Plaines River project is more than a simple restoration effort. It is an experiment in inexpensive water treatment and flood control for urban watersheds. According to Hey,

> if wetland reconstruction turns out to be a cost-effective way to reduce non-point source pollution and flood damage, as many of us believe it will, the possibilities for its future use are limitless. With a little bit of time and trouble, we could open up the hundreds of filled-in oxbows and meanders that line our rivers, flatten out old dikes and levees, and selectively and strategically bring back fragments of our former wetlands to work for us.[35]

Benefits of Restoration

Some benefits of planting trees near a river are obvious; others are less so. A recent analysis of property values of homes located on natural and channelized branches of the Portage River in Wood County, Ohio, indicates that "homes constructed on the natural stream are assessed to be worth 331% more than homes built on the channelized stream. These homes have appropriate sewage treatment for effluents and are above the floodplain."[36] Along streams not protected by state or federal wild and scenic statutes, these results have significance for riparian habitat preservation and restoration.

If we could allow our rivers to return to their natural state, American society would gain such benefits as water quality improvement, flood damage reduction, less erosion-caused land loss, and recreation and wildlife enhancement, with minimal expenditure of time and money. Until this is possible, we must take steps to protect the valuable riparian and other diminishing habitats that remain.

Creating an Endangered Ecosystems Act

The federal government is nothing more than an instrument of the public will. When it is guided by the voices of the people, the government is forced to weigh the requests of one interest group against those of another and to incorporate equanimity into its decisions and actions. When the government hears only a few voices, however, such as those of paid lobbyists representing an irrigation district or a commercial barge company, its response to those voices is unbalanced and, as a result, irreplaceable resources are destroyed.

One possible solution to the rapid loss of landscape and biological diversity in the United States is the establishment of an endangered ecosystems act. Current statutes are inadequate to protect natural communities threatened with extirpation. The National Environmental Policy Act (NEPA) creates the opportunity for interested parties to comment on federal programs but contains no provisions for prohibiting programs that are environmentally unsound. Section 404 of the Clean Water Act is limited in scope and is administered by the Army Corps of Engineers, an agency that functions primarily as a federal engineering firm. The Endangered Species Act, the nation's toothiest environmental law, protects habitat only if it is essential to the survival of an endangered species. This stopgap legislation promotes the backward process of protecting habitat after a species has reached the brink of extinction. The decline in populations of most species in modern America is related to loss of habitat; therefore, a species' becoming endangered is an indicator that its habitat has been seriously impaired by abuse or encroachment. If rare *habitats* were protected by federal statute, the number of species requiring protection under the Endangered Species Act in order to survive would be much smaller.

When a federal action is halted by implementation of the Endangered Species Act, frequently it is the endangered species' habitat that is endangered by the proposed action. When habitat loss is the true problem posed by the planned action, the action too often proceeds without being stripped of its potential menace to the environment. Before 1981, for example, changes in the Colorado River's aquatic habitat brought the Colorado squawfish, humpback chub, and bonytail chub to the brink of extinction. The Fish and Wildlife Service refused to allow any further federal development that would significantly add to the depletion of water from the Colorado River system until it had sufficient information to be certain that the water losses would not wipe out the fish. By 1981, however, pressure from western water interests was great enough to change the service's position. These water brokers argued that the Service should not hold up projects when it couldn't demonstrate that the projects would harm the endangered species. For the next 4 years, therefore, the Service allowed water development projects to proceed while it attempted to gather information on the projects' impacts and the ecological needs of the fish. Instead of instituting a more natural water management regime to restore aquatic habitat conditions, researchers yanked many of the fish from the river and bred them in captivity. Meanwhile, fish habitat in the Colorado continued to decline, riparian ecology was harmed as well, and Congress considered plans for more water development on the river.

The situation is similar on the Platte. Critical habitat has been designated for the endangered whooping crane, but the species' recovery depends to a large extent on a captive breeding program. This breeding effort, which began in 1967, has met with success; but meanwhile, populations of two more bird species that depend on essentially the same Platte River riparian habitat, the spotted sandpiper and interior least tern, have declined to the point where protection under the Endangered Species Act is warranted.

The Fish and Wildlife Service's jeopardy opinion for Cliff Dam was a move toward recognizing that habitat, rather than an individual species or population, was the resource endangered by the dam. By proposing habitat-oriented alternatives, the service offered to trade an active bald eagle nesting site for a riparian community and flows to maintain the aquatic ecosystem.

As a species nears extinction, the costs involved in recovering the species increase. Where mere restrictions on development in a certain habitat type may be sufficient to protect the species early in its decline, the expensive facilities and personnel required for feeding, breeding, and studying a chronically endangered wildlife species offer only dim hopes for its recovery later on. While the funds and energies of the responsible federal agencies are expended on trying to resuscitate the dying species, the species' habitat in the wild may continue to decline, bringing still more species to the brink of extinction. If the endangered species is successfully reared in captivity, biologists may proudly march out of their labs with a potentially growing population of the species only to find that no habitat exists to support it.

Early protection of potentially endangered species is not the only rationale for endangered ecosystems legislation. Many ecosystems harbor unique associations of plant and animal species. Although these species may exist in large numbers in other associations in different regions of the country and therefore are not candidates for the endangered species list, the associations are entities in themselves and should be preserved. The population decline of Arizona Bell's vireos, for example, is an indicator of the deteriorating health of riparian habitat on the lower Colorado River. Although the species is not in danger of extinction, the habitat is. The sturgeon and striped bass fisheries on the Apalachicola River are similar indicators of ecosystem illness. Is the existence of these fishes in other waterways sufficient justification for the death of the Apalachicola's natural ecology?

The same valuative arguments for preserving individual species, such as their importance in providing the world with future genetic resources and their values as sources of scientific knowledge, as portions of our children's rightful heritage, and even as God's creations with an inherent right to exist, apply to the preservation of ecosystems as well. These values cannot be economically quantified, so when land and water use decisions are made under pressure from participants in the national marketplace, such as irrigation equipment companies or constructors of marinas, the nonmonetary values of species and ecosystems often are not considered.

Cities are expanding, and agriculture is claiming more land. Ecosystems are being squeezed and cut into parcels incapable of supporting free-ranging animals. As the acreage of natural habitats decreases, the numbers of animals whose home range needs are satisfied by the remaining available habitat also decreases. Predators at the top of the food chain, such as mountain lions and wolves, require habitats ranging in size from 36 to 114,000 square miles. These animals often are the first link in the biological food web to be lost from an area, as the endangered status of the wolf and Florida panther (a mountain lion subspecies) indicates. The loss of predators from a region often triggers booms in populations of prey species, such as deer, which quickly outgrow the capacity of the ecosystem to feed them and often painfully starve to death in huge numbers.

Habitat shrinkage causes or contributes to the extinctions of wildlife species. The last known North American population of the ivory-billed woodpecker, a bird specifically adapted to life in mature bottomland hardwood forests, disappeared in 1948 when the 120-square-mile Singer tract in Louisiana was cut for soybean cultivation. Leadership at the federal level is necessary if we wish to preserve the natural heritage of the United States. The following pages contain a proposed legislative program to accomplish this goal.

Research

An endangered ecosystems act would appropriate federal funds to supply matching grants to the states for the purpose of surveying and designating ecosystems as endangered (in danger of complete extirpation) and threatened (close to becoming endangered). The surveying and designation work would be done on a state-by-state basis by

committees consisting of representatives from federal resource management agencies, state conservation agencies, the research community, and any interested private groups, such as conservation organizations, livestock growers, and timber companies. The committees
would address issues such as the biological richness of proposed
ecosystem types; the relative scarcity of these types on a state,
regional, and national basis; the minimum size of unit necessary to
preserve the majority of wildlife species dependent on that ecosystem; and the land and water uses that are compatible or incompatible
with the preservation of the ecosystem. The size and location of the
ecosystem and any possible connections of natural areas by corridors
would be identified in the planning stage. Once the most sensitive
ecosystem types were identified, the committees would develop maps
illustrating their locations throughout the state. The committees
would also suggest land use guidelines to be applied to threatened and
endangered ecosystems.

Protection

Committee maps depicting the location and approximate extent of
the endangered and threatened ecosystems would serve as guidelines
for the protection of those ecosystems. For threatened ecosystems,
federal resource management agencies would develop local guidelines restricting land and water uses that the committees found
incompatible with ecosystem preservation. Such guidelines for
threatened riparian habitats, for example, would create buffer zones
where logging would not be allowed, would restrict grazing, and
would prohibit the use of all-terrain cycles.

Endangered ecosystems on federal land would be managed by
guidelines more restrictive of land and water use than those for
threatened ecosystems. The guidelines would make preservation of
the ecosystem's self-sustaining biological integrity the primary management goal. In endangered riparian ecosystems, for example, no
structural alteration of streams would be allowed. The legislation
would allocate funds to federal agencies for restoration and creation of
ecosystem types that have been identified as endangered on public
lands and would provide grants to the states for restoration and
creation of these types on state and private lands. Further authorization would permit appropriations of federal funds to obtain conservation easements on endangered ecosystems on private lands.

The endangered ecosystems legislation could actually save
money for the Treasury. Restricting development on floodplains could
save billions of dollars every year in flood relief payments. Additional

incentives to take agricultural land out of production would reduce the demand for crop deficiency payments. Restrictions on structural alterations of rivers would save initial outlays for construction materials and labor as well as funds used to maintain the alterations and correct erosion problems downstream from the structures.

Prohibitions on logging in threatened and endangered ecosystem types such as riparian canyons and stands of old-growth timber would save funds that the Forest Service would otherwise spend on roads and timber landings. Finally, the Fish and Wildlife Service would save some of the funds it would otherwise spend in recovering endangered species.

The United States, a country wealthy in both knowledge and natural resources, is already a world leader in the field of conservation. To maintain this lead, our society must be able to adapt to changing conditions. Our nation has outgrown its frontier infancy, when its youthful urge to expand into and harness nature was more beneficial to the present generation and less threatening to future generations. In the sunset of the twentieth century, a social policy comprising careful stewardship of our natural resources and meticulous planning and orderly growth of our communities is more appropriate to our maturing society.

Riparian ecosystems are perhaps the best places to "test-drive" a new American conservation ethic. These ecosystems provide water quality and flood mitigation benefits to society. Preserved in their natural condition, riparian corridors can provide recreational opportunities and aesthetic pleasure to communities. Linked with larger parcels of protected natural areas, riparian zones can hold together vital wildlife habitats, allowing dispersal of animals and decreasing the genetic bottlenecks that can occur in isolated wildlife populations, while maintaining migratory corridors and seasonal shelter. If one could adequately weigh the copious benefits that could be reaped through conservation and restoration of riparian habitats, the benefit-cost analysis game would no longer be fixed. Nature would be the clear winner in a fair game.

NOTES

1. J. Fitzwilliams, *Americans Outdoors*, report no. 19 (Alexandria, VA, 1987).
2. President's Commission on Americans Outdoors, *The Report of the President's Commission on Americans Outdoors: The Legacy, the Challenge* (Washington, DC, and Covelo, CA: Island Press, 1987).

3. L. R. Johnston, "Status of Wetland and Floodplain Acquisition" (Paper presented at the annual meeting of the Association of State Wetlands Managers, Chicago, IL, 18 September 1987).
4. L. Larson, "History of Floodplain Management" (Paper presented at the annual meeting of the Association of State Wetland Managers, Chicago, IL, 18 September 1987).
5. Coastal Barriers Resources Act of 1982 (16 U.S.C. 3509).
6. Colorado River Floodway Protection Act (43 U.S.C. 1600, sec. 2a, 4, 5, 1986).
7. R. C. Hoffman and K. Fletcher, *America's Rivers: An assessment of State River Conservation Programs* (Washington, DC: River Conservation Fund, 1984).
8. President's Commission on Americans Outdoors, Report of the President's Commission.
9. A. D. Tarlock, "The Endangered Species Act and Western Water Rights," *Land and Water Law Review* 20, no. 1 (1985).
10. *Arizona* v. *California* (373 U.S. 546, 83 S. Ct. 1468, 10 L. Ed. 2d 542; decree entered 376 U.S. 340, 84 S. Ct. 755, 11 L. Ed. 2d 757, 1964).
11. 697 F.2d 851, 9th Circuit (1983); cert. denied 464 U.S. 863 (1983).
12. B. L. Lamb and H. Meshorer, "Comparing Instream Flow Programs: A Report on Current Status," in *Proceedings of the Specialty Conference on Advances in Irrigation and Drainage: Surviving External Pressures,* ed. J. Borrelli, V. R. Hasfurther, and R. D. Burman (New York: American Society of Civil Engineers, 1983).
13. Jones and Stokes Associates, Inc., R. R. Harris, and R. J. Risser, "A Review of the Mitigation Measures for Avoiding or Reducing the Impacts of Hydroelectric Development on Riparian Vegetation" (Report prepared for the Department of Engineering Research, Pacific Gas and Electric Company, San Ramon, CA, 1985).
14. P. C. Metzger and J. A. Haverkamp, *Instream Flow Protection: Adaptation to Intensifying Demands* (Washington, DC: The Conservation Foundation, 1983).
15. Jones and Stokes Associates, Inc., R. R. Harris, and R. J. Risser, "A Method for Evaluating Distribution of Plant Species on Floodplains of Headwater Streams in the Western Sierra Nevada, California" (Report prepared for the Department of Engineering Research, Pacific Gas and Electric Company, San Ramon, CA, 1984).
16. Metzger and Haverkamp, *Instream Flow Protection.*
17. Clean Water Act of 1977 (33 U.S.C.A. 1251, sec. 101g).
18. D. Ertle, *Opportunities to Protect Instream Flows in Maine,* Fish and Wildlife Service biological report 85(10) (Washington, DC: Government Printing Office, 1985).
19. Metzger and Haverkamp, *Instream Flow Protection.*
20. G. P. Nabham, "Riparian Vegetation and Indigenous Southwestern Agriculture: Control of Erosion, Pests and Microclimate," in *Riparian Ecosystems and Their Management: Reconciling Conflicting Uses,* Forest Service general technical report RM–120 (Washington, DC: Government Printing Office, 1985), 232–36.
21. G. E. Willenke and A. D. Baldwin, Jr., "A Preliminary Evaluation of the Palmiter Restoration Techniques" (Paper presented at the Twenty-third Ohio Fish and Wildlife Conference, Columbus, OH, 1983).
22. T. J. Barlow, "Why Streams Need Trees," *Garden Magazine* 6, no. 2 (March/April 1982): 2–3, 30–32.
23. Ibid., 32.
24. J. R. Sheaffer, C. R. Ford, and L. D. Mullan, "A Conceptual Framework for Formulating Non-Structural Alternatives" (Report prepared for the Water Resources Council, National Technical Information Service, by Sheaffer and Roland, Inc., Chicago, IL. 1981).

25. N. Vietmeyer, "Saving the Bounty of a Harsh and Meager Land," *Audubon* 87, no. 1 (1985): 100–106.
26. U.S. Congress, Office of Technology Assessment, *Water-related Technologies for Sustainable Agriculture in U.S. Arid/Semi-Arid Lands,* publication OTA-F0212 (Washington, DC: Government Printing Office, 1983).
27. California Department of Water Resources, *Water Conservation in California,* bulletin 198-84 (Sacramento, CA: California Resources Agency, 1983).
28. D. F. Stabler, "Increasing Summer Flows in Small Streams and Adjacent Vegetation through Management of Riparian Areas: A Synthesis," in *Riparian Ecosystems and Their Management: Reconciling Conflicting Uses,* Forest Service general technical report RM-120 (Washington, DC: Government Printing Office, 1985), 206–10.
29. L. L. Apple, "Riparian Habitat Restoration and Beavers," In *Riparian Ecosystems and Their Management: Reconciling Conflicting Uses,* Forest Service general technical report RM-120 (Washington, DC: Government Printing Office, 1985), 489–90.
30. Stabler, "Increasing Summer Flows," 209.
31. L. Kostiano, personal communication, 1985.
32. B. W. Anderson, and R. D. Ohmart, *Riparian Revegetation for Mitigation and Operational Enhancement along the Lower Colorado River* (Tempe, AZ: Arizona State University, Center for Environmental Studies, n.d.).
33. A. J. Calio and R. K. Dawson, *Cooperative Agreement between the National Oceanic and Atmospheric Administration and Department of the Army for a Pilot Study to Investigate the Practicability of a National Program for Restoring and Creating Fisheries Habitat* (Washington, DC, 1985).
34. C. J. Newling, and M. C. Landin, *Long-term Monitoring of Habitat Development at Upland and Wetland Dredge Material Disposal Sites 1974–1982* (Vicksburg, MS: Department of the Army, Waterways Experiment Station, 1985).
35. D. L. Hey, "An Experiment in River Restoration," in *Winning Strategies for Rivers: Proceedings of the 10th Conference on Rivers,* ed. C. N. Brown, P. Carlson, and R. Emeritz (Washington, DC: American Rivers Conservation Council, 1985), 2.
36. K. Schurr, R. Schurr, and P. Barker. "How a Natural River Can Increase the Community's Tax Base," *American Rivers* 14, no. 2 (1986):4.

Selected Reading List

Berkowitz, D. A., and A. M. Squires, eds. *Power Generation and Environmental Change*. Cambridge, MA: The MIT Press, 1969. This book is an overview of the environmental impacts of various methods of power production. It includes descriptions of the impacts of hydroelectric power projects on rivers and riparian habitats.

Brinson, M. M. et al. *Riparian Ecosystems: Their Ecology and Status*. Fish and Wildlife Service publication OBS-81/17. Washington, DC: Government Printing Office, 1981. This is a small overview of the extent and history of riparian ecosystems in the United States. Included is information on the current status of riparian ecosystems, discussions of their functions and properties, and an evaluation of their values.

Darnell, R. M. *Impacts of Construction Activities in Wetlands of the United States*. Corvallis, OR: Environmental Protection Agency, Office of Research and Development, Corvallis Environmental Research Laboratory, 1976. This book provides general information on direct and indirect impacts of various environmental alterations on aquatic and semiaquatic ecosystems.

Diamont, R., J. G. Eugster, and C. J. Dirksen. *A Citizen's Guide to River Conservation*. Washington, DC: The Conservation Foundation, 1984. This publication is essentially a handbook, illustrated with case studies, for groups of citizens interested in protecting a river. Some of the strategies contained herein could also be useful in persuading local governments to maintain greenways along streams or to initiate a stream protection program.

Fradkin, P. *A River No More*. New York: Alfred A. Knopf, 1983. This book describes a journey from the headwaters to the end of the Colorado River, along with descriptions of the people, industry, and history that make the river what it is today.

Hoffman, R. C. and K. Fletcher. *American Rivers: An Assessment of State River Conservation Programs.* Washington, DC: River Conservation Fund, 1984. This publication is a survey of state river protection programs throughout the United States as of 1984. It is particularly helpful to those involved in state river management, as it indicates the strengths and weaknesses of various protection strategies.

Hynes, H. B. N. *The Ecology of Running Waters.* Toronto, Canada: University of Toronto Press, 1970. This book is a classic primer on river ecology. It focuses on the aquatic ecosystem and describes in detail the functioning of river ecology, from food webs and energetics to human impacts.

Palmer, T. *Endangered Rivers and the Conservation Movement.* Berkeley, CA: University of California Press, 1986. Palmer presents a history of the movement to protect rivers in the United States. The book focuses largely on the wild and scenic rivers program but includes stories of earlier dam battles, such as the damming of the Tuolumne in Yosemite National Park's Hetch Hetchy Valley to provide San Francisco with power.

Reisner, M. *Cadillac Desert: The American West and Its Disappearing Water.* New York: Viking Penguin, 1986. This book is a startling exposé of the backstage politics that have resulted in many federal irrigation projects. Reisner's work is worth reading for pleasure as well as for information.

Ward, J. V., and J. A. Standord, eds. *Ecology of Streams.* New York: Plenum Press, 1978. This book is a compilation of works on different aspects of stream ecology. It is a good general text for anyone wanting to grasp the dynamics of fluvial ecosystems.

Glossary

acre-foot   a unit of volume of water that would cover 1 acre to a depth of 1 foot, equal to 43,560 cubic feet.

alluvial   relating to, composed of, or found in clay, silt, sand, gravel, or similar detrital matter deposited by running water.

anadromous   migrating at spawning time to deposit eggs in water of a salinity lower than that of the ocean.

anaerobic   occurring in the absence of free oxygen.

aquifer   an underground stream carrying water toward the ocean.

benthic   occurring at the bottom of a body of water.

biomass   total weight of all organisms (or of some group of organisms) living in a particular habitat or place.

biota   the flora and fauna of an area, region, or geologic period.

bosque   a small wooded area.

buteo   any of a number of species of hawks with broad, rounded wings and soaring flight.

detritus   organic matter accumulating on the soil or as a sediment from an aquatic environment.

ecotype   a locally adapted population of a species with a wide geographic range and with optima and limits of tolerance adjusted to local conditions.

emergents   plants rooted in shallow water that have most of their growth above the water.

estuarine   of, relating to, or formed in a water passage where the tide meets a river current (for example, where an arm of the ocean joins the mouth of a river).

evapotranspiration   loss of water from plant tissue by a combination of evaporation and transpiration.

floodplain   the portion of land surrounding a river or stream channel that is likely to become inundated when the river overtops its banks. For example, the 100-year floodplain is the area likely to be flooded once in 100 years, or the area with a one percent chance of flooding in any given year.

frugivore   any animal that feeds primarily on fruits.

herbaceous plant   a vascular plant that dies down to the ground level at the approach of winter.

insectivore   any organism that feeds primarily on insects.

interbasin transfer   the transport of water from one watershed or river basin to another.

lacustrine   characteristic of the ecology of a lake.

legume   any of a large family (Leguminosae) of dicotyledonous herbs, shrubs, and trees having fruits that are legumes or loments and bearing nodules on the roots that contain nitrogen-fixing bacteria.

mesic   characterized by, relating to, or requiring a moderate amount of moisture.

monoculture   the replacement of natural, mixed communities of many species with a single, dominant population of a cultigen that is to be harvested as a crop.

parasitize   to live in or on an organism of a different species and derive nutrients from it, or to be dependent on something else for existence or support without making a useful or adequate return.

phreatophyte   a deep-rooted plant that obtains its water from the water table or the layer of soil just above it.

pioneer association   the first group of plants to colonize a previously barren area, thus initiating other ecological and successional processes.

piscivore   any animal that feeds mostly on fish.

pool   a portion of a stream or river where velocity is less than the average over the stream, water depth is greater than the average, and the substrate is generally dominated by silt and fine gravel.

raptor   a bird of prey, such as a hawk or an owl.

re-aeration   the supply of oxygen to waters from which the oxygen has been largely depleted.

riffle   a portion of a stream or river where velocity is greater than the average over the stream, depth is less than average, and the substrate is generally dominated by gravel and rubble.

seral stage   a characteristic association of plants and animals during an ecological succession after colonization and before climax is reached.

streambed   the bottom of a channel occupied or formerly occupied by a stream.

substrate   the base on which an organism lives or to which it is attached.

toxin   a colloidal, proteinaceous, poisonous substance that is the specific product of the metabolic activities of a living organism.

transitional habitat   the boundary between two habitat types, where one habitat type is favored by climatic conditions on one side of the transition and the other habitat type is favored on the opposite side.

understory   the layers of vegetation beneath the canopy of a wooded area.

usufructuary   one who has the right of using or enjoying the fruits or profits of an estate or other thing belonging to another, generally treated as a servitude (for example, the water is the property of the state or of the public, and the individual owns only the right to use it, so long as it is applied to a beneficial use).

wetland   area of land inundated or saturated at a frequency and duration sufficient to support biota adapted for life in hydric conditions.

Index

Also Available from Island Press

Land and Resource Planning in the National Forests
By Charles F. Wilkinson and H. Michael Anderson
Foreword by Arnold W. Bolle

This comprehensive, in-depth review and analysis of planning, policy, and law in the National Forest System is the standard reference source on the National Forest Management Act of 1976 (NFMA). This clearly written, nontechnical book offers an insightful analysis of the Fifty Year Plans and how to participate in and influence them.

1987, xii, 396 pp., index.
Paper, ISBN 0-933280-38-6. **$19.95**

Reforming the Forest Service
By Randal O'Toole

Reforming the Forest Service contributes a completely new view to the current debate on the management of our national forests. O'Toole argues that poor management is an institutional problem; he shows that economic inefficiencies and environmental degradation are the inevitable result of the well-intentioned but poorly designed laws that govern the Forest Service. This book proposes sweeping reforms in the structure of the agency and new budgetary incentives as the best way to improve management.

1988, xii, 256 pp., graphs, tables, notes.
Cloth, ISBN 0-933280-49-1. **$24.95**
Paper, ISBN 0-933280-45-9. **$16.95**

The Forest and the Trees: A Guide to Excellent Forestry
By Gordon Robinson
Foreword by Michael McClosky

When is multiple use multiple abuse? In this detailed look at the management of our forests, Gordon Robinson provides specific information on the principles of true multiple-use forestry and on what is wrong with forestry as it is practiced today. He describes, in practical terms, "excellent forestry" — uneven-aged management for sustained yield, which safeguards the rich variety of life in the forest and protects all uses simultaneously. He offers the reader a short course in the mathematics of forestry and provides guidelines for commenting on forest plans. Includes nearly four hundred summaries of published research and expert opinions. Gordon Robinson is a well-known and respected forester with fifty years of experience in forest management.

1988. xiv, 258 pp., illustrations, tables.
Paper, ISBN 0-933280-40-8. **$19.95**
Cloth, ISBN 0-933280-41-6. **$34.95**

Last Stand of the Red Spruce
By Robert A. Mello
Published in cooperation with Natural Resources Defense Council

Acid rain — the debates rage between those who believe that the cause of the problem is clear and identifiable and those who believe that the evidence is inconclusive. In *Last Stand of the Red Spruce*, Robert A. Mello has written an ecological detective story that unravels this confusion and explains how air pollution is killing our nation's forests. Writing for a lay audience, the author traces the efforts of scientists trying to solve the mystery of the dying red spruce trees on Camels Hump in Vermont. Mello clearly and succinctly presents both sides of an issue on which even the scientific community is split and concludes that the scientific evidence uncovered on Camels Hump elevates the issues of air pollution and acid rain to new levels of national significance.

1987. xx, 205 pp., illus., references, bibliography.
Paper, ISBN 0-933280-37-8. **$14.95**

Western Water Made Simple,
by the editors of **High Country News**
Edited by Ed Marston

Winner of the 1986 George Polk Award for environmental reporting, these four special issues of *High Country News* are here available for the first time in book form. Much has been written about the water crisis in the West, yet the issue remains confusing and difficult to understand. *Western Water Made Simple,* by the editors of *High Country News,* lays out in clear language the complex issues of Western water. A survey of the West's three great rivers--the Colorado, the Columbia, and the Missouri—this work includes material that reaches to the heart of the West—its ways of life, its politics, and its aspirations. *Western Water Made Simple* approaches these three river basins in terms of overarching themes combined with case studies— the Columbia in an age of reform, the Colorado in the midst of a fight for control, and the Missouri in search of a destiny.

1987. 224 pp., maps, photographs, bibliography, index.
Paper, ISBN 0-933280-39-4. **$15.95**

The Report of the President's Commission on Americans Outdoors: The Legacy, The Challenge
With Case Studies
Preface by William K. Reilly

"If there is an example of pulling victory from the jaws of disaster, this report is it. The commission did more than anyone expected, especially the administration. It gave Americans something serious to think about if we are to begin saving our natural resources."—Paul C. Pritchard, President, National Parks and Conservation Association.

This report is the first comprehensive attempt to examine the impact of a changing American society and its recreation habits since the work of the Outdoor Recreation Resource Review Commission, chaired by Laurance Rockefeller in 1962. The President's Commission took more than two years to complete its study; the Report contains over sixty recommendations, such as the preservation of a nationwide network of "greenways" for recreational purposes and the establishment of an annual $1 billion trust fund to finance the protection and preservation of our recreational resources. The Island Press edition provides the full text of the report, much of the additional material compiled by the Commission, and twelve selected case studies.

1987. xvi, 426 pp., illus., appendixes, case studies.
Paper, ISBN 0-933280-36-X. **$24.95**

Public Opinion Polling: A Handbook for Public Interest and Citizen Advocacy Groups
By Celinda C. Lake, with Pat Callbeck Harper

"Lake has taken the complex science of polling and written a very usable 'how-to' book. I would recommend this book to both candidates and organizations interested in professional, low-budget, in-house polling." — Stephanie Solien, Executive Director, Women's Campaign Fund.

Public Opinion Polling is the first book to provide practical information on planning, conducting, and analyzing public opinion polls as well as guidelines for interpreting polls conducted by others. It is a book for anyone — candidates, state and local officials, community organizations, church groups, labor organizations, public policy research centers, and coalitions focusing on specific economic issues — interested in measuring public opinion.

1987. x, 166 pp., tables, bibliography, appendix, index.
Paper, ISBN 0-933280-32-7. **$19.95**
Companion software now available.

Green Fields Forever: The Conservation Tillage Revolution in America
By Charles E. Little

"*Green Fields Forever* is a fascinating and lively account of one of the most important technological developments in American agriculture. . . . Be prepared to enjoy an exceptionally well-told tale, full of stubborn inventors, forgotten pioneers, enterprising farmers — and no small amount of controversy." — Ken Cook, World Wildlife Fund and The Conservation Foundation.

Here is the book that will change the way Americans think about agriculture. It is the story of "conservation tillage" — a new way to grow food that, for the first time, works *with*, rather than against, the soil. Farmers who are revolutionizing the course of American agriculture explain here how conservation tillage works. Some environmentalists think there are problems with the methods, however; author Charles E. Little demonstrates that on this issue both sides have a case, and the jury is still out.

1987. 189 pp., illus., appendixes, index, bibliography.
Cloth, ISBN 0-933280-35-1. **$24.95**
Paper, ISBN 0-933280-34-3. **$14.95**

Federal Lands: A Guide to Planning, Management, and State Revenues
By Sally K. Fairfax and Carolyn E. Yale

"An invaluable tool for state land managers. Here, in summary, is everything that one needs to know about federal resource management policies." — Rowena Rogers, President, Colorado State Board of Land Commissioners.

Federal Lands is the first book to introduce and analyze in one accessible volume the diverse programs for developing resources on federal lands. Offshore and onshore oil and gas leasing, coal and geothermal leasing, timber sales, grazing permits, and all other programs that share receipts and revenues with states and localities are considered in the context of their common historical evolution as well as in the specific context of current issues and policy debates.

1987. xx, 252 pp., charts, maps, bibliography, index.
Paper, ISBN 0-933280-33-5. **$24.95**

Hazardous Waste Management: Reducing the Risk
By Benjamin A. Goldman, James A. Hulme, and Cameron Johnson for the Council on Economic Priorities

Hazardous Waste Management: Reducing the Risk is a comprehensive sourcebook of facts and strategies that provides the analytic tools needed by policy makers, regulating agencies, hazardous waste generators, and host communities to compare facilities on the basis of site, management, and technology. The Council on Economic Priorities' innovative ranking system applies to real-world, site-specific evaluations, establishes a consistent protocol for multiple applications, assesses relative benefits and risks, and evaluates and ranks ten active facilities and eight leading commercial management corporations.

1986. xx, 316 pp., notes, tables, glossary, index.
Cloth, ISBN 0-933280-30-0. **$64.95**
Paper, ISBN 0-933280-31-9. **$34.95**

An Environmental Agenda for the Future
By Leaders of America's Foremost Environmental Organizations

". . .a substantive book addressing the most serious questions about the future of our resources." — John Chafee, U.S. Senator, Environmental and Public Works Committee. "While I am not in agreement with many of the positions the authors take, I believe this book can be the basis for constructive dialogue with industry representatives seeking solutions to environmental problems." — Louis Fernandez, Chairman of the Board, Monsanto Corporation.

The chief executive officers of the ten major environmental and conservation organizations launched a joint venture to examine goals that the environmental movement should pursue now and into the twenty-first century. This book presents policy recommendations for implementing changes needed to bring about a healthier, safer world. Topics discussed include nuclear issues, human population growth, energy strategies, toxic waste and pollution control, and urban environments.

1985. viii, 155 pp., bibliography.
Paper, ISBN 0-933280-29-7. **$9.95**

Water in the West
By Western Network

Water in the West is an essential reference tool for water managers, public officials, farmers, attorneys, industry officials, and students and professors attempting to understand the competing pressures on our most important natural resource: water. Here is an in-depth analysis of the effects of energy development, Indian rights, and urban growth on other water users.

1985. *Vol. III: Western Water Flows to the Cities*
v, 217 pp., maps, table of cases, documents, bibliography, index.
Paper, ISBN 0-933280-28-9. **$25.00**

These titles are available directly from Island Press, Box 7, Covelo, CA 95428. Please enclose $2.75 shipping and handling for the first book and $1.25 for each additional book. California and Washington, DC residents add 6% sales tax. A catalog of current and forthcoming titles is available free of charge. Prices subject to change without notice.